# ROMANTIC WOMEN'S LIFE WRITING

Manchester University Press

be favourably read and widely reviewed, despite a blip in the 1830s. The 'long'-nineteenth-century scope of this book therefore helps to minimise the misinterpretation of, or overemphasis on, individual instances of reception and instead makes room for the long-term vicissitudes in women's reputations to become visible.

## Life writing in the Romantic period

In this study, I use the term *life writing* to refer to any text that has one or more historical lives as its subject, whether the work is first-person or third-person, prose or verse, non-fiction or fiction. I use the term more broadly than Sidonie Smith and Julia Watson,[6] as I include not only memoir and autobiography but also biography in its remit. In this, I follow the lead of Amy Culley and David Cook and, like them, I prefer *life writing* to *life-writing*, an older term used, for example, by James Olney.[7] Traditionally, life writing meant only biography and autobiography 'proper', that is, retrospective narratives concerning real individuals that trace the development of personality and reveal an essential self that unfolds over time.[8] Implicit in this narrower conception of auto/biography were assumptions that only certain (male, white, exceptional) people and certain (realist, unified, developmental) forms were appropriate material for life writing, or at least for the kind of life writing worthy of study. In recent decades, the work of Patricia Meyer Spacks, Lynda Thompson, Felicity Nussbaum, Anne Mellor, Liz Stanley, Laura Marcus, Sidonie Smith and Julia Watson, Daniel Cook, Amy Culley and many others has helped to interrogate definitions of, and introduce new interpretative frameworks for, life writing. The full range of self writing that existed in the eighteenth and nineteenth centuries, which included not only the linear, retrospective auto/biography emphasised by theorists like Philippe Lejeune but also travelogues, memoirs, diaries, journals, collective biographies, essays, letters, autobiographical fiction and histories, for example, has begun to receive the attention it deserves. As Daniel Cook and Amy Culley have argued, this increase in scholarship not only sheds new light on women's contributions to literary history and to the practice of Romantic auto/biography but also has 'broader implications for our understanding of literary genres, constructions of gender, the relationship between manuscript and print culture, the mechanisms of publicity and celebrity, and models of authorship in the period'.[9]

The production, consumption and discussion of life writing flourished in the Romantic period, and readers were fascinated by tales of the private lives of men and women alike. Despite the longstanding emphasis of critics like Samuel Johnson on the moral utility of life narratives, their robust sales also derived from more prurient impulses. The growing appetite for and supply of life writing was also fuelled by the expansion of the literary marketplace and the periodical press, increases in literacy rates and technologies of publication and dissemination and a burgeoning modern celebrity culture. It was at this time that biography and *autobiography*, a term which appeared in 1797 and gradually replaced the earlier designation of *self-biography*, grew into separate categories. It was also at this time that debates proliferated over the respectability of writing and reading life narratives, and according to Eugene Stelzig, it was only at the end of the Romantic period that life writing emerged as a fully 'literary' form.[10] Women's and men's life writing circulated in and was purchased by the same reading public; it responded to the same literary precursors and intertexts; it was evaluated by the same reviewers. For men and women alike, the publication of private lives involved a contradictory mixture of exposure and power: Life writing posed not only a reputational risk but also an affirmation of individual identity.

Women's life writing therefore did not comprise an intrinsically separate tradition. However, this book takes women's life writing as its focus, because the standards by which women and their work were judged, and the ways in which this work influenced its subjects' reputations, were complicated in ways different from, or at least more pronounced than, those governing men's life writing of the period. Debates about the moral respectability and literary merit of auto/ biography were intensified and complicated by the issue of gender. Women's sexual lives were held to different standards than men's, and they faced the added pressures of balancing literary labour with the cultural expectations of femininity. Moreover, personal attacks could be especially damaging to women whose dependent economic positions left them heavily reliant on literary work for their livelihoods. As Felicity Nussbaum reminds us, 'Women's real lives are made or irremediably ruined because of their public construction. ... A complex relationship develops between a woman's entry into the public sphere, through publication, publicity, and sexual representation'.[11] Women also had to negotiate the long-standing association, solidified by the scandalous memoirs of the eighteenth century, between fame and shame. Moreover, women's life writing remains a relatively under-studied genre within Romanticism, though recent volumes such as Daniel Cook and Amy Culley's edited collection *Women's Life Writing, 1700–1850* (2012) and Amy Culley's *British Women's Life Writing, 1760–1840: Friendship, Community, and Collaboration* (2014) have begun to rectify this neglect. Cook and Culley's essay collection showcases the diversity of women's contributions to the genre as well as their strategies for negotiating hostilities to the publication of life writing. Culley's monograph focuses on the collaborative and relational aspects of women's self writing, in both print and manuscript, looking at texts by female Methodist preachers, courtesans and radical women, in turn, to show how social contexts of production and alternative affiliations are embedded in the work. *Romantic Women's Life Writing* builds on the work of Cook and Culley, retaining their focus on gender and genre but looking at a later time period and paying attention to the interplay of life writing and authorial afterlives.

Scholars such as Sidonie Smith and Julia Watson, Felicity Nussbaum and Tom Mole have recognised the significance of life writing, not only in the eighteenth and nineteenth centuries but also, more broadly speaking, in the cultural production of knowledge,[12] the formation of subjectivities of gender and class[13] and the history of selfhood.[14] However, little scholarship exists on the specific impact(s) of life writing, that is, the ways that it was read and responded to, the ways that these readings and responses changed over time and the implications of these changes for the status of its subjects and/or writers. William St Clair has pointed out that text-based approaches are locked in a 'closed system' that either ignores readers or infers readers from texts and is therefore insufficient to understand 'the meanings that readers historically did construct'.[15] He thus advocates a 'systems approach' in which texts are understood not only for their intrinsic qualities but also for the ways that they were received. James Treadwell stresses the importance of this kind of approach to the study of life writing in particular: 'An attempt to write the history of autobiography in the period ... would have to be a history of reading, writing, and publishing practices; the "primary texts" would occupy a small part of its attention, because the formation and development of genre mainly takes place elsewhere.'[16] Text-based approaches also tend, as Laura Marcus notes, to overlook issues of production and circulation, isolating the individual as the 'sole producer of the life-history' and reinforcing the myth 'that authorial identity is not determined by the marketplace but is rather a function of conditions internal to the self'.[17] This book addresses these interpretive gaps by looking not only at primary life writing texts but also at the ways they were read, reviewed, responded to, reprinted and redacted over time.

## Gauging reputation

The methodological challenges of this approach are numerous and well documented. Published reviews, infamous for the inclusion of puffs, the espousal of the journal's house style and political persuasion and the unrepresentative demographic of their writers, are problematic as an index of reception. They do not always correlate with sales figures or with the opinions of readers.[18] Still, Treadwell suggests: 'Only in the major review periodicals can we see the genre being read and written about with any consistency, and they are thus the best available window on to the encounter between the world of letters and specific autobiographical acts, despite all the factors limiting the way they imagined such texts to be read.'[19] Individual reports of reading from other works of life writing, such as diaries, journals or letters, can also be useful, as can retrospective comments written at a later period.[20] However, these sources are not always reliable, nor are they necessarily representative of wider reading constituencies. Such anecdotal accounts can help us to gauge readerly expectations, interpretive frameworks and terms of debate, but they cannot be used to say, definitively, how a text was read. St Clair recommends the use, wherever possible, of quantitative information about the publication and dissemination of texts, including print runs, circulation figures, price and reprinting patterns, for example. In my efforts to assess the impact of these women's life writing on both the development of the genre and the cultural status of its subjects, I draw on all of the above types of evidence, including quantitative data, published reviews and individual accounts of reading. I also include within my remit fictionalised character portraits, responses and rewritings in novels, poetic responses, group biographies and biographical dictionaries, essays in the periodical press, illustrated serial fiction and the paratexts, reviews and reception of later reprints and scholarly volumes. This wide range of sources, most of which have received very little critical attention to date, lends originality to my approach. It also means there are, necessarily, some disparities among my chapters, with each case study harnessing different types of evidence in its analysis and favouring different moments within the long nineteenth century. However, this variety is appropriate to the unique contours of each woman's authorial career and afterlife. Furthermore, in assembling the fullest possible picture of the effects of life writing on reputation, I have found it necessary to consider any and all potential indicators of reception, evaluation or reaction, despite (though taking into consideration) their potential for bias, unreliability or generic limitation.

Each chapter discusses the authorial career of one Romantic writer, looking at how her reputation shifted after the publication of one or more key works of life writing. My case studies also attend to the ways these women attempted to shape their own public images, for example, through the strategic use of their own names, pseudonyms or anonymity; paratexts like prefaces and advertisements; the careful modulation of voice and style across their writing; and decisions about how and where to publish, price and market their work. Each chapter also analyses a range of responses to these women's public personae and to the works themselves. By looking at these women's negotiation of and reception within the literary marketplace, this book sits within the recent wave of feminist criticism that emphasises the reputations and afterlives of eighteenth- and nineteenth-century women writers. Monographs such as Ben P. Robertson's *Elizabeth Inchbald's Reputation: A Publishing and Reception History* (2013), which examines the public response to Inchbald as well as her response to the public, and Andrew McInnes's *Wollstonecraft's Ghost: The Fate of the Female Philosopher in the Romantic Period* (2017), which analyses female philosopher figures in early nineteenth-century fiction as evidence of Wollstonecraft's legacy, share my interest in using non-canonical, popular or otherwise neglected material in gauging 'reception'. Edited collections like Brenda Ayers's *Biographical Misrepresentations of British Women Writers: A Hall of Mirrors and the Long Nineteenth Century* (2017) and Amber K. Regis and Deborah Wynne's *Charlotte Brontë: Legacies and Afterlives* (2017) likewise explore reception from new angles, suggesting the ways that biography – with its distortions, biases and political or cultural agendas – as well as adaptations and/or transmediations can affect the posthumous status of women writers. However, these volumes, like most reception studies, tend to focus on a single author, whereas my book allows for the comparison of four different writers. Moreover, my chapters are not straightforward reception studies but rather seek to address more specific questions about the impact and development of life writing within the long nineteenth century.

Canvassing a wide variety of sources which are seen as not only reflecting but also influencing reputation, this study is interested in determining the effects of life writing in the three-way encounter between reader, writer and public-sphere print culture. As such, this book also fits more broadly into the trend of scholarship that interrogates Romanticism through attention to the relationship between mass market print culture, reception, public image and/or literary afterlife. It joins studies such as Andrew Bennett's *Romantic Poets and the Culture of Posterity* (1999), Lucy Newlyn's *Reading, Writing and Romanticism: The Anxiety of Reception* (2000), Claire Brock's *The Feminization of Fame, 1750–1830* (2006), and Tom Mole's edited collection *Romanticism and Celebrity Culture: 1750–1850* (2012). Brock and Mole, in particular, point to the Romantic period as a time of transition in which the authorial persona became central to the reception of a text and in which celebrity culture as we now understand it began to take shape. Both scholars pay attention to the role of public figures in the construction of gender norms, with Brock arguing that 'women were actively embracing the new forms of public self-representation' and Mole reminding us that female celebrities in the Romantic period had to negotiate the 'inherent contradiction between the norms of femininity and the experience of celebrity'.[21] My book also draws on recent work by Mary Waters, Betty A. Schellenberg, Linda Peterson and Jennie Batchelor on the professionalisation of women writers in the eighteenth and nineteenth centuries.[22] Batchelor's *Women's Work: Labour, Gender, Authorship, 1750–1830* (2010), for instance, rethinks previous assumptions about the relationship of women and literary work, and argues that although women 'register … tensions between propriety and professionalism, and between domesticity and labour … they find in these conflicting imperatives not only a subject for their writing but … a matrix within which to theorize and justify their authorial practice'.[23] My analysis builds on this premise, homing in on the importance of life writing to constructions of professionalisation, authorship and reputation. My arguments are also indebted to ground-breaking archival research, such as Peter Garside, James Raven and Rainer Schöwerling's *The English Novel 1770–1829* (2000) and William St Clair's *The Reading Nation in the Romantic Period* (2004), volumes which provide data invaluable for any attempt to gauge or compare authorial reputations in the nineteenth century.

In its focus on the contours of women writers' reputations, and in seeking to understand how these reputations were formed and transformed over time, this book sits closely alongside recent monographs by Michael Gamer, Tom Mole and H. J. Jackson. Gamer's *Romanticism, Self-Canonization, and the Business of Poetry* (2017), which assesses how authors sought to modify their reputations and shape their afterlives through reproductions of earlier works (called 're-collections'), shares my concern with highlighting a more dynamic interaction between reader and writer that goes beyond the initial moment of textual publication. In *What the Victorians Made of Romanticism: Material Artifacts, Cultural Practices, and Reception History*

(2017), Tom Mole has likewise moved past initial composition and publication (what he terms 'punctual historicism') to emphasise a 'web of reception' that takes in later re-interpretation and remediation of texts.[24] Mole's cross-period, multi-media approach allows for a more accurate evaluation of how authorial reputations fared over time and demonstrates that '[a]uthors' reputations never simply endure … and their works do not simply survive: either they are renewed or they are forgotten'.[25] Similarly, H. J. Jackson, whose *Those Who Write for Immortality: Romantic Reputations and the Dream of Lasting Fame* (2015) compares the posthumous reputations of several groups of Romantic writers to determine what contributes to the long-term literary survival of one author over another, argues that '[m]erit is only part of the reason – arguably quite a small part'.[26] According to Jackson, many other factors such as 'attract[ing] multiple audiences and bear[ing] diverse (even contradictory) meanings', the activity and effectiveness of champions or mediators working on the author's behalf (often posthumously) and 'successful remediation' remain equally significant.[27] Indeed, in Jackson's 'Scorecard' – a list of twenty-two categories affecting posthumous fame arranged in order of importance – biography not only ranks fourth but is starred as an essential factor.[28] My book follows on from the conclusions of Mole and Jackson in particular, but it focuses on investigating how and why not only biography but also life writing more generally affects the reputations of writers. Using a similarly wide-angled lens and considering a range of sources that goes beyond canonical materials like literary reviews and critical histories, my analysis nevertheless differs from theirs in its specific emphasis on life writing and the attention it pays to gender.

Reputation itself remains a slippery entity. The *Oxford English Dictionary* defines it as 'the general opinion or estimate of a person's character or other qualities; the relative esteem in which a person or thing is held'.[29] In the literary sphere, it might refer to the beliefs held about a writer's work; and in the private sphere, the beliefs held about an individual's moral, or perhaps sexual, character. Ben P. Robertson, for example, suggests that Elizabeth Inchbald's reputation rested on her successful management of these 'two distinct, yet intimately connected aspects of the idea': 'her personal reputation', which centred on 'sexual chastity', and the 'professional persona that she projected as an actor and a writer'.[30] For women, whose private lives and sexual conduct have been more heavily emphasised and regulated than men's, the professional and personal dimensions of reputation are almost always linked, if not conflated. H. J. Jackson defines reputation a little differently, using it to refer to 'posthumous fame', in contrast to 'renown', by which she designates present fame (xiii). However, Jackson's sense of reputation as 'a substitute for personal immortality' and a condition in which 'the name lives on and is carried around the world' is useful.[31] In the Romantic period, critics like William Hazlitt contrasted enduring 'fame' with its ephemeral counterpart, 'popularity': 'Fame is the recompense not of the living, but of the dead ... for fame is not popularity, the shout of the multitude, the idle buzz of fashion, the venal puff, the soothing flattery of favour of friendship; but it is the spirit of a man surviving himself in the minds and thoughts of other men.'[32] Hazlitt's distinction here is gendered, with 'popularity' in the present representing an inferior, feminised version of a masculine, posthumous 'fame' that persists over time. According to Andrew Bennett, the 'textual afterlife', or the ability of a work of art to survive beyond the death of its creator, became a new point of obsession in the Romantic period, as posthumous fame and contemporary popularity came to be seen as mutually exclusive.[33] For Bennett, this fascination with and desire for a future audience remains 'a specifically masculine phenomenon'.[34]

However, the life writings covered in this book suggest otherwise. Though ideas about reputation – and even about fame itself – were certainly gendered, each of my case studies uncovers ways in which women writers imagined and sought to influence their reputations in their lives and afterlives. The power of life writing, like fiction perhaps, lies in the bond it forges between the reader and the subject (who is sometimes, but not always, the author). Life writing is especially effective for eliciting emotional responses. It therefore wields a particular influence on reputation because readers are encouraged to identify imaginatively with its subjects. For this reason, life writing has profound implications for models and myths of authorship, authorial afterlives and canon formation. This book argues for the importance of Romantic women's life writing in shaping the reputations of its subjects. It sheds light on the dynamics underpinning the formation and evolution of these authorial reputations during the long nineteenth century. Tom Mole has urged scholars to 'move beyond individual celebrities to pay attention to the genres, media and discourses that enabled celebrity culture' in order to understand 'how the borders between celebrity and canonicity can be crossed'.[35] This book nominates life writing as one of these genres. The four women writers featured here offer case studies in the complicated and often unexpected effects of life writing on reputation and literary afterlife. They also showcase women's varied and innovative contributions to Romantic auto/biographical practice. As the remarks of Joan Didion, Roxane Gay and Chimamanda Adichie Ngozi at the beginning of this chapter remind us, life stories are still a powerful currency. It is my hope that an understanding of the complex encounter between life writing, reputation and literary reception in the long nineteenth century can help to empower writers of the current generation as well.

## Chapter breakdown

The first chapter focuses on Frances Burney (1752–1840), a figure who has often been linked with feminine diffidence, disembodiment and authorial anxiety. However, her *Diary and Letters* (1842–46) tells a different story. Burney's *Diary* presented a model of female authorship that mixed a shrewd sense of her public position with a respectable and charming feminine persona. Though the publication of diaries was popular, their dubious moral and literary status made them a reputational risk. As the first woman's diary to be published in English, the *Diary and Letters* broke new ground in its contribution both to a literary afterlife and to the genre of life writing itself. This chapter reassesses Burney's career, examining its development (via print runs, publication and sales records, reviews, essays and anecdotal responses) alongside the representation of it in the *Diary*. It argues that Burney took an active and 'professional' approach to her writing,

from the self-fashioning in the paratexts of her anonymously published
*Evelina* (1778) to the meticulous preparation for the posthumous
publication of her *Diary and Letters* (1842–46). Moreover, although
critics have lamented that the publication of her *Diary* undermined
her reputation as a novelist, an analysis of Burney's afterlife in the long
nineteenth century in literary reviews, periodical essays and scholarly
and biographical material demonstrates that in fact it strengthened
her literary status. What emerges is a reciprocal relationship by
which the publication of her *Diary* fuelled and was fuelled by the
enduring success of her fiction. By the end of the Victorian period,
Burney held a robust position in the eighteenth-century canon. This
chapter shows the potential of life writing to consolidate a woman's
literary reputation and points to the importance of Burney's *Diary*, in
particular, in bolstering the respectability of the genre itself.

The second chapter turns to Mary Wollstonecraft (1759–97),
who rose to fame with her reform-minded *Vindication of the Rights
of Men* (1790) and *Vindication of the Rights of Woman* (1792) but won
over contemporaries across the political spectrum with *Letters Written
During a Short Residence in Sweden, Norway, and Denmark* (1797). An
examination of these texts and responses to them shows her strategic
and skilful self-fashioning, which was terminated by the candid
disclosures of her husband William Godwin's *Memoirs of the Author of
a Vindication of the Rights of Woman* (1798). Critics have traditionally
seen this shocking biography as killing Wollstonecraft's reputation
and silencing discussion of her for the best part of the next century.
However, closer examination of Godwin's framing of Wollstonecraft
in the *Memoirs*, and reactions to it in the century that followed,
makes visible a complex affective response. This emotionally charged
response coexisted with ongoing engagement with Wollstonecraft's
political writing, which is traced here in the writing of Goodwyn and
Catherine Barmby, William Thompson and Anna Wheeler and John
Stuart and Harriet Taylor Mill. This chapter also considers a range of
little-studied sources that reflect Wollstonecraft's afterlife in the long
nineteenth century, including: Frances Burney's fictionalised portrayal of her as Elinor Joddrell in *The Wanderer* (1814); Percy Bysshe
Shelley's allusion to her in *Laon and Cyntha* (1817); periodical essays

by mid-Victorian critics such as George Eliot, Eliza Lynn Linton and Ann Mozley; entries in group biographies written by women such as Mary Pilkington, Mary Mathilda Betham and Anne Katharine Elwood; Charles Kegan Paul's book-length biography *William Godwin, His Friends and Contemporaries* (1876); *fin de siècle* reconsiderations of Wollstonecraft by Margaret Oliphant, Mathilde Blind and Elizabeth Robins Pennell; and first-wave feminist appropriations of her, such as that of Millicent Garrett Fawcett. Using this material, the chapter highlights unrecognised strands of Wollstonecraft's legacy and argues for Godwin's biography as an innovative contribution to Romantic life writing and a pivotal component in Wollstonecraft's affective and intellectual appeal in the nineteenth century.

The third case study looks at the actress, poet and royal mistress Mary Darby Robinson (1758–1800), who spent the bulk of her adult life transforming her public position from sex object to writing subject. Her *Memoirs of the Late Mrs Robinson, Written by Herself* (1801), edited by her daughter and published the year after her death, has been read as an apology for her life. Yet the jarring shifts in tone, gaps in narration and structural inconsistencies caused contemporary readers to doubt its veracity and have led modern critics to regard it as a flawed final attempt to rescue a tarnished reputation. However, this chapter suggests that the formal and rhetorical gaps in the *Memoirs* comprise a nuanced strategy of self-representation that allowed Robinson to straddle the contradictory identities of the victimised heroine of sensibility and the titillating actress. Through analysis of the *Memoirs*; comparison with a similar but lesser-known 'scandal memoir', *The Life of Mrs Gooch* (1792); and examination of Robinson's nineteenth-century afterlife, this chapter demonstrates that it may be the so-called failures of Robinson's *Memoirs* – its interruptions, omissions and contradictions – that made it so influential in shaping and preserving Robinson's posthumous reputation. This chapter makes use of a range of non-canonical sources for considering Robinson's posthumous reputation, including Romantic-period fictionalisations of Robinson's royal affair written by Sarah Green and Pierce Egan; coverage of Robinson in collective biographies by Mary Pilkington, Edward Robins and Mary Craven; periodical essays like Dutton Cook's

'Poor Perdita' (1865); later fictional versions of Robinson's life such as Stanley Makower's *Perdita:A Romance in Biography* (1908) and Elizabeth Barrington's *The Exquisite Perdita* (1926); responses to Robinson in the published work, private manuscripts and personal artefacts of women writers such as Charlotte Dacre, Maria Edgeworth and Violet Fane (the pseudonym of Mary Baroness Currie); and the paratexts of later reprints of the *Memoirs*. These sources show that although Robinson could not erase the scandal of her early years, she was able to reshape reactions to it by taking control of her own story.

The final case study considers Mary Hays (1759–1843), who, from the start of her career, struggled with the problem of writing as a woman. Too womanly, too scandalous or too ridiculous, Hays seemed unable to find a voice that was both authentic and acceptable. It has been suggested that by 1800, Hays had lost control of her reputation, retreated from her former radicalism and turned to didactic literature to support herself. However, this chapter contests the above narrative by examining a range of responses to Hays's early works as well as the creative ways she used fiction, essays and biography later in her career to intervene in her own reception while promoting her political, pedagogical and personal aims. The chapter first examines literary reviews, private responses to Hays in the correspondence of individuals within her Dissenting and radical networks and parodies of her such as can be found in Richard Polwhele's satirical poetry and the fiction of Charles Lloyd and Elizabeth Hamilton; it then turns to her second novel, *The Victim of Prejudice* (1799), *Monthly Magazine* contributions and biographical writings such as 'Memoirs of Mary Wollstonecraft' (1800) and *Female Biography* (1803). Detailed analysis of the structure and progressive content of *Female Biography* – along with attention to its reception and legacy in the little-known writing of her niece, Matilda Mary Hays (1820–97) – shows that Hays experimented with innovative modes of writing through which she defended her reputation; promoted long-held ideas about the representation, education, and advancement of women; and shaped the genre of life writing for decades to come.

The book ends with a Coda that draws together the analysis of the book's four case studies by turning briefly to Virginia Woolf's

*Common Reader* collections, published in 1925 and 1932. Like Samuel Johnson, whose 'common reader' becomes the central figure of these essays, Woolf envisaged reading as a conversation between reader and writer across the centuries. In these essays, Woolf's dialogue with her predecessors is often most prominent when she engages with authors of emerging genres, that is, life writing. Woolf's fascination with life writing is twofold: it allows us to be transported to another time and place, but it also encourages us to create this other world in our imagination. Offering both dissolution and affirmation of identity, life writing has an important place not only in the history of literature but in the history of women's writing. This chapter uses Woolf's dialogic engagement with past writers to reflect on the importance of women's writing and on the interaction between gender, genre and reputation in the long nineteenth century.

## Notes

1 Joan Didion, '7000 Romaine, Los Angeles 38', in *Slouching Towards Bethlehem* (London: Andre Deutsch, 1969), p. 71.

2 Roxane Gay, 'Not Here to Make Friends', in *Bad Feminist* (New York, NY: Harper, 2014), p. 85.

3 Chimamanda Adichie Ngozi, 'The Danger of a Single Story', *TED Global* (2009) www.ted.com/talks/chimamanda_adichie_the_danger_of_a_single_story (accessed 5 May 2016).

4 Patricia Meyer Spacks, *Imagining a Self: Autobiography and Novel in Eighteenth-Century England* (Cambridge, MA: Harvard University Press, 1976), p. 27.

5 Many other women engaged in life writing at this time. Lesser known life writers of the time might include bluestockings such as Mary Berry, court writers like Charlotte Bury, actresses like Sarah Siddons and Dora Jordan, scandal memoirists like Elizabeth Steele and Harriette Wilson or purveyors of spiritual autobiography like Mary Fletcher.

6 See Sidonie Smith and Julia Watson, *Reading Autobiography: A Guide for Interpreting Life Narratives*, 2nd edn (Minneapolis, MN: University of Minneapolis Press, 2001).

7 See Daniel Cook and Amy Culley, 'Introduction', in *Women's Life Writing, 1700–1850: Gender, Genre and Authorship*, ed. Daniel Cook and Amy Culley (Basingstoke: Palgrave Macmillan, 2012).

8 Philippe Lejeune, 'The Autobiographical Contract', in *French Literary Theory Today: A Reader*, ed. Tzvetan Todorov (Cambridge: Cambridge University Press, 1982), p. 193.

9 Cook and Culley, 'Introduction', p. 1.

10 Eugene Stelzig, 'Introduction', in *Romantic Autobiography in England*, ed. Eugene Stelzig (Farnham: Ashgate, 2009), p. 10.

11 Felicity A. Nussbaum, *The Autobiographical Subject: Gender and Ideology in Eighteenth-Century England* (Baltimore, MD: Johns Hopkins University Press, 1989), p. 152.

12   Smith and Watson, *Reading Autobiography*, p. 25.

13   Nussbaum, *The Autobiographical Subject*, p. xiii.

14   Tom Mole, 'Introduction', in *Romanticism and Celebrity Culture, 1750–1850*, ed. Tom Mole (Cambridge: Cambridge University Press, 2009), p. 12.

15   William St Clair, *The Reading Nation in the Romantic Period* (Cambridge: Cambridge University Press, 2004), p. 4.

16   James Treadwell, *Autobiographical Writing and British Literature, 1783–1834* (Oxford: Oxford University Press, 2005), p. 9.

17   Laura Marcus, *Auto/Biographical Discourses: Criticism, Theory, Practice* (Manchester: Manchester University Press, 1994), p. 4; Mary Jean Corbett, qtd in Marcus, *Auto/Biographical Discourses*, p. 29.

18   St Clair, for example, finds 'no correlation between reviews, reputations, and sales, or between contemporary and later reputations'. See *The Reading Nation in the Romantic Period*, p. 189.

19   Treadwell, *Autobiographical Writing and British Literature*, p. 62.

20   On the value of these kinds of sources, see Nussbaum, *The Autobiographical Subject*, p. 25.

21   Claire Brock, *The Feminization of Fame, 1750–1830* (Basingstoke: Palgrave Macmillan, 2006), p. 2; Mole, 'Introduction', p. 11.

22   See Mary A. Waters, *British Women Writers and the Profession of Literary Criticism, 1789–1832* (Basingstoke: Palgrave Macmillan, 2004); Betty A. Schellenberg, *The Professionalization of Women Writers in Eighteenth-Century Britain* (Cambridge: Cambridge University Press, 2005); Linda Peterson, *Becoming a Woman of Letters: Myths of Authorship and Facts of the Victorian Market* (Princeton, NJ: Princeton University Press, 2009); Jennie Batchelor, *Women's Work: Labour, Gender, Authorship, 1750–1830* (Manchester: Manchester University Press, 2010).

23   Batchelor, *Women's Work*, p. 150.

24   Tom Mole, *What the Victorians Made of Romanticism: Material Artifacts, Cultural Practices, and Reception History* (Princeton, NJ: Princeton University Press, 2017), p. 3.

25   *Ibid.*, pp. 2–3.

26   Heather J. Jackson, *Those Who Write for Immortality: Romantic Reputations and the Dream of Lasting Fame* (New Haven, CT: Yale University Press, 2015), p. 43.

27   *Ibid.*, p. 62; p. 106.

28   *Ibid.*, p. 111.

29   'Reputation, n', *OED Online*, Oxford University Press, June 2018.

30   Ben P. Robertson, *Elizabeth Inchbald's Reputation: A Publishing and Reception History* (London: Pickering and Chatto, 2013), p. 3.

31   Jackson, *Those Who Write for Immortality*, p. 6.

32   William Hazlitt, 'On the Living Poets', qtd in Mole, 'Introduction', p. 2.

33   Andrew Bennett, *Romantic Poets and the Culture of Posterity* (Cambridge: Cambridge University Press, 1999), p. 2.

34   *Ibid.*, p. 66.

35   Tom Mole, *Byron's Romantic Celebrity: Industrial Culture and the Hermeneutic of Intimacy* (Basingstoke: Palgrave Macmillan, 2007), p. 157.

# Chapter 1

# 'Nothing is so delicate as the reputation of a woman': Frances Burney's *Diary* (1842–46) and the reputation of women's life writing

F RANCES BURNEY (1752–1840) IS often associated with a tradition of feminine diffidence and authorial anxiety, but her *Diary and Letters* (1842–46) tells a different story. Burney's *Diary* showcased a model of female authorship that blended a sense of her position in the literary marketplace with a charming feminine persona. As the first woman's diary to be published in English, Burney's *Diary* landed at the centre of debates about the moral and literary status of publishing the 'private'. This chapter reassesses Burney's career, examining its development alongside its representation in the *Diary*. It argues that Burney took a 'professional' outlook towards her writing, from the self-fashioning in the paratexts of her anonymously published *Evelina* (1778) to the preparations for the posthumous publication of her *Diary*. Moreover, analysis of Burney's nineteenth-century afterlife – including responses to and reprints of her *Diary*, as well as a late-Victorian explosion of Burney-related scholarly, biographical and fictional material – demonstrates that the publication of the *Diary* actually strengthened her literary status. By the dawn of the twentieth century, Burney held a firm position in the eighteenth-century canon. This chapter provides a case study in the ways that life writing can enhance and consolidate a woman's literary reputation and the ways that it can likewise contribute to the respectability of the genre itself.

## Burney's 'masculine' self-fashioning

In 1778, Frances Burney's anonymously published *Evelina, or the History of a Young Lady's Entrance into the World* became a literary sensation and a source of much curiosity. Before publication, Burney had taken precautions to maintain her anonymity, keeping the manuscript secret from most of her friends and relatives, copying it out in disguised handwriting and employing her brother as a go-between with the publisher. Afterward, despite the book's success, Burney continued to keep her authorial identity a mystery. Critics have made much of this early state of namelessness, linking Burney with a tradition of feminine diffidence, disembodiment and disappearance, and regarding her as 'the ultimate eighteenth-century "Miss Nobody"'.[1] However, Burney displayed an awareness of her public standing and how she could influence it. She independently decided when and how to publish and advertise *Evelina*, making a conscious effort to shape her reception from the beginning.

Burney negotiated her entrance into the public sphere by affixing three paratexts to her novel: a dedicatory poem, a dedicatory letter and a preface. This kind of prefatory material was common in novels by writers of both genders, who followed the long-standing convention of using the preface to introduce both text and author into the public sphere. In the preface, eighteenth-century novelists tended not only to profess humility, but also to praise patrons, request critical leniency, explain authorial intentions, or otherwise instruct readers.[2] Prefatory material remained doubly important for women writers, who often apologised for the unfeminine act of writing and justified why their work merited attention in the first place.[3] Predictably, Burney's self-deprecatory verse to the 'author of my being' emphasises her 'filial love' and 'virtue' before apologising for her 'weak pow'rs' and 'feeble lines' and explaining the reason for her anonymity: she fears she 'cannot raise' her parent's 'fame'.[4] Referring to her novel as a 'trifling production of a few idle hours', Burney further underlines her status as a youthful amateur in her dedicatory epistle 'To the Authors of the Monthly and Critical Reviews'.

However, although Burney does stress her virtue, modesty and apprehension, nowhere in the three paratexts does she characterise herself as 'feminine'. Gina Campbell has situated what she terms a rhetoric of self-effacement in a 'tradition of feminine purity' by which Burney solicits the protection of male critics and reminds them of her virtue.[5] Yet readers did not assume *Evelina* was written by a woman. Burney's diary tells us that contemporary speculations included a variety of experienced, and male, writers. The publisher, Thomas Lowndes, guessed Horace Walpole to be the writer, and long-time family friend Samuel Crisp thought it might be Frances's father, Dr Charles Burney. Though the dedication professed the author's incapacity and uncertainty, readers did not necessarily take these kinds of declarations at face value. The deferential tone of the dedication and its repeated avowals of inexperience and modesty could be read as posturing and publicity mongering.[6]

Though Burney makes many of the customary prefatory gestures, she avoids the hallmarks of the 'pleading preface'. According to Leslie Thompson and John Ahrens, the 'pleading preface' was associated with women writers who exposed their 'terror and tears', along with indiscreet personal details of physical illness, financial distress and family problems, in the hopes of a more lenient critical judgement.[7] Burney distanced herself from these so-called feminine tactics. A series of negatives – she is 'No hackneyed writer … neither … a half-starved garretteer' – politely distinguishes her from the 'supplicatory author' who begs for pity on grounds of personal necessity or gender inferiority.[8] In a battlefield metaphor of the kind often seen in the *Monthly* and *Critical* Reviews, she compares herself to a 'fighting hero' who courageously courts only the 'Justice' of an unbiased judgement and wishes her work to be considered on its internal merits.[9] Furthermore, she places herself on equal footing with her reviewers, adopting their language and addressing them directly: 'Remember, Gentlemen, you were all young writers once'. If prefatory material can be understood as a space of self-fashioning, Burney here defines herself as a serious author, humble yet dignified, and, implicitly, male.[10]

Burney's preface extends this self-characterisation while also
addressing issues of genre. In a tone of self-deprecating humour,
she acknowledges the 'inferior rank' of the lowly 'Novelist' whose
books infect 'young ladies in general, and boarding-school damsels
in particular' with a 'distemper' that is 'incurable' and 'bids defiance
to the medicine of advice or reprehension'.[11] Nodding to the novels
known for inflaming the female imagination, Burney nevertheless
validates her contribution to the genre by aligning herself with
illustrious 'predecessors' that include Jean-Jacques Rousseau, Samuel
Johnson, Pierre de Marivaux, Henry Fielding, Samuel Richardson
and Tobias Smollett. Though Burney enjoyed the work of several
eighteenth-century women writers, she constructs an all-male canon
to elevate her own composition and even insinuate that it, too, was
written by a man.[12] Unlike the prefaces of female contemporaries who
apologised for their lack of formal education, Burney may have taken
cues from the rhetorically confident and even coy prefaces of her male
predecessors.[13] She not only avoided the topic of women writers but
also exhibited her learning and taste in the paratexts. Besides listing
the most widely respected male novelists of the century and nodding
to the two dominant Reviews, Burney alluded to William Shakespeare,
Alexander Pope, James Fordyce and John Sheffield, displaying her
knowledge of drama, poetry and conduct literature. The prefatory
material projects an image of the writer as a perfect young gentleman.

## Critical and commercial success

*Evelina*'s reviewers agreed with Burney's self-classification.[14] Between
February and September of 1778, Burney's first novel earned high
praise in the four reviews it received. William Kenrick's brief blurb
in the *London Review* situates *Evelina* far above the bar for its genre,
observing that 'there is much more merit, as well respecting stile,
character and incident, than is usually to be met with among our
modern novels'.[15] Quoting from Burney's preface, the *Gentleman's
Magazine* also salutes the novel's style, design and morals.[16] The
*Monthly Review* praised its 'variety of natural incidents' and 'comic'
flair, locating *Evelina* as outstanding in its genre.[17] In September of

1778, the *Critical Review* echoes this opinion and seems to answer Burney's preface by granting *Evelina* admittance into the tradition of the distinguished novelist Samuel Richardson.

> This performance deserves no common praise, whether we consider it in a moral or a literary light. It would have disgraced neither the head nor the heart of Richardson. – The father of a family … will recommend it to his daughters; they will weep and (what is not so commonly the effect of novels) will laugh, and grow wiser, as they read; the experienced mother will derive pleasure and happiness from being present at its reading; even the sons of the family will forego the diversions of the town or the field to pursue the entertainment of Evelina's acquaintance, who will imperceptibly lead them, as well as their sisters, to improvement and to virtue.[18]

The *Critical* reviewer figures every member of the family as a potential reader of this novel and installs it at the centre of the private sphere. The commendations for *Evelina* circumscribe the ideal novel of the period: it should not only instruct and amuse but also assemble the family.

In the late eighteenth century, rapid expansion of reading among people of different classes, ages and geographic locations fuelled demand for reading material as well as concerns about the suitability of such material. Of particular concern was the effect of novel reading on the minds of impressionable young ladies. As texts were often read aloud in the family home and heard by everyone, they had to be judged ethically and aesthetically sound to be purchased or borrowed.[19] The Reviews in this period offered plot summaries and made recommendations as to the moral fitness of these plots, and books deemed unsuitable for ladies were at a disadvantage commercially. All the novelists listed in Burney's preface could be safely recommended to women or read collectively as a family. Her novel, in turn, is judged by the reviews as suitable reading for all. Despite the critical attention directed at women's consumption of novels, it is important to remember that fiction was enjoyed by readers of both genders. *Evelina* meets the criteria of a respectable novel but also provides 'entertainment' and humour. The critical acclaim for *Evelina* rests, in large part, on its fulfilment of the Horatian ideal, the marriage of instruction and amusement.

Critically and commercially, *Evelina* was an instant success. Like all of Burney's novels, *Evelina* was enjoyed by readers of all ages and both genders, and some of its most famous readers included Edward Gibbon, Sir Joshua Reynolds, Horace Walpole, Mary Delany and the Duchess of Portland.[20] Despite a consistent overall increase in the number of novels published in the last three decades of the century, there was a slump in new novel production from 1775 to 1783.[21] In 1778, this downturn hit its lowest point, with only sixteen new novels issued in the entire year. These figures help to contextualise the enthusiasm with which *Evelina* was greeted in the reviews and in the market. The novel quickly passed through its first three editions, with print runs estimated at 500, 500 and 1,000, respectively, and it was soon available for one penny per volume in the circulating libraries.[22] *Evelina* went through twenty further editions by the end of the century.[23] It was translated into German, Dutch and French and was reprinted in Dublin and London as well as New York AND Philadelphia. The comprehensive historical bibliography of fiction assembled by Antonia Forster and James Raven also points to a 'flock of imitators of Frances Burney' in the wake of *Evelina* and to the practice of 'desperate and audacious' booksellers who fraudulently marketed new titles by proclaiming them to be 'by the authoress of Evelina'.[24]

Although modern scholars give different accounts of *Evelina*'s publishing history, the novel seems to have remained in print for the entirety of the Romantic and Victorian periods.[25] It was reprinted during every decade of the nineteenth century, and after going out of statutory copyright in 1810, it was frequently issued in cheap, condensed or illustrated form. The collected sets of 'classic' reprints that became popular in the nineteenth century also featured *Evelina* (and *Cecilia* as well).[26] For example, the British Novelists series, issued in 1810 and again in 1820, included *Evelina* as one of its twenty-eight titles. Whittingham's Pocket Novelists Series of 1822–23 not only included *Evelina* but also placed it as the first and second volumes in the set, indicating the novel's enduring commercial appeal. When George Bell and sons printed the Bohn's Novelists' Library Series in the 1880s, *Evelina* again featured on the list. These collections of

her indignation and anger and points to an established writer who recognises the value of her 'work'. She notes that 'work of such length and intrinsic sterling worth' should have earned better treatment in the reviews.[94] Burney's language here links the moral or 'intrinsic' worth of the novel, its critical fate and its financial yield. Ethical, artistic and economic values align in Burney's estimation of herself as a writer of merit.

The moral 'worth' of *Camilla*, however, was not lost on the reviewers. The *British Critic* identifies its 'excellent moral', the *Critical* its 'entertainment' and 'instruction' and the *Monthly* its usefulness 'as a guide for the conduct of young females'.[95] On a second perusal of the *Monthly* review, Burney herself takes comfort: 'The recommendation, at the conclusion of the book as a warning guide to youth, would recompense me, upon the least reflection, for whatever strictures might precede it.'[96] The *Monthly Mirror* summarises the general critical consensus: 'There is one beauty in the novel, however, which should recommend us to all its defects; it inculcates many valuable lessons, and the moral is perfectly unexceptionable.'[97] Richard Polwhele's *The Unsex'd Females: A Poem* (1798), published only two years later, confirmed Burney's status as a reputable author who could 'mix with sparkling humour chaste / Delicious feelings and the purest taste'.[98] Unlike revolutionary sympathisers like Wollstonecraft, whose radicalism and licentiousness Polwhele condemns (and conflates), Burney's 'moral precepts' secured her a place beside renowned bluestockings like Elizabeth Montagu, Elizabeth Carter and Hester Chapone.[99] *Camilla*'s perceived moral upshot ultimately trumped all other criticism levelled at the text, procuring for it a stamp of respectability. Although Burney's third novel was not reviewed as positively as its predecessors, the *Camilla* criticism, as well as Burney's private response to it, confirms that Burney continued to hold a reputation as a writer of distinction.

Burney's *Diary* also assesses the limited function of the Reviews in the face of expanding reading constituencies that increasingly fuelled the taste, demand and sale of novels:

> The Reviewers, as they have not made, will not, I trust, mar me. *Evelina* made its way all by itself, it was well spoken of, indeed, in all

the Reviews, compared with general novels, but it was undistinguished by any quotation, and only put in the Monthly Catalogue, and only allowed a short single paragraph. It was circulated only by the general public, till it reached, through that unbiased medium, Dr. Johnson and Mr. Burke, thence it wanted no patron. Works of this kind are judged by the many.[100]

Here Burney identifies the ascendancy of a mass market, middle-class readership that was coming into its own at the end of the eighteenth century. As traditional hierarchies of patronage gave way to softer forms such as the subscription list or the free market, the critics could be sidestepped. Word of mouth, print advertising and circulating libraries could enable a novel to skirt the reviewers, despite their best efforts to govern the genre.[101] The circulation of *Camilla* and its concomitant returns attest to Burney's enduring status as a writer of popularity and merit and her adeptness in evaluating and negotiating the literary marketplace.

## Ad feminam attacks

Nearly two decades later, the publishing arrangements, pricing and print run of Burney's final novel, *The Wanderer* (1814), suggest her ongoing fame and respect and her continued involvement in the management of her career. Refusing a substantial £2,000 lump sum offer for the sale of copyright, Burney bargained for an arrangement that she believed would be more lucrative.[102] She accepted a contract with Longman, Hurst, Rees, Orme and Brown that promised £1,500 for a first edition of 3,000 copies and another £1,500 for five subsequent editions.[103] Though very large for the period, the first print run sold out three days before publication, despite its price of 42 shillings. At what Burney herself calls a 'rapacious price', *The Wanderer* was the most expensive novel of the year, a mark of its predicted demand and the popularity of its author.[104] However, after a promising start, sales of the second edition slowed within a few months, and Longman eventually wasted the remainder.[105] Burney blamed the booksellers for outpricing readers and took comfort in the sale of over 3,500 copies.

The reviewers mostly panned the novel, though the most eminent critics – those of the quarterlies – spent far more time arraigning the author herself. This treatment can be explained, in part, by changes in the landscape of print culture in Britain. Claiming a combined readership of over 100,000, the *Edinburgh Review* and the *Quarterly Review* had clinched their positions atop the periodical press hierarchy.[106] These mandarin Reviews, along with a range of other literary magazines, negotiated the proliferation of printed material, representing themselves as mediators between authors and readers.[107] In the first half of the nineteenth century, periodicals became the dominant publishing format, which in turn helped the periodical essay to rise in status and influence.[108]

Still, Burney's harsh treatment in the press may also derive from her unique positioning as one of a handful of surviving literary celebrities of the previous generation. In 1814, at sixty-two, Burney had outlived many friends and family members, and the protection and patronage of the 'immense men' mentioned in 1796 were long gone. She represented a woman writer from an earlier era and may have offered an inviting – and vulnerable – target for rising periodical critics wishing to make a name for themselves or their journals in the early nineteenth century. Two of these critics, William Hazlitt and John Wilson Croker, writing for the *Edinburgh* and *Quarterly* Reviews, respectively, swerved towards personal criticism in their commentaries on *The Wanderer*, indicting Burney on grounds of her gender and age. It is not my intention to suggest that even reviewers as knowledgeable or influential as Hazlitt and Croker can be taken singlehandedly to characterise Burney's reception at this time. However, their criticism of Burney may indicate some of the discursive frameworks in which she was read.[109] In this sense, the reviews signal a new phase in Burney's reputation. While personal attacks in the quarterlies began to challenge, or reflect challenges to, her literary status, continuous reprints (of *Evelina* and *Cecilia*), popular demand, and large readerships perhaps reinforced it.

In February of 1815, William Hazlitt's eighteen-page article for the *Edinburgh Review* directly linked the shortcomings of *The Wanderer* with the gender of its author. Hazlitt disliked the novel's style and criticised its superficiality, sentimentality and implausibility. In comparison to *Evelina*, *The Wanderer* is 'teazing and tedious' and is predicated on an 'artifice' of always deferring the conclusion due to an imagined queue of 'female difficulties'.[110] Hazlitt, in a tone of respectful condescension, concludes:

> [W]e perceive no decay of talent, but a perversion of it. There is the same admirable spirit in the dialogues … as in her former novels. But these do not fill a hundred pages of the work; and there is nothing else good in it. In the story, which here occupies the attention of the reader almost exclusively, Madame D'Arblay never excelled.[111]

Hazlitt faults Burney for being 'a mere common observer of manners, – and also a very woman' for she writes 'with a consciousness of her sex'.[112] Hazlitt groups Burney with other women writers like Elizabeth Inchbald, Ann Radcliffe and Maria Edgeworth, all of whom he judges to be second-rate.

Hazlitt does not so much attack Burney as elucidate why she and her sister authors are inferior to their male counterparts.

> Women in general, have a quicker perception of any oddity or singularity of character than men, and are more alive to every absurdity which arises from a violation of the rules of society, or a deviation from established custom. … The surface of their minds, like that of their bodies, seems of a finer texture than ours; more soft, and susceptible of immediate impression. They have less muscular power, – less power of continued voluntary attention, of reason – passion and imagination: But they are more easily impressed with whatever appeals to their senses or habitual prejudices.[113]

Hazlitt demarcates difference along biological lines. He addresses an assumed male reader, inviting him to collude in the affirmation of women's weaknesses as distinct from 'ours'.

Hazlitt's recourse to this gendered critique needs to be read in the context of his larger historiographical enterprise. His allegation that Burney writes as 'a very woman' is not simply a sign of male self-absorption or a veiled rejoinder to the novel's feminist subtext, as some critics have suggested.[114] The *Edinburgh* article, though presented as a review of *The Wanderer*, actually describes a history of the English novel. As if to counter Burney's own self-positioning in the preface

to the Streatham circle and the success of her next two novels. This deft manoeuvre supplied the explanation and the exoneration for Burney's literary career, which was intertwined with her father's and thus sanctioned by the patriarch himself.[157] Dr Burney had chosen his daughter Frances as his amanuensis, social attendant, editor and confidante, thereby making her the rightful heir of this family mantle. Burney therefore maintained her reputation for propriety and filial piety. Though reviewers quibbled about her 'humility', most agreed with the *Monthly* reviewer's appraisal of her enduring 'filial attachment'.[158]

The reviewers tended to write about the *Memoirs* mildly and courteously, if not favourably. They pointed out defects in length, tone and style but often heralded Burney as a model of daughterly comport. However, private responses were more severe. Baroness Frances Bunsen found it all 'self-idolatry' and 'undiscriminating appetite' for 'applause', while Henry Crabb Robinson thought it simply 'ill-written'.[159] Maria Edgeworth, who had relished Burney's fiction, deplored the 'awkwardness' and 'affectation' of the *Memoirs*, pronouncing it 'tiresome and ridiculous'.[160] The book fell short of expectations, sold poorly and failed to move past a first edition.

However, only the *Quarterly* reviewer John Wilson Croker levelled any serious or sustained criticism at the *Memoirs*. For Croker, Burney had not only skewed the portrayal of her father but had contrived to mask her true intention of writing her own life story. He objects:

> [I]t is because Madame d'Arblay, with consummate art – or a confusion of ideas which has had the same effect as consummate art, – conceals from her reader, and perhaps from herself, that it is her *own Memoirs*, and *not* those of her father that she has been writing; and we confess that we have a strong suspicion, that it was *because* her father's auto-biography did not fulfil *this* object, that *it* has been suppressed – and this joint-stock history (in which, as in other joint-stock concerns, the managing partner has the larger share) has been substituted for it.[161]

The methodology of Croker's attack has not changed in the eighteen years since he reviewed *The Wanderer* in 1814. He again launches into underhand personal assault, with gender and age as Burney's primary offences. Either her vanity as a woman has induced wholesale deception, or the disorientation of her old age has initiated a pitiable strain of elderly bewilderment. Here and elsewhere in the twenty-eight-page article, he insinuates that her 'personal vanity' and 'literary vanity' drive her to suppress dates (in order to make herself seem younger when she wrote *Evelina*) and to substitute the verbatim accounts of her father for her own 'feeble, anile, incoherent' prose. [162] Using adjectives that allude to her old age, Croker suggests the 'habit of *novel-writing* has led her to colour and, as she may suppose, embellish her anecdotes with sonorous epithets and factitious details, which, however, we venture to assure her, not only blunt their effect, but discredit their authority'. [163] Ironically, it seems that all of his imputations are cast to just this purpose: to discredit *her* authority.

Croker also construes Burney as a greedy profiteer and, by extension, her (auto)biography a chronicle of the family trade. Borrowing from the lexicon of the marketplace, he charges her, the 'managing partner' in this business, with stealing her father's rightful share of the profits, a fair apportionment of copy in the biography, their 'joint-stock history'. [164] This extended imagery betrays hostility towards the upward class mobility of the Burneys. Burney designates the *Memoirs* as tracking

> the progress of a nearly abandoned Child, from a small village of Shropshire, to a Man allowed throughout Europe to have risen to the head of his profession; and thence, setting his profession aside, to have been elevated to an intellectual rank in society, as a Man of Letters. [165]

Perhaps this trajectory piqued Croker's conservatism. As Catherine Gallagher has noted:

> The family was self-consciously engaged in the project of creating [their name]. They had no rent roles, no pedigrees, no real or invented histories of military or public service; they had only talent and knowledge, copyrights and such 'symbolic capital' as Dr. Burney's degree from Oxford and (much later) Frances's place at court. ... The writings of the Burneys were the business of their lives. [166]

Croker attempts not only to expose the Burneys' precarious class footing, but also to demonstrate the insolvency of even this 'symbolic capital'.

However, even Croker was forced to make concessions to some of Frances Burney's praiseworthy characteristics. He makes a show of his esteem for her, purporting to feel 'great reluctance to give gratuitous pain to a person so respectable as Madame d'Arblay'.[167] He also reiterates in his conclusion that his

> strictures have been confined to Madame D'Arblay's errors in point of style and arrangement; – we have none other to reproach her with; – her book evinces the best feelings – the best principles – she is amiable and respectful – we may smile at her foibles, but we willingly admit that … she will go down to posterity as an exemplary woman in her private life.[168]

Such protestations of reverence illuminate the wider context of Burney's reputation even if they are difficult to accept at face value. In Croker's private correspondence with *Quarterly Review* editor John Gibson Lockhart, he writes that his review of the *Memoirs* 'amuses me & will, I think, the readers without any brutality against the poor old body'.[169] Flippantly dismissing Burney, he affects a pose of superiority. Croker appears to regard her as an insignificant source of diversion rather than a target for serious comment. This view does not square with the saccharine declarations of esteem that bookend his *Quarterly* review.

Croker's show of respect suggests that he begrudgingly tempered his criticism in the *Quarterly Review* on account of Burney's status. In 1834, Allan Cunningham's *Biographical and Critical History of British Literature of the Last Fifty Years* had included a chapter on 'Madame D'Arblay' that celebrated her talent for characterisation.[170] Her first two novels remained in print and continued to claim sizeable readerships. Perhaps Croker calculated that with Burney's respected public standing and the lingering regard for her fiction, she could not be snubbed outright.

Yet the tone of Croker's letter contradicts that of his review in another way. If Burney had become a mere figure of ridicule, Croker would not have needed twenty-eight pages to write off her biography. The length and manifest 'brutality' of his review undermine the claims he makes to Lockhart. Debasing Burney's status, even in his private correspondence, may have served somehow to bolster his own. He was no gentlemanly reviewer; his famous brand of vitriol had raged for decades. Nonetheless, he unrelentingly impugned Burney, by then in her eighties, on grounds of gender, age and even class, and on a range of charges – often contradictory – including dishonesty, egotism, immodesty and senility. Scholars have wondered if Croker bore a personal grudge against Burney or was simply a misogynist and ageist.[171] The severity of his review may also indicate hostilities to women's life writing and the challenges of self-representation in a masculine tradition of (auto)biography.[172] In the 1830s, the problematic genre of life writing was, in the words of Eugene Stelzig, 'still up for interpretive grabs', and conservative men of letters like Croker and Lockhart, his editor, may have tried to define and police it in the *Quarterly*.

Burney was incensed by Croker's review, and she and her family considered the best way to respond to it. Two of Burney's nieces, Charlotte Barrett and Fanny Raper, drafted a reply to Croker's review, which Burney referred to wryly as 'the Retort sarcastic of my own Nieces'.[173] However, Burney and her nieces decided against a public reply, partly on the basis of advice from the eminent politician, author and family friend Thomas Babington Macaulay. He assured Barrett in 1839 that 'the article in the Quarterly Review has long been utterly forgotten while Evelina and Camilla are just as much read as ever'.[174] Though he later changed his mind and defended Burney publicly (in the *Edinburgh Review*), at this point he thought 'her place in the public estimate fixed not by what other people may write about her but by what she has written herself'.[175] This exchange speaks to nineteenth-century debates about how a writer's reputation is formed and maintained and Burney's ongoing participation in them. Her discussion of Croker's essay suggests that her awareness of her public standing and involvement in shaping it continued until the end of her life.

Scholars have traditionally regarded the *Memoirs* as a failure and have attempted to account for its lack of success by placing the text in its psychobiographical context, imagining Burney's debilitating internal conflict in accepting her father's view of his family, or the guilt and ambivalence she felt towards him.[176] Others have seen the text in more sentimental terms as a loving farewell to a parent.[177] However, Burney's *Memoirs* can also be viewed as a valuable final step in a learning process about authorship and the management of reception that dates back to the author's youth. While inner turmoil may have plagued her, an overemphasis on her psychological experience distracts from her more practical considerations. Burney would not be remembered as a biographer, but nor would her reputation as a respectable woman writer suffer any damage. Even though the *Memoirs* was unsuccessful critically and commercially, it cannot be considered a complete failure. Burney had learned important lessons about celebrity status and life writing. Demand for biographical material would endure; one's children and grandchildren would face pressure to comply. At the same time, publishing private lives could invite allegations of vanity and self-promotion, or worse; one's descendants would also have to contend with these charges. Frances Burney realised that such exigencies would persist long after her death. Her father had not prepared for them, but she did.

## Diaries, respectability and gender

In the final years of her life, Burney prepared her personal records for posthumous publication. She blacked out indiscreet passages, rewrote others and cut huge sections completely.[178] She also left explicit instructions granting her niece, Charlotte Barrett, sole custody over her manuscripts, and giving Barrett leave to abridge but not to add material. These steps suggest that she anticipated the publication of her diaries, appreciated the curiosity they would arouse and guarded her legacy accordingly. Burney had always maintained a sense of her audience. Her early confessions to Nobody soon became a letter-diary intended for her sister Susan but circulated to Crisp as well as other family friends. The semi-private status of this document necessitated a level of self-censorship, and, as Patricia Meyer Spacks argues, Burney employed deft 'linguistic maneuvering … to keep her privacy intact'.[179] When the first of the seven-volume *Diary and Letters of Madame D'Arblay* reached its expectant audience in 1842, it included these letter journals interspersed with Burney's correspondence and other

personal entries. The subsequent volumes followed suit, coming out
at intervals between 1842 and 1846. The printed *Diary* had undergone
several rounds of revisions, including Burney's own self-censorship in
writing a reader-oriented letter-journal, her editing of the papers in
the last decades of her life, Barrett's two-year re-editing of the oeuvre
before its publication in 1842 and the amendments required by Henry
Colburn, the publisher.[180]

Nevertheless, Burney family anxiety abounded. Charlotte Barrett
was herself worried about the reception of the *Diary*, as was another
of Burney's nieces, her brother James's daughter Sarah Payne, who
later told her friend Henry Crabb Robinson that she was 'sensitive'
about the publication and the 'self-absorption' it showed in her
aunt.[181] Even Sarah Harriet Burney, Frances Burney's half-sister,
thought Barrett should have excised more of the diarist's self-
regarding recollections.[182] The *Diary and Letters of Madame D'Arblay*
made public a high-profile woman's personal life. Diary *keeping*
dated back to the sixteenth century at least and evolved from long-
standing traditions of household or business accounts, spiritual
diaries, family chronicles and travel records.[183] By the turn of the
nineteenth century, the diary began to take on its modern form as an
internal conversation that could, as Isaac D'Israeli described in 1793,
'render to a man an account of himself to himself'.[184] The masculine
pronoun is significant here. Maintaining a diary, with its emphasis on
privacy, introspection and self-discovery, became more problematic
when practised by women, for whom privacy was associated with
concealment.[185] As a teenager, Burney was herself warned that 'it is
the most dangerous employment young persons can have', for 'in
journals, thoughts, actions, looks, conversations – *all* go down'.[186]
However, by the nineteenth century, diary writing was often accepted
for women as a practice validated by religious precedent and made
safe by its domestic, diurnal quality.[187] Diary *publishing*, on the other
hand, only began in the nineteenth century and, before Burney, had
been limited exclusively to men. The genre came into vogue with
the publication of John Evelyn's diary in 1818 and Samuel Pepys's
in 1825.[188] As Felicity Nussbaum has argued, a woman's role in the
domestic sphere rendered self-publication a form of trespassing onto

the 'masculine domain' of producing a public textual self.[189] Burney's was the first published diary written by a woman, and her family recognised the risks.

However, the publication of diaries, or any autobiographical material for that matter, was risky not solely for women but for men as well. John Lockhart complained in 1827 of 'the mania for this garbage of Confessions, and Recollections, and Reminiscences' as 'a vile Symptom' of the 'prurient' tastes of the reading public.[190] Lockhart holds 'this garbage' in contempt for its impurity, both in its generic hybridity (it is at once confessional, historical and sentimental) and its dubious morality. This trashy, disposable material lacks the literary qualities that confer artistic integrity. In addition, Lockhart's oblique reference to Jean-Jacques Rousseau's *Confessions* (1782) reminds us that the iniquity of the genre derives not only from its association with the scandalous memoirs written by eighteenth-century women like Laetitia Pilkington, Charlotte Charke, or Constantia Phillips but also from the illicit revelations of that most notorious of literary men.[191] In its appeal to base curiosity and voyeuristic impulses, such autobiographical writing makes privacy available for public consumption, circulating it for a price. James Treadwell maintains that 'autobiographies are texts that do not know how to behave in public', and some of the most prevalent objections to them related to violations of social decorum, such as vanity and its linguistic counterpart, egotism.[192] Although such charges may have been compounded when applied to women, they were levelled at male and female practitioners alike. Treadwell argues that the most important pre-requisite for self-narration was neither gender nor class but eminence. The circulation of self-writing could be permissible if the subject occupied an elevated social standing and therefore exercised a legitimate claim on our attention. The links between generic instability, moral dubiety and mass-market consumption should not be underestimated. Diaries, and the wider species of autobiography of which they formed a part, were gaining popularity in the early decades of the nineteenth century but were not yet fully accepted as morally sound or artistically respected. Burney's *Diary and Letters* helped to elevate this genre to the status of literary and moral respectability.

It is true, however, that reviewers criticised Burney for her display of vanity and egotism. The conservative *Blackwood's Edinburgh Magazine* calls her 'profoundly, profusely, and perpetually self-admiring' and deems the text not so much a 'journal' as 'a register of all the panegyrics uttered by all the *proneurs* of her day – of all the gossip that was ever lavished on a novelist and her novel'.[193] She also seemed hypocritical, protesting her bashfulness but then meticulously recording every compliment. Figured as having the appetite and organ capacity of a man, Burney appears in the typically witty prose of *Blackwood's* as 'all swallow and digestion' for 'praise … is gulped down with the most palpable rapture'.[194] Her own great-niece, Fanny Anne Burney, echoed the sentiments and language of this extended metaphor. She was so aghast at her great-aunt's penchant for 'the most insufferable flattery' and her ability to 'swallow apparently large lumps of the poisonous drug, without … any subsequent symptoms of mental indigestion' that she gave up her own diary altogether that very year.[195] Though these comments construe Burney's *Diary and Letters* as unladylike, they nevertheless resemble the language of social offence Treadwell has observed in criticism of male self-writers as well.

Still, the *faux pas* of vanity and self-admiration were mitigated by the contents of the diary, which fulfilled the age-old Horatian criteria of being entertaining and instructive. The anecdotes and gossip about the literary and royal circles of Burney's day fascinated Victorian readers. For the *Athenaeum*, this memoir, though 'pompously announced' and self-obsessed, delivered on entertainment, divulging new tales of such well-known figures as Dr Samuel Johnson, Hester Thrale, Elizabeth Montagu, Sir Joshua Reynolds, Richard Brinsley Sheridan and Edmund Burke, not to mention the court of King George III.[196] The volumes give a fresh account of the 'wits who animated society, the social enjoyments which diversified court life sixty years ago'.[197] Predictably, the self-interested *New Monthly* ascribes to the *Diary and Letters* 'high literary, historical and social value' on par in 'value and curiosity to that which has hitherto borne the palm from all others in this class of writing (we mean of course Boswell's Johnson)'.[198] In fact, many of the reviewers agreed that Burney's portraits of the literati improved on those that came before. *Tait's Edinburgh Magazine* likewise relishes the *Diary and Letters* as a more accurate version of Mrs Thrale than Boswell's.[199] Deeming it both enjoyable and informative, the *Eclectic Review* finds 'the great interest of the diary and correspondence' in

> the light which they throw on the fashionable and literary circles of the day, and more especially in the opportunities they furnish of renewing intercourse with some old friends, by whose wit, learning, and wisdom, we have frequently been charmed and benefited.[200]

Like Boswell, to whom she was repeatedly compared, Burney offered amusing, authentic and even edifying portraits of eighteenth-century society, and they perhaps served as a reassuring foil to their own modern age.

Burney's *Diary and Letters*, however, was not easy to categorise generically. Frequent references to Boswell indicate that Burney was often seen as a memoirist or a collective biographer more than a diarist in the vein of John Evelyn or Samuel Pepys.[201] One reviewer compared her to Horace Walpole, another writer of memoirs and fiction. Other reviewers drew parallels with novelists like Maria Edgeworth and Jane Austen or Sir Walter Scott and Edward Bulwer-Lytton. Although reviewers usually called the *Diary and Letters* simply a diary or journal, they also referred to it as a play with '*dramatis personae*', as 'table-talk', as having the 'graphic power' of 'portraits', as a technology of 'photographing' and as a fictional narrative.[202] Indeed, the most frequent of all comparisons was not to Boswell's *Life of Johnson* but to her own *Evelina* and *Cecilia*.

Despite its generic indeterminacy, then, the *Diary and Letters* appeared markedly literary. Funny, moving, well-written and carefully edited, with a virtuous main character and clear narrative arc, the unmistakeably literary qualities of the *Diary and Letters* gave it artistic respectability and an internal coherence that helped to compensate for its unorthodox crossing of genres. Reviewers commented frequently on both the humour and pathos of the diary and on Burney's facility for observing and recording conversations. Some reviewers also marked her insightful study of human character. The *Tait's Edinburgh* admires the 'subtle and delicate analysis of motives of action' and the *Gentleman's Magazine* a 'maturity of judgement, quick apprehension in discovering the varieties of human character, and a lively imagination in pourtraying them'.[203] In these respects, Burney's journal resembled fiction, as the diary brought to life a well-defined and likeable protagonist. Judy Simons has described the *Diary and Letters* as 'a series of perilous episodes, with Burney the heroine of an adventure story who survives the hazards of victimisation through her hold on the solid fact of her own identity'.[204] The *Gentleman's Magazine* acknowledges the development of this 'identity', noting that the 'leading object of the Diary, however, was not only to perpetuate the pictures of society which she drew at the time, but to make it a record of her own thoughts and feelings'.[205] In an affectionately mocking tone, the *Tait's Edinburgh* likewise notes the detailed account of 'all that Miss Burney hoped, feared, and believed, about her absorbing book' in her 'honeymoon of authorship'.[206] This reviewer underscores that the 'adventure' of Burney's diary is not only personal but also professional.

Betty A. Schellenberg has argued for the significance of Burney's self-fashioning in the emergent print culture of the 1770s and 1780s as

> a reflection of, and an intervention in, late eighteenth-century shifts in the profession of letters and in the position of women writers within this profession ... Burney did not simply insert herself into a mold labelled 'female author' or 'woman novelist' which by definition forced her to transgress a gendered private-public divide. Rather, her authorial self-construction was both particularly hers and determined by her historical position, both reactive to current conditions and influential in determining subsequent conditions of authorship for female novelists.[207]

Five decades later, Burney's diary publicised this model of authorship without compromising her respectability as a woman. As we have seen, the professional narrative was embedded in a social history that not only facilitated but also seemed to sanction it. In the majority of reviews, the *Diary and Letters* received no greater criticism than cursory charges of vanity and egotism and the occasional gibe at its length. More often than not, though, Burney was eulogised as a model of feminine virtue and talent, a combination held up by editors as ideal in women's domestic memoirs.[208] The *Gentleman's Magazine* celebrated the 'splendour of her talents' along with the 'propriety of her conduct' and the New Monthly puffed her 'singleness of mind and principle' and 'feminine softness and sweetness of disposition'. Burney appeared part of a past generation often regarded as quaint or curiously outmoded. Nevertheless, in her crossing of social chronicle, personal memoir and professional history, Burney offered a new species of 'diary': entertaining and informative, morally sound and noticeably literary. The Diary and Letters helped to make autobiographical writing respectable and set an important precedent for women's contribution to the genre. Burney's diary not only shaped her own literary reputation but also that of the genre itself.

## Reputation and repertoire

Doody has suggested that the publication of Burney's journal and correspondence gradually converted her from a novelist into a diarist, and that her literary reputation would have fared better had the Diary remained unpublished.[209] However, this assessment of the Diary and Letters, and its assumption of a literary hierarchy in which life writing ranks below fiction, needs to be reconsidered. Certainly, there is evidence that by the turn of the century, some readers agree with the Saturday reviewer that Burney has 'secured a niche in the Temple of Fame' but it 'is this Diary, and not "Evelina", or "Cecilia" (still less "Camilla"), that has made Burney a classic'.[210] The Athenaeum affirms that 'her apotheosis, though secure, has been accomplished at the cost of a moiety, at least, of her literary capital', with the implication that this 'cost' resides with her novels.[211] Another Saturday reviewer posits:

> Miss Burney gives us the natural men and women with the art – but also with the minimum of art – necessary to make them acceptable. And it is for this very reason that her Diaries ... are so much better than all but the very best part of her novels.[212]

In addition, readers and reviewers also began to conflate Burney's life and her novel. William Makepeace Thackeray's Morning Chronicle review of the sixth volume of the diary provides a colourful example of this tendency:

The d'Arblay portrait is a very fine one. A noble gentleman, and a
Liberal, holding high rank in France, he quits the country when the
Constitutional King is but a puppet in the hands of the mob. Here he
and Fanny Burney give each other lessons in their native language,
and correct each others exercises. What follows from this mutual
instruction may be imagined: that indomitable virgin Fanny Burney is
conquered in a very few lessons – and Lord Orville carries off Cecilia
to love and a cottage in the country, where she writes novels and has
a little baby.[213]

Thackeray's characteristically affectionate, entertaining style converts
Burney's life into a fairy tale wherein the hero tames the prudish
bluestocking and delivers her into happy domesticity. Burney is
conflated with one of her heroines, obscuring the line between fiction
and history and encouraging readers to enjoy Burney's life just as they
do her novels. The haphazard references to the novels (Lord Orville
is the romantic interest of *Evelina*, not *Cecilia*) contain a playful
irreverence. Thackeray transposes writer and protagonist in a gambit
to liven up his review. However, this nonchalant swap eclipses other
parts of Burney's life: her diligence and success as a writer, her travels,
her position at court. Thackeray encourages readers to envisage her as
another interesting heroine for dramatic abstraction but muddies her
agency as an author and her place in literary history.

There is also evidence that people began to read her novels as
thinly veiled autobiography. One reviewer appraised her novels as
'supplementary to her own records' for 'Fanny Burney is the heroine
of each. She is both Evelina and Cecilia, and Evelina and Cecilia
are Fanny Burney in a series of imaginary situations'.[214] Burney's
biographer, Austin Dobson, also saw *Evelina* as an autobiographical
representation of Burney's 'younger self'.[215] These reductive blend-
ings of the life and the work facilitated distortions and elisions in the
readings of both. This practice was not unique to readers of Burney,
and nineteenth-century reviewers often assumed that women were
only able to write about what they had experienced personally.[216]
However, though this kind of conflation encouraged speculation
about the connection between a writer's work and life, it also
increased interest in both.

In Burney's case, what emerges is a reciprocal process in which the publication of the *Diary* (and its four subsequent reprints) both fuelled and was fuelled by the enduring success of the fiction. Burney's literary reputation needs to be reconsidered in light of the complex dynamics of reception, publication and re-imagination that played out in the wake of the *Diary and Letters*. As mentioned earlier, both *Evelina* and *Cecilia* continued to be reprinted and purchased throughout the nineteenth century, even after the publication of the diary. Both novels were selected for various series of 'classics', where they often occupied prime positions. Moreover, there is nearly as much evidence in the Victorian reviews of enduring esteem for Burney's fiction as dismissal of it.[217] Though *Evelina* was in print throughout the nineteenth century, with new editions appearing in every decade, *Cecilia* was rereleased (in Britain) in clusters: a spate of reprints in the 1810s and 1820s, two more in the 1840s, a couple of Bohn's Novelists' Library editions in the 1880s and 1890s and another wave of reprints in the early twentieth century. The timing of these waves coincided, roughly, with the publication of the diary in the 1840s, its later editions and the release of related biographical material.

At the same time, the popularity of the *Diary and Letters* contributed to an explosion in Burneyana, including *Memoirs of Madame D'Arblay* (1844), Anne Raine Ellis's edited volumes of Burney's previously unreleased early journals, *The Early Diary of Fanny Burney* (1889), L. B. Selley's *Fanny Burney and Her Friends* (1890) and Burney's inclusion in the prestigious *English Men of Letters* (second) series with Austin Dobson's *Fanny Burney* (1903).[218] This biographical material, along with the reprints of her fiction (including Ellis's important scholarly editions of *Evelina* and *Cecilia* in the 1880s), provided ample opportunities for biographers, editors, reviewers and readers to reassess Burney. The regular reprinting of Macaulay's 1843 *Edinburgh* review of Burney's *Diary and Letters* as part of his collected *Essays* also contributed to ongoing reassessments of Burney, with reviewers debating whether Burney owed her reputation to him or to her own novels. These re-evaluations continued in the reviews, and although they remain too varied to suggest a critical consensus, their frequency and number attest to her continued relevance. As Tom Mole has argued, 'authors' reputations never simply endure ... either they are renewed or they are forgotten'.[219] In the early decades of the twentieth century, Burney's two most popular novels were in print, as was her own *Diary and Letters* and several other biographical works.[220] Her biographical and fictional works continued to be debated and reviewed in the periodical press. Scholarship on Burney was prevalent among eighteenth-centuryists. Though it is possible that these facts are in spite of, rather than because of, the *Diary*, it appears that Burney's afterlife involved a complex, reciprocal relationship between the reading of the novels and the life writing. On balance, the reception of Burney's fiction, diary and related biographical material, shown via publication and republication patterns, circulation, literary reviews, contemporary scholarship and anecdotal evidence, suggests that the *Diary and Letters* helped to promote her standing.

What seems even more certain is Burney's contribution to life writing. Burney's *Diary*, the first woman's to be published in Britain, proved a popular and a critical success, contributing to the literary and moral respectability of this genre and, at the same time, introducing a new subgenre in women's life writing: the journal as social, personal and professional history. Nineteenth-century readers of women's life writing actively looked for links between subjects' lives and works. Women, especially, craved knowledge of and intimacy with these life writers and were eager to uncover the person behind the fiction they enjoyed.[221] Many women readers also sought role models and examples of female writing lives compatible with their own.[222] In Burney's *Diary*, they found elements of both. Much women's life writing neglected the writing life in favour of the domestic; certain other works, though more rare, offered serious, professional accounts of women writers, but they seemed masculine models incompatible with the texture of most women's lives.[223] Burney's diary offered a middle ground, embedding her professional history within the record of family, personal and social life.

Burney's *Diary and Letters* influenced and inspired later memoirists such as Anne Thackeray, Julia Kavanagh and, most notably, Virginia Woolf, to whom I will turn to in my conclusion.[224] In her admiration of Burney's *Diary*, Woolf followed generations of readers before her, though perhaps for different reasons. Writing in her own diary in August of 1929, Woolf emphasised the genre's capacity to recover someone from across the centuries, making her feel 'as if some dead person were said to be living after all'.[225] In this respect, Woolf's response to Burney suggests the importance of the *Diary and Letters* not only to Burney's afterlife but also to life writing and literary history more generally. Woolf admires the *Diary* as an artistic achievement, for it brings to life its subject, absorbs the imagination and affections and rivals the best of fiction. An avid reader of diaries, letters and biographies, Woolf often celebrates texts that revive their subjects in the reader's mind. To enable this communion of selves, life writers have to invent textual forms as extraordinary as their subjects. In structure, storytelling and personal expression, the best life writing often comprises an 'experiment' of sorts, which can obtain popularity and respectability as in the case of Burney's diary or, as in the case of Godwin's *Memoirs*, invite controversy and scandal.[226]

## Notes

1 Catherine Gallagher, *Nobody's Story: The Vanishing Acts of Women in the Marketplace, 1670–1820* (Oxford: Clarendon Press, 1994), p. xviii; Claire Brock, *The Feminization of Fame, 1750–1830* (Basingstoke: Palgrave Macmillan, 2006), p. 110.

2 Julie A. Eckerle, 'Prefacing Texts, Authorizing Authors, and Constructing Selves: The Preface as Autobiographical Space', in *Genre and Women's Life Writing in Early Modern England*, ed. Michelle M. Dowd and Julie A. Eckerle (Aldershot: Ashgate, 2007), pp. 99–101.

3 Cynthia L. Nixon, '"Stop a Moment at this Preface": The Gendered Paratexts of Fielding, Barker, and Haywood', *Journal of Narrative Theory*, 22:2 (2002), p. 124.

4 Frances Burney, *Evelina*, ed. Edward A. Bloom (Oxford: Oxford University Press, 2002), p. 3.

5 Gina Campbell, 'How to Read Like a Gentleman: Burney's Instructions to Her Critics in *Evelina*', *ELH*, 57 (1990), p. 558.

6 Leslie M. Thompson and John R. Ahrens, 'Criticism of English Fiction 1780–1810: The Mysterious Powers of the Pleading Preface', *Yearbook of English Studies*, 1:1 (1971), p. 126. See also Gerard Genette, *Paratexts: Thresholds of Interpretation*, trans. Jane E. Lewin (Cambridge: Cambridge University Press, 1997), p. 293.

7 Thompson and Ahrens, 'Criticism of English Fiction', p. 127. Some male authors who published anonymously also employed a 'pleading preface'.

8 Burney, *Evelina*, p. 6.

9 In *The Fame Machine: Book Reviewing and Eighteenth-Century Literary Careers* (Stanford, CA: Stanford University Press, 1996), Frank Donoghue suggests that the *Critical Review* adopted military metaphors to bring it more in line with the *Monthly* (p. 29).

10 On the preface as a self-fashioning space, see Eckerle, 'Prefacing Texts', and Nixon, '"Stop a Moment at this Preface"'.

11 Burney, *Evelina*, p. 9.

12 For other considerations of Burney's exclusion of women writers, see Donoghue, *The Fame Machine*, p. 170; Jennie Batchelor, '"[T]o Strike a Little Out of a Road Already so much Beaten": Gender, Genre, and the Mid-Century Novel', in *The History of British Women's Writing, 1750–1830*, ed. Jacqueline Labbe (Basingstoke: Palgrave Macmillan, 2010), p. 84; Betty A. Schellenberg, *The Professionalization of Women Writers in Eighteenth-Century Britain* (Cambridge: Cambridge University Press, 2005), p. 160.

13 Genette, *Paratexts*, p. 233.

14 Here I differ from Donoghue, who concludes that her 'ingenious dedication simply did not have its desired effect' (*The Fame Machine*, p. 173).

15 [William Kenrick], 'Evelina', *London Review*, 7 (February 1778), p. 151.

16 '89. Evelina', *Gentleman's Magazine*, 48 (September 1778), p. 425.

17 [William Enfield], 'Art. 49. Evelina', *Monthly Review*, 58 (April 1778), p. 316.

18 'Evelina', *Critical Review*, 46 (September 1778), pp. 202–3.

19 William St Clair, *The Reading Nation in the Romantic Period* (Cambridge: Cambridge University Press, 2004), p. 189; pp. 282–4; p. 394.

20 Catherine M. Parisian, *Frances Burney's Cecilia: A Publishing History* (Aldershot: Ashgate, 2012), p. 25. According to Burney's *Diary*, most of her family and friends, including those she met at the Streatham abode of the Thrales, also read it.

21 James Raven, 'Historical Introduction: The Novel Comes of Age', in *The English Novel 1770–1829: A Bibliographical Survey of Prose Fiction Published in the British Isles*, ed. Peter Garside, James Raven and Rainer Schöwerling, 2 vols (Oxford: Oxford University Press, 2000), I, pp. 26–7.

22 Frances Burney, *Diary and Letters of Madame D'Arblay, 1778–1840*, ed. Charlotte Barrett, rev. Austin Dobson, 7 vols (London: Macmillan, 1904), I, pp. 23–4.

23 Scholars give different figures. I follow Garside, Raven and Schöwerling, who list twenty-three editions published in London and Dublin before 1800 (*The English Novel*, p. 269) though Vivien Jones and Edward A. Bloom cite only eleven British editions in the same period ('Note on the Text', in *Evelina*, p. xxxv). Even Vivien Jones's smaller count of eleven editions represents a huge figure for the period.

24 Raven, 'Historical Introduction', p. 34; p. 102.

25 Again, scholars' figures differ slightly. See Garside, Raven and Schöwerling, *The English Novel*, p. 269; Joseph A. Grau, *Fanny Burney: An Annotated Bibliography* (London: Garland, 1981), pp. 3–7; Jones and Bloom, 'Note on the Text', pp. xxxv–xxxvi; St Clair, *The Reading Nation*, p. 584.

26 On these collections of reprinted novels, see Parisian, *Frances Burney's Cecilia*.

27 Jennie Batchelor, *Women's Work: Labour, Gender, Authorship, 1750–1830* (Manchester: Manchester University Press, 2010), p. 2. See also Michelle Levy, 'Women and Print Culture, 1750–1830', in *The History of British Women's Writing, 1750–1830*, ed. Jacqueline M. Labbe (Basingstoke: Palgrave Macmillan, 2012), pp. 30–1.

28 Anonymity may also have held this appeal for some male writers. Some men postured as women by writing 'pleading prefaces' that would secure critical leniency, and others signed their novels with the ubiquitous moniker 'By a Lady' for similar reasons. Reviewers were well aware of both ploys. See Thompson and Ahrens, 'Criticism of English Fiction', pp. 127–8 and Raven, 'Historical Introduction', p. 42.

29  Raven, 'Historical Introduction', pp. 47–9; Levy, 'Women and Print Culture', p. 40; St Clair, *The Reading Nation*, p. 174.

30  Jan Fergus, 'The Professional Woman Writer', in *The Cambridge Companion to Jane Austen*, ed. Edward Copeland and Juliet McMaster (Cambridge: Cambridge University Press, 2010), p. 2; St Clair, *The Reading Nation*, p. 174.

31  Burney, *Diary and Letters*, I, p. 24; p. 27; p. 30.

32  *Ibid.*, p. 24; p. 26; p. 27; p. 29.

33  *Ibid.*, p. 29.

34  *Ibid.*, p. 33.

35  *Ibid.*, p. 25; p. 34; p. 30.

36  I draw on work by several critics in adopting the term 'professional'. See Betty A. Schellenberg, 'From Propensity to Profession: Female Authorship and the Early Career of Frances Burney', *Eighteenth-Century Fiction*, 14:3–4 (2002), p. 348; Janice Farrar Thaddeus, *Frances Burney: A Literary Life* (London: Palgrave Macmillan, 2000), p. 3; p. 6; George Justice, 'Suppression and Censorship in Late Manuscript Culture: Frances Burney's Unperformed *The Witlings*', in *Women's Writing and the Circulation of Ideas*, ed. George L. Justice and Nathan Tinker (Cambridge: Cambridge University Press, 2002), p. 202; Levy, 'Women and Print Culture', pp. 37–8. Burney's model of authorship influenced other women writers. See Jacqueline Pearson, 'Mothering the Novel: Frances Burney and the Next Generation of Women Novelists', *Corvey CW3 Journal*, 1 (2004), www2.shu.ac.uk/corvey/CW3journal/Issue%20one/pearson.html (accessed 10 June 2013).

37  Burney claims this offer 'was accepted with alacrity; and boundless surprise at its magnificence' (*Memoirs of Doctor Burney*, 3 vols (London: Edward Moxon, 1832), II, p. 132).

38  Burney, *Diary and Letters*, I, p. 44.

39  *Ibid.*, p. 41.

40  Kate Chisholm, 'The Burney Family', in *The Cambridge Companion to Frances Burney*, ed. Peter Sabor (Cambridge: Cambridge University Press, 2007), p. 14.

41  She records, for example, the details of how her father published each work (by commission, subscription, etc.), when foreign translations were issued, and how his work was received by the likes of Jean-Jacques Rousseau and Samuel Johnson. See Frances Burney, *Early Journals and Letters of Fanny Burney*, ed. Lars E. Troide, 6 vols (Oxford: Oxford University Press; Montreal: McGill-Queen's University Press, 1988), I, p. 146; p. 152; p. 217; p. 241; p. 244; p. 252.

42  Stephanie Eckroth, 'Celebrity and Anonymity in the *Monthly Review*'s Notices of Nineteenth-Century Novels', in *Women Writers and the Artifacts of Celebrity in the Long Nineteenth Century*, ed. Ann R. Hawkins and Maura Ives (Aldershot: Ashgate, 2012), p. 24; p. 30.

43  Dr Burney originally wanted to release the second volume of his *General History of Music* together with *Cecilia*, presumably so that the timing would maximise visibility of both. See Parisian, *Frances Burney's Cecilia*, pp. 1–2.

44  Chisholm, 'The Burney Family', p. 10.

45  Gallagher, *Nobody's Story*, p. 216; Barbara Eaton, *Yes Papa! Mrs Chapone and the Bluestocking Circle* (London: Francis Boutle Publishers, 2012), pp. 201–2.

46  Burney, *Diary and Letters*, I, pp. 24–5; pp. 35–6; p. 46. Dr Burney learned in July 1778 from his son Richard, who had known since January.

47  Eaton, *Yes Papa!*, pp. 201–2; pp. 204–5.

48  Gallagher, *Nobody's Story*, pp. 224–5.

49  Burney, *Diary and Letters*, I, p. 24.

50  *Ibid.*, p. 24; p. 36.

51  *Ibid.*, p. 37.

52  *Ibid.*, p. 128.

53  *Ibid.*, p. 162.

54  My interpretation tallies, broadly, with Schellenberg's discussion of the 'poten-
    tial for balancing' the claims of these 'two distinct identity categories' in *The
    Professionalization of Women Writers*, p. 151.

55  Burney, *Diary and Letters*, I, p. 97.

56  Schellenberg, 'From Propensity to Profession', p. 347; p. 352.

57  Felicity A. Nussbaum, 'Sociability and Life Writing: Hester Lynch Thrale Piozzi', in
    *Women's Life Writing, 1700–1850: Gender, Genre and Authorship*, ed. Daniel Cook and
    Amy Culley (Basingstoke: Palgrave Macmillan, 2012), p. 58.

58  See Parisian, *Frances Burney's* Cecilia, p. 10.

59  Burney, *Diary and Letters*, I, p. 97.

60  Parisian, *Frances Burney's* Cecilia, pp. 17–18; Thaddeus, *Frances Burney*, p. 24; Burney,
    *Diary and Letters*, II, pp. 481–2.

61  Burney, *Diary and Letters*, II, p. 75.

62  Parisian (*Frances Burney's* Cecilia, p. 1) and Donoghue (*The Fame Machine*, pp. 173–4)
    make this claim. See also Peter Sabor and Margaret Anne Doody, 'Introduction',
    in *Cecilia*, ed. Peter Sabor and Margaret Anne Doody (Oxford: Oxford University
    Press, 1988), p. xi.

63  There were an impressive six presses at work for a print run of this magnitude. See
    Parisian, *Frances Burney's* Cecilia, p. 14.

64  'Art. II. Cecilia', *British Magazine and Review*, 1 (July 1782), p. 48; 'Cecilia', *European
    Magazine, and London Review*, 2 (September 1782), p. 208; 'III. Cecilia', *London
    Magazine*, 52 (January 1783), p. 39; [Samuel Badcock], 'Art. X. Cecilia', *Monthly
    Review*, 67 (December 1782), p. 453.

65  'Cecilia', *Critical Review*, 54 (December 1782), p. 414.

66  *Ibid.*, p. 416.

67  [Samuel Badcock], 'Art. X. Cecilia', *Monthly Review*, 67 (December 1782), p. 457.

68  'Cecilia', *European Magazine, and London Review*, 2 (September 1782), p. 208.

69  *Ibid.*, p. 210.

70  [Samuel Badcock], 'Art. X. Cecilia', *Monthly Review*, 67 (December 1782), p. 453.

71  'Art. II. Cecilia', *British Magazine and Review*, 1 (July 1782), p. 48.

72  'Domestic Literature, Of the Year 1782', *New Annual Register* (January 1783), p. 247.

73  Samuel Johnson, *Rambler*, 4 (31 March 1750), reprinted in *The Norton Anthology of
    Theory and Criticism*, ed. Vincent B. Leitch *et al.* (New York, NY: Norton, 2001), p. 463.

74  'Cecilia', *Critical Review*, 54 (December 1782), p. 420.

75  'Art. II. Cecilia', *British Magazine and Review*, 1 (July 1782), p. 49.

76  Katherine Soba Green, *The Courtship Novel 1740–1820: A Feminized Genre* (Lexington,
    KY: University Press of Kentucky, 1991), p. 80.

77  Emma E. Pink, 'Frances Burney's *Camilla*: "To Print My Grand Work…by
    Subscription"', *Eighteenth-Century Studies*, 40 (2006), pp. 58–9. The previous
    standard was set by Elizabeth Carter's 1758 translation of Epictetus, which had
    1,031 subscribers.

78  Pink, 'Frances Burney's *Camilla*', p. 58.

79  Eckroth, 'Celebrity and Anonymity', p. 27.

80  St Clair, *The Reading Nation*, p. 19.

81  Justice suggests Burney was continually 'outfoxed' by publishers ('Burney and the Literary Marketplace', p. 150; p. 157). On Burney's profits from *Camilla*, see Thaddeus, *Frances Burney*, pp. 132–4.

82  Burney, *Diary and Letters*, V, p. 262.

83  *Ibid.*, pp. 293–4.

84  Batchelor, *Women's Work*, p. 2.

85  Jane Spencer stresses the difficult position of women writers. *The Rise of the Woman Novelist: From Aphra Behn to Jane Austen* (Oxford: Basil Blackwell, 1986), p. 80. Scholars like Schellenberg have argued, in contrast, that 'the 1770s and 1780s were not predominantly hostile to women's literary and dramatic activity' (*The Professionalization of Women Writers*, p. 145). See also Levy, 'Women and Print Culture', p. 30.

86  'Art. XXV. Camilla', *English Review*, 28 (August 1796), p. 180.

87  See Justice, 'Burney and the Literary Marketplace', p. 158 and Derek Roper, *Reviewing before the Edinburgh: 1788–1802* (Newark, DE: University of Delaware Press, 1978), p. 165; p. 167. The *Camilla* reviews averaged five pages each, a length which has been seen as a mark of critical esteem. See Joseph F. Bartolomeo, *A New Species of Criticism: Eighteenth-Century Discourse on the Novel* (London: Associated University Presses, 1994), p. 115.

88  'Art. XIII. Camilla', *British Critic*, 8 (November 1796), p. 536.

89  [William Enfield], 'Art. IX. Camilla', *Monthly Review*, 21 (October 1796), p. 62.

90  Raven, 'Historical Introduction', p. 120.

91  Burney, *Diary and Letters*, V, p. 297.

92  *Ibid.*, pp. 296–7.

93  Julia Epstein, *The Iron Pen: Frances Burney and the Politics of Women's Writing* (Madison, WI: University of Wisconsin Press, 1989), p. 195; Thaddeus, *Frances Burney*, p. 146.

94  Burney, *Diary and Letters*, V, p. 297.

95  [William Enfield], 'Art. IX. Camilla', *Monthly Review*, 21 (October 1796), p. 163.

96  Burney, *Diary and Letters*, V, p. 301.

97  'Camilla', *Monthly Mirror*, 2 (August 1796), p. 227. Particularly 'moral' extracts featured in *Universal Magazine*, 99 (September 1796), pp. 201–5; *Scots Magazine*, 58 (October 1796), pp. 691–7; and *Analytical Review*, 24 (August 1796), pp. 142–8, where a notoriously harsh Mary Wollstonecraft praised many aspects of the novel.

98  Richard Polwhele, *The Unsex'd Females: A Poem, Addressed to the Author of the Pursuits of Literature* (London: Cadell and Davies, 1798), ll. 195–6.

99  Eleanor Ty, *Unsex'd Revolutionaries: Five Women Novelists of the 1790s* (Toronto: University of Toronto Press, 1993), p. 13.

100  Burney, *Diary and Letters*, I, p. 298.

101  Bartolomeo, *A New Species of Criticism*, p. 114.

102  Peter Sabor, 'Journal Letters and Scriblerations: Frances Burney's Life Writing in Paris', in *Women's Life Writing, 1700–1850*, p. 83. Sabor emphasises that Burney hoped the novel would secure enough profit to allow her husband to stop working.

103  St Clair, *The Reading Nation*, p. 584; Justice, 'Burney and the Literary Marketplace', p. 149.

104  Burney, *Diary and Letters*, VI, p. 102; Eckroth, 'Celebrity and Anonymity', p. 27.

105  St Clair, *The Reading Nation*, p. 199; p. 584.

106  Thaddeus, *Frances Burney*, p. 170.

107  David Higgins, *Romantic Genius and the Literary Magazine: Biography, Celebrity, Politics* (New York, NY: Routledge, 2005), p. 15.

108 Lee Erickson, *The Economy of Literary Form: English Literature and the Industrialization of Publishing, 1800–1850* (Baltimore, MD: Johns Hopkins University Press, 1996), p. 6; p. 72. Erickson pinpoints 1815–1835 as the pinnacle of prestige in periodical essay writing. On the competition between the essay and book as literary forms, see Hilary Fraser and Daniel Brown, *English Prose of the Nineteenth Century* (London: Addison Wesley Longman, 1996), p. 7.

109 I follow William St Clair in using reviews as evidence of 'horizons of expectations' rather than transparent markers of reception (*The Reading Nation*, p. 6).

110 [William Hazlitt], 'Art. III. The Wanderer', *Edinburgh Review*, 24:48 (February 1815), p. 336.

111 *Ibid.*, p. 338.

112 *Ibid.*, p. 336.

113 *Ibid.*, p. 337.

114 Thaddeus, *Frances Burney*, p. 174; Epstein, *The Iron Pen*, p. 195.

115 [William Hazlitt], 'Art. III. The Wanderer', *Edinburgh Review*, 24:48 (February 1815), p. 334.

116 *Ibid.*, p. 335.

117 Kathryn Temple, *Scandal Nation: Law and Authorship in Britain, 1750–1832* (Ithaca, NY: Cornell University Press, 2003), p. 124.

118 *Ibid.*, p. 128.

119 [William Hazlitt], 'Art. III. The Wanderer', *Edinburgh Review*, 24:48 (February 1815), p. 335.

120 [John Wilson Croker], 'Art. IX.—The Wanderer', *Quarterly Review*, 11: 21 (April 1814), p. 124.

121 *Ibid.*, p. 126.

122 Devoney Looser, *Women Writers and Old Age in Great Britain, 1750–1850* (Baltimore, MD: Johns Hopkins University Press, 2008), p. 32; p. 35; p. 41.

123 Margaret Anne Doody, *Frances Burney: The Life in the Works* (New Brunswick, NJ: Rutgers University Press, 1988), p. 386.

124 Fraser and Brown, *English Prose of the Nineteenth Century*, p. 301.

125 Frances Burney, *The Wanderer* (London: Pandora, 1988), p. xviii.

126 *Ibid.*, p. xviii.

127 [John Wilson Croker], 'Art. IX.—The Wanderer', *Quarterly Review*, 11:21 (April 1814), p. 130.

128 *Ibid.*, p. 129. See Chapter 2 for more on Elinor Joddrell as a version of Mary Wollstonecraft.

129 *Ibid.*, p. 126.

130 'The Wanderer', *Anti-Jacobin Review* (April 1814), p. 347.

131 Burney, *Diary and Letters*, VI, p. 102. Late in 1814 Burney was still grieving for her father, who had died in April. She claims not to have read the reviews yet.

132 *Ibid.*, p. 103.

133 *Ibid.*, p. 102.

134 *Ibid.*, p. 395.

135 Joyce Hemlow, *The History of Fanny Burney* (Oxford: Clarendon Press, 1958), p. 455.

136 *Ibid.*, p. 449.

137 *Ibid.*, p. 452; Doody, *Frances Burney*, p. 377.

138 See, for example, 'Memoirs of Doctor Burney', *Gentleman's Magazine* (February 1833), p. 142.

139   On the vicious *ad hominem* attacks that appeared in early nineteenth-century periodicals, see Mark Parker, *Literary Magazines and British Romanticism* (Cambridge: Cambridge University Press, 2001), p. 4.

140   Irma Lustig, 'Fact into Art: James Boswell's Notes, Journals, and *The Life of Johnson*', in *Biography in the Eighteenth Century*, ed. J. D. Browning (London: Garland, 1980), p. 142; A. O. J. Cockshut, *Truth To Life: The Art of Biography in the Nineteenth Century* (London: Collins, 1974), p. 12.

141   James Treadwell, *Autobiographical Writing and British Literature, 1783–1834* (Oxford: Oxford University Press, 2005), p. 13.

142   On Mary Shelley and Sara Coleridge in similar roles as family editors, see Michelle Levy, *Family Authorship and Romantic Print Culture* (Basingstoke: Palgrave Macmillan, 2008), p. 144.

143   On Thrale's market orientation, see Nussbaum, 'Sociability and Life Writing', p. 62.

144   Stuart Sherman, 'Diary and Autobiography', in *The Cambridge History of English literature, 1660–1780*, ed. John Richetti (Cambridge: Cambridge University Press, 2012), p. 666.

145   'The Memoirs of Dr. Burney', *The Examiner* (2 December 1832), p. 774.

146   Burney, *Memoirs of Doctor Burney*, III, p. 110.

147   'Memoirs of Dr. Burney (Second Notice)', *Athenaeum* (24 November 1832), p. 757.

148   Hermione Lee, *Body Parts: Essays on Life-Writing* (London: Chatto & Windus, 2005), p. 3.

149   Burney, *Memoirs of Doctor Burney*, II, p. 121.

150   'Memoirs of Dr. Burney', *The Examiner* (2 December 1832), p. 774.

151   Thaddeus, *Frances Burney*, p. 188.

152   Linda Peterson, *Traditions of Victorian Women's Autobiography: The Poetics and Politics of Life Writing* (Charlottesville, VA: University Press of Virginia, 1999), p. 220.

153   Daniel Cook and Amy Culley, 'Introduction', in *Women's Life Writing, 1700–1850*, p. 4.

154   Daniel Cook, 'An Authoress to Be Let: Reading Laetitia Pilkington's *Memoirs*', in *Women's Life Writing, 1700–1850*, p. 39; Lynda M. Thompson, *The 'Scandalous Memoirists': Constantia Phillips, Laetitia Pilkington, and the Shame of 'Publick Fame'* (Manchester: Manchester University Press, 2000), p. ix; pp. 225–6.

155   Thaddeus, *Frances Burney*, p. 189.

156   Janice Carlisle, qtd in Peterson, *Traditions of Women's Autobiography*, p. x.

157   The *Memoirs of Doctor Burney* also prefigured political biographies written by radical Victorian women whose public sphere activism was legitimated as continuing the values of their fathers. See Helen Rogers, 'In the Name of the Father: Political Biographies by Radical Daughters', in *Life Writing and Victorian Culture*, ed. David Amigoni (Aldershot: Ashgate, 2006), p. 147.

158   'Art. II.—Memoirs of Dr. Burney', *Monthly Review*, 4:1 (January 1833), p. 20.

159   Frances Bunsen to Mrs Waddington, 24 August 1833. *The Life and Letters of Frances Baroness Bunsen*, ed. Augustus J. C. Hare (London: George Routledge & Sons, 1879), pp. 400–2, qtd in Grau, *Fanny Burney*, p. 66; Henry Crabb Robinson, *Henry Crabb Robinson: On Books and Their Writers*, ed. Edith J. Morley, 3 vols (London: J. M. Dent & Sons, 1938), I, p. 137.

160   Maria Edgeworth, 27 June 1833. *The Education of the Heart: The Correspondence of Rachel Mordecai Lazarus and Maria Edgeworth* (Chapel Hill, NC: University of North Carolina Press, 1977), qtd in Grau, *Fanny Burney*, p. 82.

161 [John Wilson Croker], 'Art. V.—Memoirs of Dr. Burney', *Quarterly Review*, 49:97 (April 1833), p. 107, italics in original.

162 *Ibid.*, p. 98; p. 100.

163 *Ibid.*, p. 125.

164 *Ibid.*, p. 107.

165 Burney, *Memoirs of Doctor Burney*, I, p. ix.

166 Gallagher, *Nobody's Story*, p. 217.

167 [John Wilson Croker], 'Art. V.—Memoirs of Dr. Burney', *Quarterly Review*, 49:97 (April 1833), p. 97.

168 *Ibid.*, p. 125.

169 John Wilson Croker to John Gibson Lockhart, qtd in Grau, *Fanny Burney*, p. 152.

170 Allan Cunningham, *Biographical and Critical History of the Last Fifty Years* (Paris: Baudry's Foreign Library, 1834), pp. 129–32.

171 Looser suggests Croker had an obsessional hatred for older women (*Women Writers and Old Age*, p. 39).

172 Cook and Culley argue that cultural anxieties about life writing were 'compounded by an author's sex' ('Introduction', p. 4).

173 Frances Burney, *The Journals and Letters of Fanny Burney (Madame D'Arblay)*, ed. Joyce Hemlow, 12 vols (Oxford: Clarendon Press, 1984), XII, p. 797.

174 *Ibid.*, p. 797. For a useful account of this exchange, see Catherine Delafield, 'Barrett Writing Burney: A Life among the Footnotes', in *Women's Life Writing, 1700–1850*, pp. 26–7.

175 Burney, *Journals and Letters*, XII, p. 797.

176 Doody, *Frances Burney*, p. 377; Thaddeus, *Frances Burney*, p. 202.

177 Hemlow, *The History of Fanny Burney*, p. 466.

178 Lars E. Troide, 'History of the Manuscripts and Earlier Editions', in *Early Journals and Letters of Fanny Burney*, I, p. xxv.

179 Patricia Meyer Spacks, *Privacy: Concealing the Eighteenth-Century Self* (Chicago, IL: University of Chicago Press, 2003), p. 194.

180 Harriet Blodgett uses the term 'reader-influenced' to distinguish between diaries like Burney's that circulated to family or friends, and those that remained private. See *Centuries of Female Days: Englishwomen's Private Diaries* (New Brunswick, NJ: Rutgers University Press, 1988), pp. 14–15. For detailed discussions of Barrett's revisions, see Delafield, 'Barrett Writing Burney', p. 27, and Delafield, *Women's Diaries as Narrative in the Nineteenth-Century Novel* (Aldershot: Ashgate, 2009), p. 46.

181 Claire Harman, *Fanny Burney: A Biography* (London: Flamingo, 2000), p. 382.

182 *Ibid.*, pp. 383–4. On Sarah Harriet Burney's reaction, see Delafield, 'Barrett Writing Burney', pp. 29–30.

183 Blodgett, *Centuries of Female Days*, p. 35; Delafield, *Women's Diaries*, p. 23.

184 Isaac D'Israeli, 'Diaries Moral, Historical and Critical', in *Curiosities of Literature*, new edn (London: Warne, 1881), II, p. 206, qtd in Delafield, *Women's Diaries*, p. 11.

185 See Spacks, *Privacy*, p. 11; pp. 169–70; Delafield, *Women's Diaries*, p. 13; Sherman, 'Diary and Autobiography', pp. 666–7.

186 Burney, *Early Journals and Letters of Fanny Burney*, I, p. 22.

187 Judy Simons, *Diaries and Journals of Literary Women from Fanny Burney to Virginia Woolf* (Basingstoke: Palgrave Macmillan, 1990), pp. 3–4; Felicity A. Nussbaum, *The Autobiographical Subject: Gender and Ideology in Eighteenth-Century England* (Baltimore, MD: Johns Hopkins University Press, 1989), pp. 201–5; Delafield, *Women's Diaries*, pp. 14–16.

188  Delafield, *Women's Diaries*, p. 26.
189  Nussbaum, *The Autobiographical Subject*, p. 223.
190  [John Gibson Lockhart], 'Autobiography', *Quarterly Review*, 35:69 (January 1827), p. 164.
191  For more on scandal memoirs, see Thompson, *The 'Scandalous Memoirists'*; Nussbaum, *The Autobiographical Subject*; Cook, 'An Authoress to be Let'; Peterson, *Tradition of Victorian Women's Autobiography*.
192  Treadwell, *Autobiographical Writing and British Literature*, p. 12; p. 16; p. 55; p. 57.
193  'Madame D'Arblay', *Blackwood's Edinburgh Magazine* (June 1842), p. 784.
194  *Ibid.*, p. 784.
195  Blodgett, *Centuries of Female Days*, pp. 35–6.
196  'Diary and Letters of Madame D'Arblay', *Athenaeum* (29 January 1842), p. 101.
197  'Diary and Letters of Madame D'Arblay. Vol II', *Athenaeum* (5 March 1842), p. 205.
198  'Madame D'Arblay's Diary and Letters', *New Monthly Magazine*, 64:254 (February 1842), p. 271.
199  'Miss Burney's Diary and Letters', *Tait's Edinburgh Magazine*, 9:100 (April 1842), p. 246.
200  'Madame D'Arblay's Diary,' *Eclectic Review*, 11 (April 1842), p. 453.
201  Macaulay is one of the few commentators to mention Pepys and Evelyn. See 'Art. IX—Diary and Letters of Madame D'Arblay', *Edinburgh Review*, 76:154 (January 1843), p. 551. For comparisons with Boswell, see 'Madame D'Arblay's Diary and Letters', *New Monthly Magazine*, 64:254 (February 1842), p. 271; 'Diary and Letters of Madame D'Arblay. Vol. 1–5', *Gentleman's Magazine* (December 1842), p. 566; 'Diary and Letters of Madame D'Arblay', *Literary Gazette* (29 January 1842), p. 73; 'Miss Burney's Diary and Letters', *Tait's Edinburgh Magazine*, 9:100 (April 1842), p. 246.
202  'Diary and Letters of Madame D'Arblay. Vol II', *Athenaeum* (5 March 1842), p. 205; 'Diary and Correspondence of Madame D'Arblay', *New Monthly Magazine*, 64:255 (March 1842), p. 405; 'Diary and Letters of Madame D'Arblay. Vol. 1–5', *Gentleman's Magazine* (December 1842), p. 566; p. 582; W. P. Courtney, 'The Early Diary of Frances Burney, 1768–78', *Academy* (22 February 1890), p. 125.
203  'Miss Burney's Diary and Letters', *Tait's Edinburgh Magazine*, 9:100 (April 1842), p. 246; 'Diary and Letters of Madame D'Arblay. Vol. 1–5', *Gentleman's Magazine* (December 1842), p. 563.
204  Simons, *Diaries and Journals*, p. 197.
205  'Diary and Letters of Madame D'Arblay. Vol 1–5', *Gentleman's Magazine* (December 1842), p. 563.
206  'Miss Burney's Diary and Letters', *Tait's Edinburgh Magazine*, 9:99 (March 1842), p. 185.
207  Schellenberg, *The Professionalization of Women Writers*, pp. 144–5.
208  Peterson, *Traditions of Victorian Women's Autobiography*, p. 24.
209  Doody, *Frances Burney*, pp. 1–2.
210  'Fanny Burney's Diary', *Saturday Review* (8 April 1905), p. 458.
211  'Fanny Burney (Madame D'Arblay)', *Athenaeum* (2 January 1904), p. 5.
212  'Fanny Burney and Her Friends', *Saturday Review* (30 November 1889), p. 620.
213  [William Makepeace Thackeray], 'Diary and Letters of Madame D'Arblay Vol. 6', *The Morning Chronicle* (25 September 1846), p. 6.
214  'Fanny Burney, Her Diary and Her Days', *Edinburgh Review*, 203:415 (January 1906), pp. 86–7.
215  Austin Dobson, *Fanny Burney* (London: Macmillan, 1903), p. 72.

216 Joanne Shattock, 'The Construction of the Woman Writer', in *Women and Literature in Britain 1800–1900*, ed. Joanne Shattock (Cambridge: Cambridge University Press, 2001), p. 8. Michelle Dowd and Julie Eckerle suggest this practice continues among scholars today. See 'Introduction', in *Genre and Women's Life Writing in Early Modern England*, p. 4.

217 For more on Burney's treatment in the Victorian Reviews, see Susan Civale, 'The Literary Afterlife of Frances Burney and the Victorian Periodical Press', *Victorian Periodicals Review*, 44:3 (2011), pp. 236–66.

218 Shattock identifies a similar process at work in the afterlives of Brontë and Austen ('The Construction of the Woman Writer', p. 20; p. 25).

219 Tom Mole, *What the Victorians Made of Romanticism: Material Artifacts, Cultural Practices, and Reception History* (Princeton, NJ: Princeton University Press, 2017), pp. 2–3.

220 According to J. Paul Hunter, Burney's status changed by mid-century, however: 'early in the twentieth century, ... scholarship on Burney far exceeded in quantity that on Tobias Smollett, but by the 1950s Smollett had for some reason become a "major" figure and Burney a "minor" one'. See 'The Novel and Social/Cultural History', in *The Cambridge Companion to the Eighteenth-Century Novel*, ed. John Richetti (Cambridge: Cambridge University Press, 1996), p. 35n1, qtd in Betty A. Schellenberg, 'Writing Eighteenth-Century Women's Literary History, 1986 to 2006', *Literature Compass*, 4:6 (2007), p. 1547.

221 See Shattock, 'The Construction of the Woman Writer', p. 12; Joanne Wilkes, *Women Reviewing Women in Nineteenth-Century Britain: The Critical Reception of Jane Austen, Charlotte Brontë and George Eliot* (Aldershot: Ashgate, 2010), p. 161.

222 Shattock, 'The Construction of the Woman Writer', p. 28.

223 Shattock sees Elizabeth Gaskell's *Life of Brontë* (1857) and James Edward Austen-Leigh's *Memoirs of Jane Austen* (1870) as examples of the first kind, and J. W. Cross's *George Eliot's Life* (1885) as an example of the second.

224 According to Doody, Anne Thackeray was 'inspired to become a diarist and novelist' after reading Burney's *Diary and Letters* (*Frances Burney*, p. 425n8). Julia Kavanagh's *English Women of Letters* (Leipzig: Bernhard Tauchnitz, 1862), pp. 38–90, shows evidence of a careful reading of Burney's *Diary and Letters*. See also Virginia Woolf, 'Dr. Burney's Evening Party', in *The Second Common Reader*, ed. Andrew McNeillie (London: Harcourt, 1986).

225 Virginia Woolf, *The Diary of Virginia Woolf*, ed. Anne Olivier Bell, 5 vols (London: Hogarth Press, 1978–84), III, p. 238.

226 See Virginia Woolf, 'Four Figures', in *The Second Common Reader*, pp. 156–63. Woolf uses the word 'experiment' five times in the essay: to describe Wollstonecraft's life, her relationship with Godwin, and her ideas, though implicitly also to refer to the *Memoirs* itself.

# Chapter 2

# 'A man in love': Revealing the unseen Mary Wollstonecraft

MARY WOLLSTONECRAFT ROSE TO prominence with her *Vindication of the Rights of Men* (1790) and *Vindication of the Rights of Woman* (1792), but she won over readers' hearts in her confessional travelogue *Letters Written During a Short Residence in Sweden, Norway, and Denmark* (1797). Despite her unorthodox personal life, Wollstonecraft's careful self-fashioning ensured that she died in 1797 as a respected writer and the most widely known political thinker of her day. Only a few months later, however, the disclosures of her husband William Godwin's *Memoirs of the Author of a Vindication of the Rights of Woman* (1798) confounded the public image she had crafted so skilfully. This chapter traces Wollstonecraft's reputation in her lifetime, looking at her early reception and her self-construction in her *Vindications* and *Letters*, before turning to Godwin's *Memoirs* and its aftermath. Critics have often asserted that the scandal surrounding the *Memoirs* silenced Wollstonecraft for nearly a century. However, close attention to a range of little-studied nineteenth-century responses to Wollstonecraft – in reviews, fiction, poetry, multibiographies, biographical dictionaries, book-length biographies, essays and political writing – suggests that while the *Memoirs* did take a toll, it also imbued her afterlife with a unique emotional and intellectual appeal. Her *Rights of Woman*, moreover, continued to attract readers and influence political thinking throughout the century. By the *fin de siècle*, Wollstonecraft had received renewed attention as journalists, novelists, biographers and activists drew her life and work into the public eye, not only to champion her achievements but also to associate themselves with her legacy. Though successive generations have rewritten Wollstonecraft to suit their own values and agendas, throughout the long nineteenth century, the flawed yet principled heroine of Godwin's *Memoirs* continued to resurface. Like Burney's *Diary and Letters*, Godwin's *Memoirs* was a pivotal influence on Wollstonecraft's reputation and an important innovation in the genre of life writing itself.

## Self-fashioning and the 'profession' of writing

In her early years as an author in 1787–89, Wollstonecraft did not experience the popularity or critical acclaim that marked Burney's authorial debut in 1778. However, she wrote prolifically and profitably, developed her authorial voice and style and established herself as a writer. Wollstonecraft's early career was, in some ways, typical of her period. Most writers at this time published anonymously, struggled to earn critical or financial rewards and made only transitory appearances in print.[1] Educated women, in particular, had few options for employment, and Wollstonecraft, like many of her female contemporaries, turned to literary work (after being employed as a governess, schoolmistress and lady's companion) to discharge debts and earn a living. She began in one of the most popular and profitable genres for women writers: instructional literature.[2] Her first publication, *Thoughts on the Education of Daughters; with Reflections on Female Conduct* (1787), earned £10 and was considered by reviewers as 'correct' and 'judicious', if 'trite'.[3] Excerpts soon appeared in the *Lady's Magazine*, a pirated edition was published in Dublin and copies were still available for purchase in 1794.[4]

Wollstonecraft alternated between publishing anonymously, pseudonymously and under her own name, experimenting with genres and authorial styles. Her first novel, the anonymous *Mary*

(1788), garnered only cursory reviews and did not move past a first edition.[5] Wollstonecraft's 'Advertisement' declared that *Mary*'s heroine would be 'different from those usually portrayed' by Rousseau and Richardson, but some reviewers nevertheless felt she was 'imitating Rousseau'.[6] Still, the novel was approved as a source of 'reflection' and a 'moral' fiction designed to inculcate virtues in readers.[7] Appearing in the same year, her anonymous *Original Stories* (1788), a collection of children's tales accompanied by illustrations by William Blake, was greeted more enthusiastically. The *Critical Review*'s reviewer found it 'highly proper' in developing 'moral virtues and religious conduct' in the 'youthful mind'.[8] *Original Stories* saw six reprints before the end of the century, as well as a German translation. The *Monthly Review*'s reviewer guessed that it was written by the author of *Thoughts* and pronounced it likewise 'agreeable and useful'.[9] Wollstonecraft employed a didactic style that linked *Thoughts* and *Original Stories* but made her unidentifiable as the author of *Mary*, which reviewers assumed to have been written by a man.[10] The style of *Thoughts* and *Original Stories* differed from that of her translation of Jacques Necker's *Of the Importance of Religious Opinions* (1788), a political work that also appeared the same year. The following year, her anthology *The Female Reader* (1789), published under the pseudonym of 'Mr. Cresswick', became a widely used educational text for female readers.[11] The generic diversity of Wollstonecraft's early publications allowed her to turn a profit, to try out different authorial styles and to build confidence in negotiating the literary marketplace.

However, as most of these texts did not bear her name, this success did not translate into a consolidated literary reputation. Wollstonecraft's anonymous contributions to her radical publisher Joseph Johnson's *Analytical Review* in 1788–89 did little more to raise her public profile. Though these articles reached a more diverse audience than her instructional works or fiction, they were not generally associated with Wollstonecraft. Thus, even though Wollstonecraft was writing regularly for the *Analytical* and had published five other texts to varying degrees of success, in the late 1780s, she remained an obscure figure.

Unlike Burney, who had risen quickly to critical esteem and fame with her bestselling *Evelina* ten years earlier, Wollstonecraft's career profile seems more akin to that of a 'hack', a jobbing writer associated with short-term, paid work of mediocre quality.[12] Some critics have emphasised that women who engaged in hack work, or who wrote for profit more generally, were seen as disreputable, and that women could only maintain propriety by publishing as genteel amateurs.[13] Certainly, it was difficult for women to balance domestic duty with paid labour, and the literary marketplace could be hostile to women writers. Still, Wollstonecraft's so-called 'hack' work does not seem to have met with hostility, and if anything, it projected an image of decorum and decency.[14] Women had long justified the importance of their writing for instilling virtue in (female) readers, and Wollstonecraft's first five works were generally reviewed in this light. Moreover, many women wrote highly esteemed conduct books and educational literature.[15] Like her contemporary Hannah More and successors such as Harriet Martineau, Mary Howitt and Charlotte Elizabeth Tonna, Wollstonecraft emerged as a writer of instructive works and children's literature, acceptable genres for women which could also guarantee a return.[16]

Wollstonecraft's steady progress through the ranks of didactic, advice and periodical writing might seem to mark her as a more 'professional' writer than a contemporary like Burney. However, labelling women as amateurs or professionals is complicated because so few authors at this time earned enough to subsist on writing alone.[17] Despite the obvious differences in their early careers, Burney and Wollstonecraft were both part of a minority of writers of the period who enjoyed popular success, frequent reprints and substantial profits.

Wollstonecraft and Burney also developed similar strategies in self-fashioning which surface in their anonymous work. Wollstonecraft's period at Joseph Johnson's *Analytical Review*, during which she wrote hundreds of unsigned articles on every topic from natural history to political science to prose fiction, contributed to her development as a writer and cultural critic. Her range of writing in different genres and stylistic registers was also formative. In her early years, Wollstonecraft refined her ideas of education, gender and literature, and she recognised the language that could tag writing as feminine. According to Mitzi Meyers, Wollstonecraft understood the ways in

man. He admits that he did not personally 'discover this Defender of the Rights *Man* to be a *Woman*'.[40] Using italics to stress the humour and irony of this gender reversal, he suggests that by stepping out of her traditional role, Wollstonecraft has forced him to do the same: 'if she assumes the disguise of a man, she must not be surprised that she is not treated with the civility and respect that she would have received in her own person'.[41] Anonymity becomes a duplicitous 'disguise' by which Wollstonecraft forfeits his 'respect'. Predictably, the conservative *Critical Review* also objects to her definition of 'the birthright of man' and the 'liberty' it should confer and disputes her conclusion that 'innovation cannot introduce greater evils than have already been felt'.[42] The criticism of Wollstonecraft's anonymous identity serves to undercut her credibility and her argument.

Other reviewers mocked Wollstonecraft's gender outright in order to undermine her politics. The *Gentleman's Magazine*, for example, scoffs:

> The *rights of men* asserted by a fair lady! … We should be sorry to raise a horse-laugh against a fair lady; but we were always taught to suppose that the *rights of women* were the proper theme of the female sex.[43]

This raillery funnels into an assault on her lack of 'reason' and her radical programme of 'equalization' which comprises the bulk of the three-page article. Accusing her of 'inspir[ing] the poor of this country with jealousy and resentment against the rich', the reviewer aligns her with 'the French reformers [who] are groping blindfolded in the chaos of their reason'.[44] The final sentences expose the fear latent in the reviewer's opposition:

> [The reformers'] last shift is to poison and inflame the minds of the lower class of his Majesty's subjects to violate their subordination and obedience. Mrs. W. if she be a real and not a fictitious lady, is engaged in a service wherein their great leaders have run themselves aground. … But reflecting minds will see through their stale and shameful tricks, and not involve themselves in the ruin of their country.[45]

The reviewer, despite his earlier jocularity, engages with Wollstonecraft in earnest. So seriously does he take her, in fact, that he doubts she is actually a woman and suspects her 'supposed' gender as a 'trick' to manipulate readers into undermining British constitution and country. This accusation confirms the efficacy of Wollstonecraft's rhetorical skill, while also signalling more general concerns about the dynamics of self-fashioning in a rapidly expanding public sphere of letters.

In spite of these pointed responses, many reviewers treated the *Rights of Men* with respect. The *General Magazine*, calling his fellow reviewers 'prurient wags' on account of their 'jokes, low, lascivious, and poor', even complains that such 'pointless sarcasm' obscures the merits of the work.[46] The *English* and *Monthly* reviews praised Wollstonecraft's argument warmly, and even the oppositional *Critical Review* spent two pages discussing it. The *Monthly* reviewer defends Wollstonecraft's vigorous and unfeminine style, finding her 'air of eager warmth and positiveness ... fully compensated by the ardent love of liberty, humanity, and virtue, which evidently actuates her heart'.[47] The *English Review* likewise exonerates Wollstonecraft:

> The language may be thought by some too bold and pointed for a female pen; but when women undertake to write on masculine subjects, and reason as Miss Wollstonecraft does, we wish their language to be free from all female *prettiness*.[48]

This defence of Wollstonecraft invokes her own indictment of Burke's configuration of women as '*little, smooth, delicate, fair* creatures' who lack the rational powers necessary for the attainment of virtue.[49] According to Skolnik, Wollstonecraft's rhetoric performs a 'stylistic dislocation of sex and gender' as a form of 'empowerment', which some of the reviewers, especially those sympathetic to her politics, seem to accept.[50] None of the reviewers, however, allude to Wollstonecraft's earlier pedagogical writing, suggesting that they either had not read or had not remembered it. By 1791, Wollstonecraft had emerged as a leading radical polemicist and rising figure in the Revolution Controversy.

### Fame secure

Just two years later, Wollstonecraft published *A Vindication of the Rights of Woman* (1792), an immediate bestseller that secured her fame in Britain and abroad. In this 300-page pamphlet, written in only a few months, Wollstonecraft recruited the human rights discourse of the American and French Revolutions to suggest that women were intellectually and spiritually equal to men and therefore deserved the same freedoms and rights. Her argument against women's exclusion from education flowed out of a long-standing debate that looked back to Mary Astell's *A Serious Proposal* (1694) and *A Serious Proposal, Part II* (1697) and to Catharine Macaulay's more recent *Letters on Education* (1790). As many modern scholars have noted, much of its argument was familiar to liberal thinkers and was less revolutionary than its attempt to join women's rights to a larger campaign about civil rights.[51] Priced at seven shillings, *Rights of Woman* sold out quickly, and a revised second edition was published later that year. Circulating libraries, such as Hookham's in London, ordered dozens of copies for lending, and a third edition was released in 1796 with further revisions. The first three print runs comprised roughly 1,500–2,000 copies in total, and there is evidence that some of these copies became available at reduced prices, and thus potentially to an expanded readership, over time.[52] The *Rights of Woman* was immediately republished in America, appearing in Philadelphia and Boston in 1792, with a second Philadelphia edition in 1794. It was also translated into French and German, and a Dublin edition was printed in 1793.[53] The *Rights of Woman* was reviewed widely, both in England and abroad, and journals frequently featured free-standing extracts. It prompted verse and fictional responses, and it loomed large in private correspondence as well.[54] Some of its most famous readers included Hester Chapone, Jane Austen, Maria Edgeworth and Anna Seward, along with most of Wollstonecraft's own circle.[55]

In the *Rights of Woman*, Wollstonecraft developed many of the arguments of the *Rights of Men*, critiquing the binary opposition between the beautiful and the sublime, and interrogating gender as a product of social conditioning, not nature. Wollstonecraft's *Rights of Woman* also builds on her early educational texts, exposing the paradoxes within traditions of female improvement; promoting rational independence through right conduct, duty and intellectual development; and rejecting the idea of 'sexual virtues'.[56] Wollstonecraft's *Rights of Woman* capitalises on the range of authorial personae she had cultivated through her expertise in writing across different genres. Fiore Sireci identifies in the *Rights of Woman* several narrative personae, including the educational writer, moral philosopher, literary critic and republican citizen, all of which contribute to Wollstonecraft's political and philosophical argument.[57] Wollstonecraft fashions a powerful and nuanced authorial voice that moved from informing, to admonishing, to exhorting, but never resorted to pleading.

Again, the reviews indicate that Wollstonecraft continued to command respect, though, predictably, party affiliations tended to determine responses. The two *Critical Review* articles that appeared in February and April of 1792, which levelled almost twenty pages of criticism at the text's radicalism, logic and literary style and addressed Wollstonecraft paternalistically as 'dear young lady', seem obviously politically motivated. The *Critical* reviewer objects to her premise that there is no difference in the minds of men and women, pronouncing her reasoning 'imperfect' and 'inconclusive'. The *Critical* then reinstates sex as a central element in its critique. In defending the current system, the reviewer not only *reacts* to Wollstonecraft's ideas about the relations between the sexes, but, with a droll wink at the male Tory reader, *enacts* his own:

> We must contend then with this new Atalanta; and who knows whether, in this modern instance, we may not gain two victories by the contest? There is more than one batchelor [sic] in our corps; and, if we should *succeed*, miss Wollstonecraft may take her choice.[58]

The *Critical Review* not only attacks Wollstonecraft's analysis, but also undermines her political rhetoric with the language of sexual conquest. The *Critical* reviewer refocuses attention on her status as a woman, both to distract from and to ridicule her argument. However, the *Critical* commentary stretched to nearly twenty pages and spanned two separate issues, suggesting the reviewer took her seriously nonetheless.

In contrast, the left-leaning Reviews praised Wollstonecraft's reasoning and her language. Writing in the *Monthly*, William Enfield casts Wollstonecraft alternately as 'Wisdom' and 'Philosophy', and extols her contribution in the 'progress toward perfection'.[59] His warm tone celebrates Wollstonecraft's ideas and conveys optimism for future change. The revolutionary ideals of Wollstonecraft's *Vindications* appealed to like-minded reformists and gained added momentum from a historical moment that saw rapid change as well as the expectation of more change to come.[60] Although there was some hostility to the *Rights of Woman*, reviewers generally greeted it with approbation in 1792, applauding its basic impulse towards the improvement of women's education and ignoring its more extreme elements, such as the demand for women to participate in government.[61]

Despite growing conservative ferment after France declared war on England in 1793, Wollstonecraft published another explicitly political text and continued to advance her rhetorical and stylistic range. Though written while she was in France in 1793, Wollstonecraft's *Historical and Moral View of the Origin and Progress of the French Revolution* (1794) traces events up to 1789, reading the early phases of the Revolution in a way that supports her political optimism.[62] Amy Culley points to this text as an early attempt at connecting personal and political narratives, using feelings and historical memories to discuss Revolution, strategies which would come to fruition in her *Letters* (1796).[63]

Wollstonecraft maintained the reputation that she initiated with the *Vindications*, and although support for the *Historical and Moral View* did not approximate that of her two previous political texts, it was reviewed widely and treated seriously. Critiques of Wollstonecraft's work generally remained grounded in considered analysis of her arguments and examples. Predictably, left-wing journals continued to support her, and the *Analytical* and *Monthly* Reviews praised her judicious approach, her attempt to be impartial and her cerebral bent. They celebrated her as an enlightened female philosopher. The *Analytical* reviewer applauds her 'correct ideas' and 'liberal spirit' and suggests that her 'understanding' might 'appear to male vanity highly astonishing'.[64] The smooth transition here between the discussion of her intellectual merits and the threat they pose to certain men may be directed as a come-back to the *Critical* or as a pre-emptive defence against future assaults.

Even the conservative reviewers made an immense concession to Wollstonecraft. Their solemnity of tone connoted a genuine engagement with Wollstonecraft's ideas as those of a serious political writer. The *English* admits that 'this lady has attained to a very considerable degree of celebrity by the publication of various tracts' and the *Critical* alludes to readers' familiarity with the 'the strong mind of Mrs Wollstonecraft, and the high tone of her sentiments'.[65] Although conservative agitation accelerated during the 1790s, even Wollstonecraft's most trenchant critics still nodded to her renown and treated her as a serious political writer.

## Audience, reputation and life writing

The final text Wollstonecraft published in her lifetime, *Letters Written During a Short Residence in Sweden, Norway, and Denmark* (1796), steered away from the overtly political content of her previous three texts. In the anti-Jacobin scare that reached its height in the late 1790s, radicalism came to be almost synonymous with treason. After war began with France in 1793, the British government tightened controls on leftist publication through the Treason Trials of 1794, the Gagging Acts of 1795 and the Seditious Societies Act of 1799. Writers, publishers and booksellers could be prosecuted, fined and jailed for seditious libel, as had happened in the case of Thomas Paine.[66] In publishing the twenty-five semi-private letters written during her three-month tour of Scandinavia in 1795, Wollstonecraft opted for a new genre, one which was not only different from her previous writing but also a formal innovation in its own right.

*Letters* was Wollstonecraft's most popular text with her contemporaries. It earned favourable reviews in conservative and radical periodicals alike. It was translated into German, Dutch, Swedish and Portuguese, and an American edition was issued in Wilmington, Delaware in 1796. Johnson printed a second edition in 1802, a remarkable occurrence given the moral outrage that followed the *Memoirs* and the reactionary political climate in Britain more generally. Richard Holmes has demonstrated the text's influence on later Romantics, such as William Wordsworth, Samuel

Taylor Coleridge and William Hazlitt.[67] The appeal of the *Letters* lay, in part, in its uniqueness as a travel book by a solitary woman. Topics such as war, history and voyages to distant lands did not often feature in women's writing in any genre, and travel narratives by women were particularly rare. Only one prominent travelogue, Lady Mary Wortley Montagu's *Letters from Constantinople* (1763), had been published in England by a woman before *Letters*.[68] Even men's travel books, of which there were many, did not often include journeys so far afield; Sterne, Smollett, Gray and Walpole, for example, all limited their travels to areas of Europe farther south and west than those navigated by Wollstonecraft.[69] Moreover, Wollstonecraft's *Letters* details an exploration of the remote countries of Scandinavia alongside a journey into an equally remote internal hinterland. Replacing the language of the geographical survey or picturesque description with a register of philosophical reflection and emotional confession, Wollstonecraft's voice also differs from standard travel accounts. The hybrid form of the *Letters*, Holmes suggests, amounts to nothing less than a 'revolution in literary genres', an unprecedented amalgamation of social commentary, wounded sensibility and remote locales.[70]

Several other recent critics have echoed this claim, and many now explicitly discuss the *Letters* as a contribution to Romantic life writing. Amy Culley sees *Letters* as a mixture of 'sentimental travelogue and correspondence' that allows Wollstonecraft 'to assert her continuing faith in revolutionary progress, social connection, and personal relationships in the aftermath of the Terror'.[71] Christine Chaney regards *Letters* as an example of Michel Beaujour's 'literary self-portrait' that represents the 'dialogic nature' of Wollstonecraft's selfhood through a combination of essay, confession and conversation.[72] Treadwell highlights the *Letters* as a text as much interested in dialogue and negotiation as in interiority and subjectivity.[73] Building on these critical appraisals, I suggest that Wollstonecraft's innovative form allows her to reshape her public persona and to cultivate a more affective connection with her reader. This new dimension to her public face contributed to her popularity in the final years of her life and influenced her posthumous reputation as well.

As a travelogue-journal-letter hybrid, *Letters* frees Wollstonecraft to traverse landscapes at once natural, political and personal, yet also to circumnavigate politicised topics she wishes to avoid or intimate details she wishes to keep private. At the same time, she makes the reader an eavesdropper as well as a confidante. Wollstonecraft creates a genre, narrative and authorial persona 'calculated' to win over the reader.[74] In 'Letter XII', for example, Wollstonecraft admits:

> At Gothenburg I shall embrace my Fannikin; probably she will not know me again – and I shall be hurt if she do not. How childish this is! Still it is a natural feeling ... Yet I never saw a calf bounding in a meadow, that did not remind me of my little frolicker. A calf, you say. Yes; but a capital one I own.[75]

Wollstonecraft confides in her interlocutor, and by proxy her reader, disclosing fears at once 'childish' and maternal. Her 'natural' feeling of parental solicitude prompts empathy with the animal world, and the comparison of her daughter and the calf is both endearing and ridiculous. By anticipating the unconvinced response of her addressee ('A calf, you say'), and then answering it ('Yes'), she plays out an imagined conversation, suggesting familiarity and good humour as well as emotional honesty. In the next section, she ruminates on 'friendship and domestic happiness' and concludes that 'a degree of simplicity, and of undisguised confidence, which, to uninterested observers, would almost border on weakness, is the charm, nay the essence of love or friendship'. Wollstonecraft shows us such 'simplicity' and 'weakness' to establish a 'friendship' with the reader. In doing so, she transforms her reader from an 'uninterested observer' into a companion, cultivating a rapport characterised by esteem and affection.[76]

The persona she projects complements the public image fostered by her earlier works in two important ways. First, this new authorial Wollstonecraft possesses an exquisite sensibility. 'Letter XV', one of the most frequently quoted by contemporaries, represents the crescendo of the collection. In this epistle, Wollstonecraft narrates her experience of the waterfall near Fredericstadt, displaying her acute receptivity to the natural world:

Reaching the cascade, … my soul was hurried by the falls into a new train of reflections. The impetuous dashing of the rebounding torrent from the dark cavities which mocked the exploring eye produced an equal activity in my mind. My thoughts darted from earth to heaven, and I asked myself why I was chained to life and its misery. Still the tumultuous emotions this sublime object excited were pleasurable; and, viewing it, my soul rose with renewed dignity above its cares.[77]

Though the 'torrent' and 'dark cavities' of the cataract inspire fear and awe, they invigorate her imagination. Her response to this sublime scene is shown in the 'activity' and 'reflections' of her mind. In this process, her soul is renewed and can transcend the pain of its earthly cares by contemplating something higher than itself. The regenerating power of the imagination does not cancel out her emotional vulnerability but uses these sentiments to project beyond the narrow world of her interaction.

Wollstonecraft exposes an interior self that keeps the reader emotionally engaged. It is no coincidence that reviewers of the *Letters* nicknamed her 'a female Rousseau', connecting her with a philosopher whose confessional autobiography *The Confessions of Jean-Jacques Rousseau* (1782) detailed the progression of his inner soul towards total self-expression.[78] According to Jane Darcy, the appeal of the *Letters* lies in Wollstonecraft's 'semi-fictional' self-portrayal as a melancholic whose refined sensibility allows her to experience grief and loss as pleasure.[79] In 'Letter X', Wollstonecraft turns from the people of Norway to the landscape:

Adieu! I must trip up the rocks. The rain is ever. Let me catch pleasure on the wing – I may be melancholy to-morrow. Now all my nerves keep time with the melody of nature. Ah! let me be happy whilst I can. The tear starts as I think of it. I must flee from thought, and find refuge from sorrow in a strong imagination – the only solace for a feeling heart.[80]

The interjections are loaded with emotion, mixing an appreciation of nature with sensations of pleasure and pain. Elsewhere, Wollstonecraft discusses these digressions as 'the effusions of a sensibility wounded almost to madness', but the effect on the reader, throughout, is not horror but sympathy. Both revelatory *and* performative, these interludes made a profound impression on readers, which can be seen in the language of affect that laces nearly every review. The *Monthly* reviewer suggests that readers will 'regret the circumstances which excited the writer's emotions' but 'will never be inclined to withhold their sympathy'.[81] The *Analytical* is 'certain that no reader, who possesses any portion of sensibility, will be able to peruse the preceding passage, without deeply deploring the state of society, in which it is possible that such a mind should be loaded with distress'.[82] The reaction to Wollstonecraft here becomes a litmus test of the reader's own emotional responsiveness.

In addition to sensibility, Wollstonecraft also emphasised her femininity.[83] As Stuart Curran has discussed, even though she continues to challenge 'the gendered opposition between the masculine sublime and the feminine beautiful by locating them within the same perspectival frame', she presents her acute sensibility in a highly 'feminized' mode.[84] Wollstonecraft's rhetoric moves beyond the rationalism of her earlier work into sentimentality.[85] Contemporary readers responded warmly to this previously unseen, feminine side of Wollstonecraft. Amelia Alderson, for example, compares the effect of the *Letters* with that of the *Vindications*:

> I remember the time when my desire of seeing you was repressed by fear – but as soon as I read your letters from Norway, the cold awe which the philosopher has excited, was lost in the tender sympathy called forth by the woman. I saw nothing but the interesting figure of feeling and indignation.[86]

Reviewers, likewise, praised the balance between what the *Analytical* terms 'strength of understanding' and 'delicacy of sensibility'.[87] The gendering of these attributes is made plain by the *Monthly* reviewer who admires the 'strong – or if the fair traveller will accept the epithet as a compliment, the *masculine* – mind of this female philosopher'.[88] For a writer whose early work was couched in the masculine house style of the *Analytical Review*, who became prominent in 'male' genres of politics and philosophy and who had garnered criticism for her unladylike style, the recognition of this feminine side was new. Even the conservative *Critical Review*, which had reviled her want of delicacy and flawed political agenda in 1794, found her full of 'taste and feeling' and applauded her 'artless' and 'unstudied' composition.[89] In addition to her 'strong' and 'masculine' mind and 'refined' sense, Wollstonecraft was associated with 'tender' sensibility and 'beautiful' prose.[90] Peter Swaab has contended that critics of the *Letters* began to see her negatively, as a 'martyr' to sensibility.[91] However, the mixture of masculine and feminine descriptors suggests that her womanly appeal did not replace but instead merged with her manly reason, reflection and strength of mind.

Wollstonecraft's narrative persona gained added ideological sway and affective power from her self-portrayal as a mother. Having embarked on her Scandinavian journey unattended by any male escort, with only her daughter and her French maidservant Marguerite, Wollstonecraft appears free and independent. 'Letter I' establishes Wollstonecraft in opposition to the nursemaid who accompanies her:

> The day was fine, and I enjoyed the water till, approaching the little island, poor Marguerite, whose timidity always acts as a feeler before her adventuring spirit, began to wonder at our not seeing any inhabitants. I did not listen to her.[92]

The contrast between the two women announces Wollstonecraft as a confident, self-sufficient adventurer, interrupted in her fair-weather reverie by the panicky Marguerite. She empathises with Marguerite's misgivings but does heed them. A few paragraphs later, Wollstonecraft mentions her infant daughter. Though for Wollstonecraft the local flora invoke a 'cruel remembrance', her child reacts differently, remaining on a wholly sensory level and experiencing an unadulterated enjoyment that Wollstonecraft cannot. She describes how '[t]he gaiety of my babe was unmixed; regardless of omens or sentiments, she found a few wild strawberries more grateful than flowers or fancies'.[93] Whereas Wollstonecraft's sensations are saddled with painful recollections, her infant daughter remains unencumbered by such emotional burdens. The motherly appreciation of the baby's pure state vicariously imbues her with a tinge of that purity.[94] The pathos of these observations of her daughter lends her a further dimension of sensibility and at the same time reinforces her independence.

This glimpse of parent—child interaction also operates on another level. Granting the reader a peek at a private family moment and revealing herself as a mother, Wollstonecraft asks the reader to accommodate this altered persona. However, Wollstonecraft refers to her daughter without mentioning a husband or marriage and without abandoning her maiden name. In fact, she gives no account of her situation. She alludes to a painful separation from the father of the child: 'I was returning to my babe, who may never experience a father's care or tenderness'.[95] However, such passing laments often appear at the end of her letters and invariably go unexplained. Scholars have verified that the eponymous journey to Scandinavia was actually a business trip organised by Gilbert Imlay, Wollstonecraft's lover and the father of her illegitimate child.[96] Both the aim of the voyage (the recovery of Imlay's missing cargo ship) and its scandalous back story (her betrayal at his hands and subsequent suicide attempt) are screened deftly by Wollstonecraft.[97] The window into Wollstonecraft's personal life is half shaded, maintaining privacy and yet adding an air of mystery. Holmes stresses the 'extraordinary skill with which she transformed a prosaic business venture into a poetic revelation', and notes that various mysteries hover over the text, lending it 'tension and atmosphere', 'urgency' and a 'haunting' quality.[98] The hybrid form of the *Letters* accommodates such gaps in narrative exposition, camouflaging them in the rhetoric of confession and feminine sensibility. Wollstonecraft's literary 'skill', in this respect, also indicates a keen awareness of the importance of personal reputation and her efforts in shaping it.[99]

The 'mystery' of the *Letters* seems to have provoked curiosity among readers, and the reviews reveal an unprecedented attention to Wollstonecraft's personal life. A range of speculations and suspicions co-existed, however awkwardly, with rising regard for Wollstonecraft as a writer. Sympathetic critics like William Enfield were prone to explain away the missing details to safeguard Wollstonecraft's reputation. Enfield, writing in the *Monthly*, consigns the matter to an early footnote, where he wonders 'why the writer, a married lady, has here chosen to retain her maiden name'. He then offers a plausible explanation: Wollstonecraft's 'name' may be 'more advantageously known in the literary world, than that of her husband'.[100]

Other journals entertained less flattering possibilities. The *English* reviewer notes this 'singular circumstance':

> We are not told whether Mary Wollstonecraft be maid, widow, or wife; yet we find her accompanied by her infant daughter! Licentious imaginations will be apt to indulge conjectures concerning the point to which she may have carried her claim to the rights of women. But, for our part, we conclude, from the circumstance just mentioned, that she is a married lady.[101]

Though the final sentence ostensibly gives Wollstonecraft the benefit of the doubt, the reviewer in fact insinuates the worst. The interjection of surprise, the use of the exclamation point and the poetic parallel structure ('maid, widow, or wife') not only register the possibility of a child outside marriage but also suggest that this illegitimate child may represent the indecent end of Wollstonecraft's radical politics. Though brief, this surmise prefigures the deluge of abuse that followed Godwin's *Memoirs* two years later. It is possible that some reviewers knew of Wollstonecraft's affair with Imlay, for although she signed the text 'Wollstonecraft', she had already adopted Imlay's name privately and remained candid with friends about not being legally married.[102] Gossipy (though accurate) suppositions like the two cited here appeared in several of the reviews. In contrast, reviews like the *Critical* simply replaced the appellation of 'Miss', which had previously been used in articles about Wollstonecraft, to 'Mrs'. This substitution registers unease with Wollstonecraft's ambiguous status, yet circumvents discussion of it. Whatever their suspicions, the reviewers appear unwilling to precipitate a scandal. This unwillingness may seem peculiar given the enthusiasm with which the press embraced this scandal when it did break in 1798. In 1796, though, the situation was different. As the best-known female political writer in Europe, Wollstonecraft had attained widespread recognition and respect. More importantly, although her unconventional personal life raised eyebrows, the *public* persona of her written texts had not stepped out of line.

Parallels in the public reception of Wollstonecraft in 1796 and that of the poet Laetitia Landon (the self-styled L.E.L.) four decades later may help to explain the dynamics at play here. Landon, who published poetry and fiction and worked as a paid periodical reviewer, lived in London and was known for her illicit affairs. Nevertheless, as Linda Peterson explains, Landon enjoyed a surprisingly favourable representation in the press:

> Maginn knew the material aspects of Landon's literary life, including her penury and sexual impropriety; but *Fraser's* evades or suppresses the dubious features of a woman's professional life because Landon remains feminine in her public persona and literary productions. For women in the 1830s, as for men, the key aspects of professional authorship were respectable social status, genius or genial wit, and silence about earnings.[103]

Like Landon, Wollstonecraft could maintain public esteem as long as she seemed convincingly 'feminine' in her 'public persona and literary productions'.

Moreover, the changing status of the periodical press is also important in understanding Wollstonecraft's reception in 1796. As discussed in Chapter 1, the literary review came into its own by the end of the eighteenth century and began to hold considerable sway in the early nineteenth. However, reviewers still had to negotiate the prejudices surrounding hack work. In this new market where people were starting to write for a living, what Mary Waters calls 'the illusion of elite dilettantism' still held importance.[104] Reviewers may have attempted to sidestep the stamp of the professional artisan, stretching instead for the ranks of the gentleman intellectual.[105] Those reviewing Wollstonecraft had to tread carefully to distance themselves from the vulgarity associated with the hack and to avoid offences to the taste of readers. It seems that both Wollstonecraft's and Landon's reviewers toed this line. By the 1790s, the reputation of the review(er) and that of the author being reviewed were becoming intertwined. In this overlapping of interests, candour may have been sacrificed for an impression of polite gentility, allowing the public image of a writer like Wollstonecraft – despite rumours about her private life – to remain unsullied. Wollstonecraft herself was in a position to understand the exigencies faced by the reviewer, and professional experience in the field may have informed her self-presentation in *Letters*.

The autobiographical persona in *Letters* was hugely successful. Godwin himself preferred this persona to that of Wollstonecraft's polemical works.[106] To many, the voice of *Letters* seemed more vulnerable, likeable or authentic. However, this persona, though it differed from that of her reviews, didactic writing and *Vindications*, relied on the same skilful handling of tone, rhetoric, syntax and form. Like all autobiographical performances, it derived as much from self-concealment as self-disclosure. In *Letters*, Wollstonecraft delicately beckoned her audience in – to sympathise with her distress, to reflect with her on foreign cultures, to catch sight of her maternal side – only to draw the shades in time to sustain her privacy. The air of mystery lingering over Mary Wollstonecraft might never have endangered her reception had her husband not terminated this performance with his *Memoirs* in 1798.

## From fame to infamy

Godwin's *Memoirs of the Author of a Vindication of the Rights of Woman* (1798), published by fellow radicals Joseph Johnson and George and John Robinson, disclosed all the intimate details of the private life Wollstonecraft had so artfully veiled from her public. Most notably, it included accounts of her love for the married artist Henry Fuseli; her affair, unwed pregnancy and subsequent abandonment by the American businessman Gilbert Imlay; her two suicide attempts, one of which post-dated the birth of her illegitimate daughter, Fanny Imlay; her embrace of atheism; her relationship and subsequent marriage to William Godwin; and her death in childbirth. The public was shocked. The reviewers singled out, in particular, her impropriety in 'sexual intercourse' and the 'versatility' of her attachments as 'disgusting'.[107] Attempting suicide as a mother was seen as morally depraved and inconsistent with Wollstonecraft's self-portrayal in the *Letters*. Godwin issued a revised second edition at the end of 1798, with several modifications in phrasing and added paragraphs but no substantial change to the narrative. Editions were published in Dublin in 1798 and in America in 1799 and 1804, and translations into German and French appeared in 1799 and 1802, respectively, but no further editions were published in Britain for nearly 130 years.[108]

Nonetheless, the *Memoirs* had a huge impact both on contemporaries and the generations that followed.

Predictably, political affiliations shaped responses, though reviewers across the spectrum struggled to reconcile Wollstonecraft's scandalous behaviour with the principled persona that had emerged in her work. The conservative journals seized on the implicit construction of Wollstonecraft as a courtesan and connected political radicalism with personal licentiousness.[109] The counter-revolutionary *Anti-Jacobin Review* framed Wollstonecraft as the superlative in cautionary tales of Jacobin immorality, calling her a 'concubine'.[110] Some put it down to the existence of such an 'undaunted and masculine spirit' in a woman.[111] Others proceeded to 'question' Godwin's account. The *Monthly Review*, for example, suspects that 'Mr. G. rather gives his own opinions than those of his wife; or he exhibits her's [sic] with the colouring of his own system thrown over them'.[112] John Evans's six-page *Monthly Visitor* essay compared the religious beliefs found in *Thoughts on the Education of Daughters* and *Letters* with the 'irreligion' of the *Memoirs*, reminding readers (and Godwin himself) of Wollstonecraft's faith 'at an uncontaminated period of her life'.[113] The *British Critic* similarly disparages her 'false philosophy'. Wollstonecraft's inconsistencies were matched only by the turpitude of a deranged husband who could publish such 'ravings' about his late wife.[114]

Like this *British* critic, other reviewers were horrified that a husband would wish to publicise these transgressions. Godwin had long been known for the revolutionary doctrine of sincerity proposed in *Political Justice* (1793). With the *Memoirs*, though, he seemed to take this doctrine to an obnoxious extreme. Even a respectful *Monthly* reviewer who readily grants Godwin's 'abilities' as 'indisputable' confesses:

> Blushes would suffuse the cheeks of most husbands, if they were *forced* to relate those anecdotes ... which Mr. Godwin voluntarily proclaims to the world.[115]

As was often the case in the genre of life writing, the breach of privacy seemed as much a scandal as the events relayed.[116]

To contemporary readers, Godwin's biography bore an uneasy resemblance to the scandalous memoirs that flourished earlier in the eighteenth century, in which women revealed illicit histories to make money or vindicate their actions. In the *Memoirs of Laetitia Pilkington* (1748), for example, Pilkington revealed her own indecorous conduct, but there was a clear rationale behind such 'extraordinary self-assertion'. Spacks explains:

> By it, Pilkington acquires both money and revenge. The self-exposure of her privacy constitutes an aggressive tactic. … She restores her self-ownership by taking public possession of her story.[117]

Portraying herself as the victim, Pilkington implicitly justified her transgressive self-violation. Scandalous memoirists like Pilkington and her contemporary, Constantia Phillips, often used autobiographical revelation to protest injustice and positioned themselves as warnings rather than examples. Drawing on stock figures such as the sentimental courtesan and the libertine whore, these memoirs alternated between postures of penitence and defiance.[118] These narratives were also connected with a vulgar commodification of intimate details, and courtesan autobiographies epitomised the dubious standing of the genre.[119] Putting scandalous escapades in print risked undermining the literary aspirations of the autobiographer altogether.[120] Godwin, however, appeared to take this risk willingly, compromising Wollstonecraft's reputation by placing her in the light of a courtesan. The *Memoirs* seemed a fanatic break with biographical practice and a breach of spousal duty as well. Readers were unable to place the memoir within any discernible genre. With Godwin's twin violations of literary and family protocol and Wollstonecraft's countless indelicacies, husband and wife appeared to collude in collective defiance of social decorum and morality.

Still, Wollstonecraft was not without her defenders. Her loyal friend and fellow feminist author Mary Hays published a sympathetic obituary in the *Monthly Review* three months before the release of the *Memoirs*. She then followed Godwin's biography with her own fifty-page 'Memoirs of Mary Wollstonecraft' in 1800.[121] Hays's 'Memoirs' did not depart substantially from Godwin's version of events. However,

Hays did place greater emphasis on Wollstonecraft's importance for the 'emancipation of her own sex', and at points addressed female readers in particular.[122] Wollstonecraft had already paid the price for her own mistakes, Hays suggests, and therefore need only awaken 'sympathy' for her failings and 'gratitude' for her intrepid efforts at reform. Like other men of 'genius' she may have been 'imprudent', but she was not vicious: 'her errors and her sufferings arose out of the vices and prejudices of others'.[123] The anonymous *A Defence of the Character and Conduct of the Late Mary Wollstonecraft Godwin* (1803) likewise championed Wollstonecraft as a brave pioneer of reform.[124] Yet this apologist lacked Hays's tone of 'sublimest feeling', which had impressed the *Critical* reviewer with Wollstonecraft's 'powerful feelings', 'vigorous genius' and 'resolution'.[125] However, neither Hays's 'Memoirs' nor the anonymous *Defence* enjoyed more than fleeting recognition among contemporary readers.[126]

## Radical politics and personal sentiment

Modern scholars have tended to view the *Memoirs* as ushering in the demise of Wollstonecraft's reputation for nearly a century. They have seen Godwin's biography as a cautionary tale impeding the development of feminism and the public discussion of Wollstonecraft for decades. Harriet Jump contends, for example, that 'for almost fifty years after the publication of Godwin's *Memoirs*, no criticism or commentary on Wollstonecraft's writings appeared in print'.[127] Janet Todd has speculated that Mary Wollstonecraft's reputation would have fared far better had Godwin foregone his experiment in radical sincerity.[128] Shattock calls the biography a 'double murder of Wollstonecraft's reputation, firstly by his misguided candour and secondly by his unwitting undermining of her intellectual credentials'.[129]

Recent studies by Culley and Spongberg, however, have moved away from binary interpretations of the *Memoirs*, situating it as a landmark contribution to life writing, feminism and genre formation. Culley, Spongberg and Darcy have also looked beyond the scandalous content of the *Memoirs* to attend to its style and form. None of these scholars focuses on the longer-term effects of the *Memoirs* in shaping Wollstonecraft's reputation, though. Responses to the *Memoirs* in nineteenth-century fiction, life writing and periodical essays point to a more complex engagement with Wollstonecraft. Situating these responses alongside nineteenth-century engagement with Wollstonecraft's political writing creates a different picture of Wollstonecraft's nineteenth-century reputation. Though Godwin's decision to publish the *Memoirs* mystified contemporary reviewers, he had both political and personal motivations for doing so. Examining his rationale for the *Memoirs* and the 'reading' of his wife that it inculcates not only flags the literary achievement of this biography but also opens up a confluence of implications for Wollstonecraft's authorial reputation that go beyond its mere suppression or survival.

Godwin's attitudes to life writing can be traced back to the radical ideas of sincerity he proposed in *Political Justice* (1793) and the theories of biography and personal reputation he put forward in *The Enquirer* (1797). Godwin believed in the study of 'individual man' as a means to promote change. In his 'Essay of History and Romance', he professes that '[i]t is the contemplation of illustrious men ... that kindles into flame the hidden fire within us.'[130] The most eligible subject for this 'contemplation' is the person who has contributed to bettering society, though Godwin is famously 'not contented to observe such a man upon the public stage, [but] would follow him into his closet'.[131] Understanding this person's intimate history can inspire readers to fulfil their potential. The *Memoirs* opens with an authorial mission statement that echoes this philosophy:

> Every benefactor of mankind is more or less influenced by a liberal passion for fame; and survivors only pay a debt due to these benefactors, when they assert and establish on their part, the honour they loved.[132]

Godwin justifies his memoir of Mary Wollstonecraft, one such eminent 'benefactor', on grounds of the utility of his narrative in animating readers toward reform.[133]

Furthermore, Godwin does not think a 'reputation for talents' sufficient for literary distinction, for he defines fame more fully, as a welding of intellectual and emotional regard:

> I am not contented to be admired as something strange and out of the
> common road; if I desire anything of posthumous honour, it is that I
> may be regarded with affection and esteem by ages yet unborn.[134]

To achieve such 'affection and esteem' can be difficult, even arbitrary,
and subject to change over time. Godwin distinguishes between 'the
fame of literature' and 'moral fame'. If the author's complete oeuvre
is in print, then the readers of posterity are equipped to evaluate his
or her literary fame. Without 'the entire evidence' of the author's
private character, an author's moral fame may be decided unfairly.
Such a fallacy is pivotal because the 'fame of literature' is contingent
on 'moral fame':

> Men will not allow force to the advice, they will not listen to the
> arguments, often they will even decline the practical good offices, of a
> person they disesteem.[135]

The honour secured by moral fame necessarily underpins the appraisal
of literary merit. Both moral and literary fame are requisite for the
'esteem and affection' of posterity. For Godwin, the stakes of the
'want of facts' remain high indeed.

Without recapitulating this theory in the *Memoirs*, his opening lines
allude to the 'duty incumbent on survivors' of providing a faithful
record so as to offer 'animation and encouragement to those who
would follow them'.[136] This statement indicates his political rationale
for publishing the *Memoirs*. Clemit and Walker argue that the *Memoirs*,
'never purely inward-looking or private', functions polemically as a
'vindication of a woman's entitlement to the type of moral and political
education advocated by Wollstonecraft in her public writings' and 'an
indictment of present-day social corruption'.[137]

Nevertheless, the book manifests, at the same time, a cathartic
leave-taking of and testimonial to his beloved. Like Boswell in his
*Life of Samuel Johnson* (1791), which has been identified as 'a personal
book, almost as much his autobiography as a biography of Johnson',
Godwin too seems 'to satisfy some need of his own'.[138] Godwin even
aligns himself with Boswell by grounding his claims for authenticity in
his direct communication from his subject.[139] Godwin has a political

agenda as well as a personal, even narcissistic, desire to explain Wollstonecraft's transformative effect on him, and he conceives of their relationship as a 'catalyst for further changes in his thought'.[140] He emphasises, in particular, how her superior 'imagination' and 'intuition' balanced out his 'oscillation and scepticism'.[141] He figures her as a 'light that was lent' temporarily 'and is now extinguished for ever', mourning her in an economy of intellectual loss:

> The loss of the world in this admirable woman, I leave to other men to collect; my own I well know [is] the improvement I have for ever lost.[142]

The concluding pages of the *Memoirs* home in on Wollstonecraft's absence and the grievous deficit Godwin faces in the wake of her death. The implications of this focus are significant. It projected a version of Godwin's masculinity that inscribed him into the eighteenth-century tradition of sensibility. This period saw a revolution in style that stressed the role of emotion in abetting reason and produced what Jerome McGann has called a 'discourse of sensibility [that] typically develop[ed] through an ethics of loss and suffering'.[143] Godwin performed his feelings in textualising his grief.[144]

The conclusion of Godwin's biography also inclined towards specular autobiography, that species of life writing that 'sees, comprehends, even creates the self by mirroring (often with distortions) the life of another'.[145] Although he justified appending this final chapter as necessary to explain Wollstonecraft's intellectual character, Godwin also assimilated his own emotions into the narrative. This self-expression may have comprised part of his bereavement process, but it risked articulating Wollstonecraft in relational terms. In the domestic memoir tradition, the trope of situating women within their socially sanctioned, affective roles as mother, wife, daughter or sister had emerged to mitigate editorial and authorial anxieties surrounding the publication of women's private histories. Godwin's *Memoirs* lapses into the 'relational' mode discussed by Peterson, whenever the account of Wollstonecraft's life digresses into a discussion of the ways she affected *him*: through her 'conjugal love', 'fortitude under calamity' and 'exemplar status'.[146]

This shift in affective focus emerges clearly in Godwin's amendments to the closing paragraph in the second version of the *Memoirs*, published in August of 1798:

> The improvement I had reason to promise myself, was however yet in its commencement, when a fatal event, hostile to the moral interests of mankind, ravished from me the light of my steps, and left to me nothing but the consciousness of what I had possessed, and must now possess no more.[147]

In a dramatic re-rendering of these final lines, the 'light' Wollstonecraft once 'lent' to Godwin is transfigured into an object that he 'possessed'. The 'improvement' he had anticipated is pilfered in an act of aggression which is envisioned here as a violent assault on Godwin's person. The revision of this passage accentuates William Godwin as a bereft victim, robbed of the love of his life.

This slippage in the climax of the *Memoirs* shows how Godwin undermines Wollstonecraft's vigilant self-representation. He allowed a sentimental sub-plot to creep into what was commenced as a politically pointed narrative. He highlighted Wollstonecraft's formative effect on him and her affective role as the 'light' of his life. Though he may have aimed to honour her intellectual influence, he succeeded, rather, in drawing attention to the pain he suffered in losing her. As the sensible, sentimental male narrator, he enclosed the *Memoirs* within a lyric that traded as both elegy and love song.

Godwin's *Memoirs* romanticised Wollstonecraft as a legendary love object. Modern critics have argued that the text instates Wollstonecraft, alternatively, as an 'exemplary public fiction', a 'Rousseauvian romantic heroine', a 'flawed hero' or a 'tragic heroine'.[148] Favret and Culley both find that Wollstonecraft herself had already, in the *Letters* (1796), sown 'the suggestion of intimacy' in a way that led readers to fictionalise her as an epistolary heroine.[149] For Favret, this configuration muffled Wollstonecraft's political critique, and Godwin only reinforced this effect in the *Memoirs* when he privileged 'Wollstonecraft the feeling woman over the radical thinker'.[150] Like Wollstonecraft's autobiographical *Letters*, Godwin's biography is a cross-pollination.[151] It brings together radicalism, tragedy and taboo and ultimately raises Wollstonecraft up as *his* beloved, the heroine of their real-life love story.

Godwin's *Memoirs* initiated a mode of 'reading' Wollstonecraft: as an affective, transcendent signifier whose meaning rested, ultimately, with the beholder. This mode may contribute to what Cora Kaplan sees as 'most enduring but also most troubling' in Wollstonecraft's afterlife: 'the aura of unreconciled emotion that hovers around her shifting reputation'.[152] She became not only a political polemicist but also the tragic heroine in a story of star-crossed lovers. From this point on, Wollstonecraft became a female philosopher associated with radicalism and personal scandal, but also imbued with an emotional currency in the imaginations of her readers. Tom Mole has discussed celebrities as 'spectacles of subjectivity' integral to the construction of Romantic-period gender norms and individuality.[153] The *Memoirs* helped to make Wollstonecraft into one of these 'spectacles'. Rather than forcing her into a bipolar interpretation as the angel or the whore,[154] Wollstonecraft became a figure with a protean capacity for meaning.

## 'Characterising' Wollstonecraft

As a mark of this imaginative preoccupation, Wollstonecraft was often likened to fictional characters in the Reviews. The *Analytical Review* and the *British Critic* compare her with 'Heloise' or 'Eloisa', the twelfth-century nun and scholar whose illicit affair with Abelard was preserved in his writings.[155] The *Anti-Jacobin Review* assigns her to the whorish 'sisterhood' that includes 'Mary Flanders', the protagonist of Daniel Defoe's novel *Moll Flanders* (1722), as a harlot whose 'adventures' are antithetical to Christian virtue.[156] Godwin himself, in the 'Preface' to the *Posthumous Works*, had described Wollstonecraft's letters as

> the finest examples of the language of sentiment and passion ever presented to the world. They bear a striking resemblance to the celebrated romance of Werther.[157]

These reviewers seem to respond to Godwin's reference to Wollstonecraft as a female 'Werther' by reincarnating her in other fictional characters.

Wollstonecraft also appeared as a thinly disguised character in a number of novels of the period, such as Charlotte Smith's *The Young Philosopher* (1798), Elizabeth Hamilton's *Memoirs of Modern Philosophers* (1800), Maria Edgeworth's *Belinda* (1802), Amelia Opie's *Adeline Mowbray* (1804), Godwin's own *St. Leon* (1799) and *Fleetwood* (1805), Frances Burney's *The Wanderer* (1814) and Susan Ferrier's *Marriage* (1818). However, it is not the number but the complexity of these portrayals which bears significance. Though one-dimensional caricatures existed, many of these novelists produced multi-faceted reinventions of Wollstonecraft. Harriet Jump explains this proliferation in Wollstonecraftian characters by the fact that 'novels became one of the few sites open for a debate on her life and principles, whether overt or covert'.[158] Andrew McInnes has examined contrasting female philosopher characters in nineteenth-century fiction to show how women writers, in particular, engaged with and reinterpreted Wollstonecraft's life and work.[159] These reinventions are also significant, however, in following Godwin's use of biography for political ends, and as McInnes suggests, in 'creat[ing] a space … on the faultline between literary production and political action, exploiting this position to broaden the scope of women's role in the private sphere … as the conservative press sought to narrow concepts of women's domestic role'.[160] The fictional Wollstonecrafts that abounded in early nineteenth-century novels thus in part speak to the significance of Godwin's framing mechanism in the *Memoirs*.

Burney's *The Wanderer* (1814) contains a particularly complex recasting of Wollstonecraft in the radical yet virtuous Elinor Joddrell. Elinor returns from abroad having imbibed the principles of the French Revolution, and renounces her fiancé, Dennis Harleigh, who does not share her views. Burney circumvents the most problematic aspects of Wollstonecraft's biography by having Elinor terminate the engagement *before* any physical relationship occurs. An educated woman with no intellectual outlet suitable for her 'energies', Elinor personifies a plight at the heart of Wollstonecraft's *Rights of Woman*:

> He delighted to … ask my opinions. I always took the opposite side to that which he was employed to plead, in order to try his powers, and prove my own. The French Revolution had just then burst forth … I began canvassing with him the Rights of Man. … The truth is,

our mutual vanity mutually deceived us: he saw my pleasure in his company, and concluded that it was personal regard: I found nothing to rouse the energies of my faculties in his absence, and imagined myself enamoured of my vanquished antagonist.[161]

Burney encourages the reader to sympathise with Elinor's situation. She depicts a flawed Wollstonecraft, but one whose restrictions as a woman have contributed to the formation of these flaws.

As the story progresses, Elinor's vanity combines with her lawless emotions, prompting a new attachment to the brother of her former betrothed. She melodramatically declares her feelings for him and then repeatedly attempts suicide, casting herself as the tragic victim of this unrequited love, but revealing, as McInnes has shown, the 'selfishness underneath her revolutionary polemic'.[162] Elinor confounds principle and passion, allowing the latter to dictate her actions. Alternately comic, grotesque and pathetic, her penchant for drama spurs her to ever-grander performances. Elinor's childlike compulsion towards performance and applause affords countless opportunities for her unbridled sensibility to creep onto her face with a 'crimson hue' and to emanate from her 'lustrous' eyes.[163] Her body physically registers the crazed feelings on which she acts. In Elinor, Burney ties revolutionary fervour and excessive sensibility, tragicomically suggesting suicide as one of the most dangerous outcomes.

Yet Burney keeps Elinor alive to become the cogent mouthpiece of controversial opinions that no other character can effectively repudiate. In Elinor's discussions with Harleigh about suicide, it is *his* sentences that go unfinished, while hers assemble a pointed, intelligent defence.[164] If Burney mocks or censures Elinor's (and Wollstonecraft's) attempts to take her own life, she also grants Elinor the eloquence to justify her convictions. Just as Ellis observes Elinor 'with mingled censure and pity', so Burney considers Wollstonecraft multi-dimensionally.[165] Elinor serves as a foil for the story's heroine, Ellis. Yet it is ultimately Elinor who becomes Ellis's protector. Without endorsing Wollstonecraft wholesale, Burney recognises merit in her ideas and sympathises with her difficulties.

Wollstonecraft also figured in poetry of the period. She influenced the work of Wordsworth and Coleridge, as Holmes has shown, and appeared in other poems, including Blake's 'Mary' (c. 1803), the

anonymous 'Ode to the Memory of Mary Wollstonecraft' (1804),
Anna Laetitia Barbauld's 'Rights of Woman' (1825) and Percy Bysshe
Shelley's *Queen Mab* (1813), *Laon and Cyntha* (1817) and *The Revolt of
Islam* (1818). In the 'Dedication' of *Laon and Cyntha*, Shelley writes of
Wollstonecraft in relation to her daughter, Mary Shelley:

> I wonder not – for One then left this earth
> Whose life was like a setting planet mild,
> Which clothed thee in the radiance undefiled
> Of its departing glory; still her fame
> Shines on thee, through tempests dark and wild
> Which shake these latter days; and thou canst claim
> The shelter, from thy Sire, of an immortal name.[166]

In this eulogy, as Susan Wolfson notes, Wollstonecraft appears as 'a
lost light and a continuing inspiration'.[167] The simile recalls Godwin's
own figurative language at the end of the *Memoirs*. Whereas Godwin
lamented Wollstonecraft's death as a 'light' that was 'lent' to him 'for
a very short period, and is now extinguished for ever', Shelley sees
her 'radiance' living on in her daughter. Throughout the Dedication,
Mary Shelley herself, 'the child of love and light' and the 'lamp
of vestal fire', bears the same light – and enlightenment – of her
mother.[168] By the end of the poem, Percy and Mary assume this light,
as 'lamps' and 'stars' that illuminate the 'tempestuous night', in stark
contrast to the 'fury blind' of those who ignore the voice of truth.[169]
Shelley reworks Godwin's metaphor, allowing Wollstonecraft's light
to shine on into the next generation. In the early decades of the
nineteenth century, the sophisticated and impassioned portrayals of
Wollstonecraft indicate that she remained a source of anxiety and
interest, and that some writers were already starting to respond to
the version of Wollstonecraft proffered by Godwin.

## Wollstonecraft's political legacy

According to scholars like Jump, Godwin ensured that Wollstonecraft's
name disappeared from published writing and became detached
from her work, which in turn fell out of print until her late-century

recuperation by Charles Kegan Paul's biography and the women's movement. This interpretation implies that Wollstonecraft's political writing was lost for much of the nineteenth century. William St Clair's publication history of the *Rights of Woman* seems to confirm this conclusion. He finds that after sizeable print runs for the first three editions of the 1790s, the text fell out of print in Britain until the 1890s, except for one cheap, re-edited version issued by the radical bookseller Strange in 1841 (of which there is only one known surviving copy).[170] The *Rights of Woman* did not join the radical canon which included Paine, Godwin, Volney, Shelley and Byron. St Clair concludes that, 'with only a few thousand copies of the book manufactured during the whole of the first century after first publication ... it would have been difficult, and unusual, for anyone, woman or man, to find and read the book'.[171]

However, access to the text may have been wider than St Clair allows. John Windle lists two editions in the 1840s (one in 1841 and another in 1844), both published by Strange and linked to the Chartist agitation of this decade.[172] The cheap price and stereotyped, paper-cover format of these 1840s editions, moreover, suggest large print runs. The preface to the 1844 edition confirms that the intent of the 'portable form' and 'low price' is politically motivated: 'to procure for it a wide circulation, and a proportionate inculcation of the important principles it enunciates'.[173] St Clair himself acknowledges elsewhere that commonly available, inexpensive printed texts often correlate with substantial readerships and poor survival rates over time.[174] The existence of these 1840s *Rights of Woman* editions shows that the book continued to be read, and it is possible that there were other 'disposable' editions of the *Rights of Woman* which have not survived.[175] St Clair concedes that the 1841 edition 'shows that the *Vindication* was not entirely forgotten by the Chartists' and 'may have been the most widely read edition before the twentieth century'.

Limited access to the text certainly prevented its wider dissemination and influence in nineteenth-century Britain, but this was not an obstacle for all reading constituencies, especially those actively in search of literary and political precedents for their work.

Political writing in periodicals also affirms that Wollstonecraft's *Rights of Woman* continued to be read and discussed throughout the

century, especially among the reform minded. Early nineteenth-
century radical groups, such as left-wing Unitarians, Owenite socialists
and equal-rights Chartists, reprinted Wollstonecraft frequently in
their publications.[176] In the 1830s, Owenite journals like the *New Moral
World* and the *Pioneer* – especially on its 'Woman's Page' – frequently
featured extracts from the *Rights of Woman*.[177] As the Chartist movement
developed in the 1830s and 1840s, many of its supporters promoted
the economic and political rights of women alongside those of the
working class, and they looked to the *Rights of Woman* for inspiration.
In 1841, Goodwyn Barmby, a leading Chartist, and his wife, Catherine
Barmby, wrote the 'Declaration of Electoral Reform' (1841), which
argued for the inclusion of women's suffrage in the Chartist movement.
Catherine Barmby later defended women's suffrage again in her
tract 'The Demand for the Emancipation of Women, Politically and
Socially' (1843). Early feminist activist Barbara Leigh Smith Bodichon
(and other ladies of Langham Place) applauded the *Rights of Woman*.[178]
Wollstonecraft's ideas influenced Bodichon's *Brief Summary, in Plain
Language, of the Most Important Laws Concerning Women* (1854), a pamphlet
which objected to women's unfair legal and social restrictions. The
widespread reference to Mary Wollstonecraft within feminist and
other progressive debates, as Kathryn Gleadle argues, 'calls into
question the extent to which Wollstonecraft's fire had ever been
truly quenched'.[179] Despite the alarm produced by Godwin's
*Memoirs*, Wollstonecraft's *Rights of Woman*, enjoyed a healthy, if
minority, readership.

The legacy of Wollstonecraft as a political polemicist can also
be traced in the two most significant nineteenth-century responses
to her work, William Thompson's *Appeal of One-Half the Human
Race* (1825) and John Stuart Mill's *The Subjection of Women* (1869).[180]
The *Appeal*'s 'Introductory Letter to Mrs. Wheeler' reveals Anna
Wheeler, a reform-minded writer who lived with Thompson in a free
union, as the pamphlet's co-author. The *Appeal* counters the assertion
of James Mill's *Essay On Government* (1820) that women did not need
political rights, as their interests were already represented sufficiently
by their fathers or husbands. At the outset of the *Appeal*, Thompson
and Wheeler invoke Wollstonecraft's 'neglected banner' and outline
their intention to 'equally elevate both sexes'.[181] Their calls for sex

and class equality form a radical programme of social reform that extends the ideas of predecessors like Mary Wollstonecraft (and Mary Hays).[182]

Four decades later, *The Subjection of Women* (1869) followed in this trajectory of liberal feminist discourse. Like Thompson, John Stuart Mill's feminist ideas emerged from a lengthy and intimate collaboration. His wife, Harriet Taylor Mill, was also a political radical who wrote and campaigned on topics discussed by Wollstonecraft, such as the inequality of the sexes, the customs and laws of marriage and women's rights.[183] Although neither husband nor wife seemed comfortable naming Wollstonecraft explicitly, they shared many of her social and political concerns.

Harriet Taylor Mill's *Westminster Review* essay 'Enfranchisement of Women' (1851), John Stuart Mill's *The Subjection of Women* (1869) and their early essays on marriage and divorce all bore traces of Wollstonecraft's thinking and rhetoric. The Mills echoed Wollstonecraft's claim that the education and legal rights of women are intimately connected with the progress and welfare of mankind. Wollstonecraft describes her 'main argument' in the *Rights of Woman* as 'built on this simple principle, that if she be not prepared by education to become the companion of man, she will stop the progress of knowledge and virtue; for truth must be common to all, or it will be inefficacious with respect to its influence on general practice'.[184] In the *Westminster Review* (1851), Harriet Taylor Mill argues:

> For the interest, therefore, not only of women but of men, and of human improvement in the widest sense, the emancipation of women, which the modern world often boasts of having effected ... cannot stop where it is.[185]

Nearly two decades later, John Stuart Mill reiterated this ideology in his *Subjection of Women* (1869).

> That the principle which regulates the existing social relations between the two sexes – the legal subordination of one sex to the other – is wrong in itself, and now one of the chief hindrances to human improvement; and that it ought to be replaced by a principle of perfect equality, admitting no power or privilege on the one side, no disability on the other.[186]

Even if Wollstonecraft is constructing 'a plea for the better education of women rather than a political manifesto', her *Rights of Woman* can be seen as a precursor to the campaign for suffrage and legal equality which was upheld by the Mills in the mid-nineteenth century.[187] Wollstonecraft had argued for a 'REVOLUTION' – a complete overhaul in women's education – from which emancipation would follow.[188] Building on this call, the Mills supported women's voting rights, and Harriet Taylor Mill also emphasised women's entitlement to work outside the home. As McLay explains, both husband and wife came 'full circle to Mary Wollstonecraft's concerns'.[189] The Mills used Wollstonecraft's ideas to support their arguments for legal, political, social and professional reform.

Wollstonecraft's presence in political texts, whether named or implied, means that some assumptions about the impact of the *Memoirs* need to be reconsidered. I follow Gleadle in finding that the 'conventional narrative' that Godwin's scandalous biography closed down 'the articulation of revolutionary feminism' and induced 'female authors ... to forget the lessons Wollstonecraft had taught' seems inaccurate.[190] Sapiro appears mistaken in her suggestion that 'there is little indication that anyone who played a key role in women's history or feminism ... read Wollstonecraft's work seriously after her death until the twentieth century'.[191] As has been shown, readers in progressive movements engaged with the *Rights of Woman* throughout the century and built on Wollstonecraft's work in their own. Nor is it entirely accurate to say, as Barbara Caine has, that Wollstonecraft 'was rarely even mentioned, let alone venerated, for most of the nineteenth century'.[192] Certainly, as Taylor shows, many budding feminists 'balked at claiming a free-living revolutionary as their political ancestor'.[193] The Mills, for example, did not refer to Wollstonecraft directly, and in order to protect their own reputations, many women avoided naming a woman whose sexual transgressions could be damning by association.[194] Yet even if Wollstonecraft's ideas were often raised anonymously or implicitly, she was read, referenced, and often respected, nonetheless. Godwin's *Memoirs* did not silence the voice of Wollstonecraft's *Vindication of the Rights of Woman*.

## A political life

In addition to influencing political tracts, Wollstonecraft had also become a topic in periodicals by the 1850s. Amidst debates sparked in part by the Seneca Falls Convention in New York in 1848, three sizeable articles exemplify mid-Victorian discussions of Wollstonecraft and women's rights: Eliza Lynn Linton's 'Mary Wollstonecraft' (1854), which appeared in the *English Republic*; Anne Mozley's 'Rights of Women' (1855), in the *Christian Remembrancer*; and George Eliot's comparative essay in *The Leader*, 'Margaret Fuller and Mary Wollstonecraft' (1855).[195] Both Linton, a well-known Victorian reviewer and prolific writer of fiction, and esteemed novelist and journalist George Eliot praised Wollstonecraft's ideals and admired her politics, whereas the conservative, High Church Mozley remained much more critical. However, all three showed familiarity with Wollstonecraft's life and works, as well as her relevance to contemporary women's rights discourse and activism. Linton mentions not only the *Rights of Woman* but the *Wrongs of Woman* as well; Mozley refers specifically to her copy of *Rights of Woman* being published in New York (probably the American edition of 1833, which included a biographical sketch) before quoting from it at length; Eliot peppers her essay with shorter extracts from the *Rights of Woman*.

These articles suggest that although the *Memoirs* rendered Wollstonecraft a symbol of impropriety and immorality for some, it fashioned her into a figure for study and inspiration for others. Godwin believed that the 'account of the life of a person of eminent merit … converts into the fairest source of animation and encouragement to those who would follow them'.[196] After the *Memoirs*, Sapiro contends, Wollstonecraft's life itself

> became a text of political theory and a practice that [was] interpreted and reinterpreted by later writers and activists. From the time Godwin revealed something of the private Wollstonecraft in the *Memoirs*, her life-events and choices have been read and studied in much the same way that political-theory texts, more conventionally defined, are read and studied.[197]

This effect can be seen in George Eliot's *Leader* essay, 'Margaret Fuller and Mary Wollstonecraft' (1855). At first, Eliot skirts around

Wollstonecraft's life by emphasising the text of *Rights of Woman* rather than its infamous author. This evasion has been attributed to Eliot's own dubious circumstances: she had entered into a scandalous common-law marriage with George Henry Lewes the previous year. Yet the essay reveals more than the 'compliment' of taking Wollstonecraft's work seriously or Eliot's own wish to be respected as a writer regardless of her decisions in her private life.[198] Her interpretation of the *Rights of Woman* figures Wollstonecraft's life as the prime example of her own progressive ideas on women's social status.

Eliot compares Wollstonecraft and Fuller to segue from a discussion of women's work and education into a pointed critique of the disparity between the sexes in marriage. Fuller, the true 'literary woman', takes up the pen as an intellectual enterprise for its own sake, while Wollstonecraft 'writes from the pressure of other motives'.[199] Here Eliot veers away from textual analysis into personal life, suggesting that unlike Fuller, Wollstonecraft's writing resulted from financial necessity. Having implied Wollstonecraft's professional and material self-reliance, Eliot then reflects on the philosophical argument of the *Rights of Woman*.

Far from ignoring Wollstonecraft's personal reputation, as some critics have suggested, Eliot invokes it as the tacit substructure of her exposition. She reiterates Wollstonecraft's argument for educating women as sentient beings: 'Business of various kinds they might likewise pursue, if they were educated in a more orderly manner. ... Women would not then marry for a support'.[200] Eliot then links women's lack of rational education with the debasement of marriage.

> Men pay a heavy price for their reluctance to encourage self-help and independent resources in women. The precious meridian years of many a man of genius have to be spent in the toil of routine ... for a woman who can but understand none of his secret yearnings, who is fit for nothing but to sit in her drawing-room like a doll-Madonna in her shrine.[201]

The implicit antithesis of this scenario is Wollstonecraft's union with Godwin. If Wollstonecraft wrote for a living, not purely for intellectual pleasure, as Eliot proposes, it follows that she chose her romantic partner *not* materialistically for 'a support' but for companionship and affection. Eliot, perhaps, was thinking of Godwin's famous declaration of his courtship of Wollstonecraft as 'friendship melting into love' or of his conviction that 'no two persons ever found in each other's society, a satisfaction more pure and refined'.[202]

Eliot invokes Wollstonecraft's life here without explicitly reciting it.[203] This circuitous strategy has been viewed as usual fare for mid-century authors who dealt with Wollstonecraft's questionable past by simply ignoring it.[204] However, Wollstonecraft's life is not ignored here; it is the implied subtext of Eliot's essay. Trusting that her readers already knew the details of this 'questionable past', Eliot suggested it as another example of Wollstonecraft's visionary politics.

Eliza Lynn Linton's 'Mary Wollstonecraft' (1854) also reads private life as political praxis, though she gives a more explicit account of Wollstonecraft's history. Calling the decision not to marry Imlay a 'social experiment', Linton praises Wollstonecraft's consistent adherence to her 'morality' and her ability to 'appeal to God for judgement, not to man for approbation'.[205] Linton also apparently agrees with Godwin about the significance of Wollstonecraft's life as a text that will live on for posterity:

> She was one of the priestesses of the future; and men will yet gather constancy and truth from her example: so true it is that a good deed never dies out, but extends its influence as far as Humanity can reach.[206]

Yet this interpretation also leads Linton to conflate text and life, confusing the reception of *Rights of Woman* with that of the *Memoirs*. Linton incorrectly suggests that 'Mary's great work' caused 'the very class she had defended [to turn] the most bitterly against her'.[207] She assumes that Wollstonecraft's *Rights of Woman* was as controversial as the *Memoirs*. This assumption signals one dangerous consequence of Godwin's *Memoirs*: her political writing could be collapsed into her life.

Anne Mozley's 'Rights of Women' (1855) illustrates how this same blurring was used to condemn Wollstonecraft. Her discussion of Elizabeth Oakes Smith's feminist novel *Bertha and Lily* (1854), and its controversial philosophy of free love, is swiftly brought back to

Wollstonecraft. Mozley pronounces Smith's idea of free love 'a very unsettling theory' before bemoaning:

> Nor, alas! Can we speak of these views as mere theory. Already ... they are bearing their natural fruits, as all theories on so vital a point must very soon do.[208]

This lament segues into an indictment of Wollstonecraft, who, Mozley implies, set the precedent for such 'unsettling' theories and the immoral behaviour they foster.

> One main end of the 'Vindication of the Rights of Women,' [sic] is to persuade them that the sentiment of warm, devoted, conjugal affection, all 'exclusive affections,' prevent women fulfilling the duties of their station with dignity, by preoccupying and narrowing the mind.[209]

Here Mozley either misreads the *Rights of Woman* or misrepresents it. Her interpretation speaks to a prevalent misconception about the *Rights of Woman* that derived from reading (or imagining) it via the *Memoirs*. It also evidences a problem that had long plagued Wollstonecraft's posthumous reputation. Since its publication in 1798, the greatest liability of the *Memoirs* had been that, as Nicola Trott articulates, it 'present[ed] Wollstonecraft's enemies, not just with the material, but with the very method – that of reducing 'theory' to 'practice' – by which she is to be anathematized'.[210] Nevertheless, critics have perhaps privileged this 'unfortunate' consequence of the *Memoirs* at the expense of other, more positive effects.[211]

## Affective response

One of the most powerful – and least documented – effects of the *Memoirs* is the emotional connection it forged between Wollstonecraft and her posthumous readers. Godwin not only encouraged readers to admire Wollstonecraft's life as a revolutionary model but also invited them to identify with her personally. Scholars have questioned Godwin's emphasis on his wife's 'feminine qualities of imagination, emotive force, and maternal softness' and his privileging of her love life over the life of her mind.[212] Although Godwin has been faulted for writing the 'memoir of a woman, not a writer, or a feminist', it may be in part this 'feminine' emphasis that affected readers so deeply.[213]

The accounts of Wollstonecraft in nineteenth-century group biographies and biographical dictionaries illustrate this personal, emotionally charged response.[214] Wollstonecraft appeared in several such volumes published in Britain in the first half of the nineteenth century, most of which predated the 'boom' in collective biography that began in the 1830s and peaked at the *fin de siècle*.[215] Wollstonecraft featured in William Boyd's *Eccentric Biography* (1803), Mary Pilkington's *Memoirs of Celebrated Female Characters* (1804), Mary Mathilda Betham's *Biographical Dictionary of Celebrated Women* (1804), Alexander Chalmers's *A New and General Biographical Dictionary* (1814) and Anne Katharine Elwood's *Memoirs of the Literary Ladies of England from the Commencement of the Last Century* (1843). An equal number of similar volumes from this period omitted Wollstonecraft.[216] Gleadle finds that merely including Wollstonecraft may already 'signal a feminist sympathy',[217] and this is evident in the entries by Pilkington and Betham. Yet the coverage of Wollstonecraft in these multibiographies reveals more than a feminist leaning.

Like Godwin's *Memoirs*, these collective biographies reimagine Wollstonecraft as a real-life heroine. Pilkington explains that although Wollstonecraft possessed 'vigour of understanding', she was ever 'influenced by feeling, humanity, and love'.[218] Lamenting that such a gifted and noble woman had ultimately 'deviated from the path of purity and rectitude' in her involvement with Imlay and her suicide attempts, Pilkington separates her from those 'who glory in their vice'. Moreover, she reads into Wollstonecraft's narrative the hand of 'providence', which ensured the failure of her suicide attempt and also restored her to domestic peace. Pilkington explains that soon after this difficult period, Wollstonecraft met and married Godwin, 'became a mother, and completely fulfilled the duties both of a parent and a wife'.[219] Here, Wollstonecraft's life reads like the plot of a novel.

The *Eccentric Biography* goes further, dressing Wollstonecraft in all the trappings of a sentimental heroine. The editor's parenthetical aside adds emotional force to his argument.

> The history of this singular woman ... has been that of one continued
> struggle with adverse circumstances, cares, and sorrows, combated,
> in every instance but one (over which humanity sheds its softest tear),
> with heroic fortitude.[220]

Though Wollstonecraft was 'a victim to the vices and prejudices
of mankind', she eventually 'triumph[ed] over her malignant
destiny' and found herself at last 'a wife, a mother, surrounded by
tender, admiring, intelligent friends'.[221] Boyd not only emphasises
Wollstonecraft's happy ending but also follows the main construct of
the *Memoirs*: that there was a heroic relationship between her life and
work.[222]

Alexander Chalmers's *Biographical Dictionary*, despite its
denunciation of Wollstonecraft, nevertheless also responds to
Godwin's framing. Chalmers's tone is contemptuous as he chronicles
Wollstonecraft's transgressions and does his best to prove her 'a
voluptuary and a sensualist'. Still, in stressing that 'her history indeed
forms entirely a warning, and in no part an example', Chalmers
acknowledges the affective power of Godwin's narrative.[223] As a
rejoinder, he advises that her writings be suppressed and fashions
a scathing five-page account as a deterrent to readers.[224] Chalmers
perhaps feared that reading Wollstonecraft as the romantic heroine of
her own life was moving enough to be dangerous.

Anne Katharine Elwood's decision to include Wollstonecraft
in her *Memoirs of the Literary Ladies of England* (1843) has surprised
some modern critics, yet it is likely that she, too, felt an affinity with
her predecessor.[225] Elwood supposedly undertook her *Memoirs of the
Literary Ladies of England* because she could not locate a work of this
kind.[226] She wrote it from a

> partiality to the literary performances of her own sex, and from her
> anxiety to obtain information concerning the lives and characters of
> those individuals in whom she took an interest, without, in general,
> being able to gratify that curiosity.[227]

Elwood's decision to include Wollstonecraft, then, signals 'curiosity'
and 'interest' – both her own and her readers' – which trumped the
risks of associating herself with such a figure.

Though Elwood hails Wollstonecraft's 'virtues and talents' as well as her 'bold and original way of thinking', she seems most of all to relish the junction of bliss and tragedy that characterised the end of her subject's life. Dreamily reiterating the romantic confession Godwin disclosed in the *Memoirs*, of having fallen for his wife from the perusal of her *Letters*, Elwood emphasises the happy ending of the Godwin–Wollstonecraft union:

> The Godwins seemed for a short time to have enjoyed happiness as unalloyed as it is possible to meet with in this transitory world.[228]

Even in celebrating their tranquillity and joy as a pair, though, these lines warn of the misfortune that awaits the lovers. Elwood's 'for a short time' foreshadows Wollstonecraft's death days after giving birth to her second child, Mary Godwin.

Even if, as Jump suggests, Elwood's 'final verdict on Wollstonecraft is decidedly mixed', her regard for Wollstonecraft as an ancestor in the history of women remained unequivocal.[229] Joan W. Scott has defined women's historiography as 'a story of discontinuity that was repeatedly sutured by feminist activists in the eighteenth and nineteenth centuries into a vision of uninterrupted linear succession: women's activism on behalf of women'.[230] Despite their differences, Elwood finds her a compelling prototype of their sex:

> If error even in a Mary Wollstonecraft could not be overlooked, what woman can hope to offend with impunity against the laws of society?[231]

The curiosity, admiration and sympathy that infuse Elwood's text attest not only to Wollstonecraft's enduring presence in the hearts and minds of posthumous readers but also to the lasting power of Godwin's exposition of Wollstonecraft in the *Memoirs*.

The emotional investment of readers in Wollstonecraft led to a preoccupation with her romantic relationship with Godwin. Mary Shelley's unfinished memoir of her father, begun in 1836, tenderly rehearsed the meeting and marriage of her parents. Paying homage to her father's description of these events and their effect on him, she affectionately explains:

> As time proceeds a considerable change appears to have been
> operated in Mr Godwin's mind; more in manner than in substance
> certainly – but there was a softening attendant on his having quitted
> his independent position & making one of the family of mankind.[232]

Shelley's tone, with its mix of reverence, fondness and regret, is
perhaps unsurprising. After all, she was writing about her own
mother, who had died in childbirth. Yet similarly affective undertones
pervaded responses to Wollstonecraft by writers with no familial
connection to her.

Even those women writers who went to great lengths to distinguish
themselves from Wollstonecraft betrayed an affective connection to
her. In her *Autobiography*, written in 1855 but not published until 1877,
Harriet Martineau distances herself from the lack of discipline and
unbridled sensibility she perceives in Wollstonecraft.

> I never could reconcile my mind to Mary Wollstonecraft's writings,
> or to whatever I heard of her. ... Women who would improve the
> condition and chances of their sex must, I am certain, be not only
> affectionate and devoted, but rational and dispassionate. ... But Mary
> Wollstonecraft was, with all her powers, a poor victim of passion,
> with no control over her own peace, and no calmness or content
> except when the needs of her individual nature were satisfied.[233]

The best advocates for the advancement of women's position, for
Martineau, are those morally and intellectually sound women who
'have no injuries of their own to avenge' and who thus do not 'injure
the cause by their personal tendencies'. Unlike Godwin, Martineau
does not view the personal as a category of political protest. Instead,
unorthodox 'personal tendencies' erode women's credibility, tarring
them with the 'suspicion' of passion rather than securing for them
the 'consideration' that leads to 'rational treatment'. The scandal
of Wollstonecraft's life undermines her integrity as a promoter of
women's rights.

In spite of the demarcation she draws between women like
Wollstonecraft and herself, though, Martineau admits to an
'admiration' for her. Moreover, Martineau's letters reveal esteem for
Wollstonecraft as a pioneer in the 'hard work' of effecting women's

'liberty'. Meditating on the 'the woman question' in 1840, Martineau wrote to Mrs Chapman in America:

> You will live to see a great enlargement of our scope, I trust; but, what with the vices of some women and the fears of others, it is hard work for us to assert our liberty. I will, however, till I die, and so will you; and so make it easier for some few to follow us than it was for poor Mary Wollstonecraft to begin.[234]

This passing reference reveals Martineau's assumption that Wollstonecraft marked the origin of the contemporary women's 'movement'. The adjective 'poor', which Martineau repeats several times, conveys sympathy for Wollstonecraft, even if it is mixed with a sense of superiority. Still, Martineau seems to harbour an emotional and intellectual regard for Wollstonecraft. It may thus not be entirely fair to say, as Taylor has, that for Martineau, 'Wollstonecraft's sexual history … contaminated her writings and diseased her politics'.[235] Wollstonecraft, simply, was not 'a safe example'. That Martineau wished to sequester herself from Wollstonecraft's behaviour does not mean that she had no regard for her political predecessor. Her *Autobiography* and correspondence corroborate that Martineau recognised Wollstonecraft's contribution and felt compassion for her even if she did not condone her lifestyle.

## Rehabilitation and respectability

Charles Kegan Paul's two-volume *William Godwin, His Friends and Contemporaries* (1876) marks a turning point in Wollstonecraft's posthumous reception.[236] Much recent scholarship has concluded that the recuperation of Wollstonecraft was only truly accomplished when Sir Percy Shelley, the grandson of Wollstonecraft and Godwin, commissioned this official biography to clear the family name. The clergyman-turned-author Paul was given access to the Shelley family archive to accomplish the task. Entertaining and well researched, Paul's biography added detail and intimacy to the family history, while at the same time carefully modifying the most controversial episodes. His biographical rehabilitation project did not end here, either. In

1878, *Fraser's Magazine* featured his fifteen-page 'Mary Wollstonecraft. A Vindication', which the following year became the 'Prefatory Memoir' to his edition of *Mary Wollstonecraft: Letters to Imlay* (1879). Together, these pieces of life writing helped to make Wollstonecraft respectable, rewriting the record on three counts: her involvement with the painter Henry Fuseli, her cohabitation with Imlay outside marriage and her radical religious and political beliefs.

Paul dismissed the Fuseli incident as outright slander. Godwin's *Memoirs* had briefly mentioned Wollstonecraft's 'personal and ardent affection' for her married friend, Henry Fuseli, the unrequited love for whom eventually induced her to move to France at the end of 1792.[237] In his *Life and Writing of Henry Fuseli* (1831), John Knowles claimed to have used extant letters to fill in the gaps of Godwin's account: Wollstonecraft had fallen in love with Fuseli and subsequently suggested moving in with his family. According to Knowles, she believed:

> Although Mrs. Fuseli had a right to the person of her husband, she, Mrs. Wollstonecraft, might claim … a place in his heart; for "she hoped," she said, "to unite herself to his mind."[238]

Paul, however, insisted that Godwin 'knew extremely little of his wife's earlier life' and probably heard the story 'second-hand'.[239] In response to the 'extremely inaccurate' Knowles, Paul reminds us 'that Mary remained to the end the correspondent and close friend of Mrs. Fuseli'.[240] Paul concludes that the relationship between Fuseli and Wollstonecraft was platonic: she left for Paris 'heart-whole'.[241]

Paul also rationalised Wollstonecraft's decision not to marry Imlay. The 'high-minded' Wollstonecraft was living out a 'moral theory gravely and religiously adopted' when she consented to reside with Imlay out of wedlock, for she felt that 'mutual affection was marriage, and that the marriage tie should not bind after the death of love'.[242] Besides, Wollstonecraft's precarious status as an English woman in a Parisian war zone meant that a legal marriage would have been practically 'impossible'. The decision not to marry Imlay, then, was occasioned by a combination of misguided philosophy and unfortunate logistics, not vice or religious unbelief. Paul stressed her piety and morality, and the tragedy that 'living and dying as a Christian, she

has been called an atheist'. Changes in the contemporary position
of women, moreover, made many of Wollstonecraft's views about
the equality of the sexes and the importance of co-education, for
example, seem commonplace. Her so-called 'subversive' opinions,
Paul reminded readers, were 'those which most cultivated women
now hold'.[243]

Paul thus attempted to sanitise a reputation tainted by the
publication of the *Memoirs* in 1798. Yet despite the instrumental
modifications made in constructing his version of Wollstonecraft,
he also took many cues from Godwin. Like his predecessor, Paul
humanised Wollstonecraft by including her letters and focused more
on showcasing her womanly character than discussing her writing.[244]
He also, like Godwin, celebrated Wollstonecraft for leading a life in
accordance with her beliefs. It is perhaps not surprising, then, that
Paul's life writing evoked a sympathy reminiscent of so many earlier
nineteenth-century responses to Wollstonecraft. Leslie Stephen's
1876 *Fortnightly Review* article indicates one contemporary reaction:

> Mr. Paul has a warm admiration for this lady, and vindicates her
> triumphantly … She was plainly a woman of much noble feeling and
> high aspirations: if her conduct was not irreproachable … we must
> forgive much to a woman thrown from an early age on her own
> resources.[245]

A familiar Wollstonecraft emerges: the heroine of sensibility, the
high-minded pioneer in a real-life romance – but now, her conduct
has been 'forgive[n]'. Wollstonecraft had lived on in the nineteenth-
century imagination, and Leslie Stephen even acknowledges that
'Godwin is probably remembered at the present day chiefly as the
husband of Mary Wollstonecraft'.[246] According to Stephen, Godwin
was 'wanting in the force and richness of character that keeps the dead
alive'; Wollstonecraft, by implication, was not.[247] She had only been
'wanting' in virtue, which Paul helped to restore. His life writing
in the 1870s indeed marked a 'turning point', but not because he
radically refashioned her persona. He just made her respectable.

Paul's newly revised Wollstonecraft soon saw coverage in a range
of biographical works, including essays as well as monographs. His

writing certainly paved the way for these texts, but the timing was also crucial. It is no coincidence that the era of the New Woman, which saw the rise of the female professional journalist and an increased attention to women's political, economic and cultural status, witnessed a renewed interest in Wollstonecraft. Female aesthete and New Woman writer Mathilde Blind published her version of 'Mary Wollstonecraft' in the *New Quarterly* in 1878; Scottish novelist, historical writer and established reviewer Margaret Oliphant's *The Literary History of England in the End of the Eighteenth and Beginning of the Nineteenth Century* (1882) included a healthy entry on Wollstonecraft; and in 1885, the art critic, biographer and journalist Elizabeth Robins Pennell contributed her *Mary Wollstonecraft Godwin* to John H. Ingram's 'Eminent Women' series, creating the first book-length biography of Wollstonecraft since the *Memoirs*. These texts tended to regard Wollstonecraft's persona much as Godwin had in 1798, but they incorporated Paul's reconditioned version of events. With her indecencies vindicated, they were free to discuss her literary contributions.

Mathilde Blind carefully establishes Wollstonecraft as a female 'Werther' with a 'lovely face [and] a countenance essentially feminine'.[248] Yet she also characterises Wollstonecraft as one of the few female 'professional authors' of her day. Acknowledging that the *Rights of Woman* 'has enjoyed the doubtful privilege of looming in the imagination of the reading world as a *terra incognita* of the most daring and subversive speculations', Blind analyses its arguments about women's duties and rights and lists the reforms proposed alongside sizeable extracts.[249] Unlike Paul, Blind's purpose is not just to remove the prejudice by displaying the book's 'moderate character'. Blind also endeavoured to position her forebear in relation to the 'present movement for securing to women certain professional privileges and political rights'.[250] She weaves lengthy discussions of Wollstonecraft's literary works into a chronicle of her life.

Oliphant also considers Wollstonecraft's life and work in tandem, urging readers to revise their impressions of her and situating her *Rights of Woman* in the context of contemporary debates on women's rights. Yoking the personal and the political, Oliphant discusses the effect of Wollstonecraft's early struggles to protect and provide for her family in the face of a 'disreputable' and 'drunken' father on the development of her views about women.[251] She suggests that Wollstonecraft's situation in this respect is not singular, because 'the strong protestations in favour of … the Rights of Women … have risen almost invariably from women compelled by hard stress of circumstances to despise the men around them'.[252] Oliphant goes on to remind readers, however, that Wollstonecraft's 'plea for women is of the mildest description': she argues for 'their right to be considered as human creatures', asks for 'common education, of boys and girls together' and touches only momentarily on suffrage when she mentions that 'women ought to have representation instead of being arbitrarily governed'.[253] Oliphant stresses that the *Rights of Woman* is a 'book … free from revolutionary principles' and 'full of the warmest religiousness'.[254]

Pennell's sentimental tone differs from the intellectual tenor of Oliphant and Blind, but she likewise aims to combat the 'infamy attached to [Wollstonecraft's] name' and to produce a biography as a 'refutation' of the malignant attacks on her character.[255] She introduces Wollstonecraft as a martyr to a cause, one who 'devoted herself to the relief of her suffering fellow-beings with the ardour of a Saint Vincent de Paul' but 'was considered by them a moral scourge of God'.[256] With full chapters on 'First Years of Work', 'Literary Life', 'Literary Work, 1788–1791', 'Vindication of the Rights of Woman' and 'Literary Work, 1793–1796', a third of Pennell's biography is dedicated to Wollstonecraft's literary and political significance. She names Wollstonecraft's *Rights of Woman* as 'the first word in behalf of female emancipation', explicitly situating Wollstonecraft as 'the forerunner' of the contemporary women's movement.[257] At the same time, like Oliphant, she reminds readers that 'her propositions are, to the present advocates of the cause, foregone conclusions'.[258]

As part of the 'Eminent Women' series, Pennell's *Mary Wollstonecraft Godwin* (1885) also positions Wollstonecraft within an emerging canon of literary women. Edited by John Henry Ingram and published by W. H. Allen between 1883 and 1895, this series paired contemporary biographers with deceased women writers. The biography of Wollstonecraft thus sat alongside volumes on Emily Brontë (written by A. Mary F. Robinson), Elizabeth Barrett Browning (written by Ingram), Harriet Martineau (written by Florence Fenwick Miller),

Mary Shelley (written by Lucy Madox Brown Rossetti), Hannah More
(written by Charlotte Mary Yonge), George Eliot (written by Mathilde
Blind) and Jane Austen (written by Sarah Fanny Malden). Except
for the volume on Barrett Browning, which he undertook himself,
Ingram exclusively commissioned women to pen the biographies in
the 'Eminent Women' series. It thus not only showcased the most
prominent female authors of the period but also put them in dialogue
with earlier women writers. The series allowed its writers not only
to champion their literary predecessors but to write themselves into
the canon as well.[259] Pennell's *Mary Wollstonecraft Godwin*, like the texts
by Oliphant and Blind, thus exemplifies how this renewed attention
to Wollstonecraft's life and work offered her posthumous readers
– among them journalists, novelists, aesthetes and activists – an
opportunity to use her legacy as a means to participate in literary
historiography, contemporary cultural debates and self-promotion.

## Wollstonecraft and first-wave feminism

The last decade of the nineteenth century saw a surge in Wollstonecraft
reprints and her apotheosis in the women's rights movement. Professor
Henry Morley reissued the *Letters Written During a Short Residence in
Sweden, Norway and Denmark* (1889); Millicent Garret Fawcett and
Elizabeth Robins Pennell edited reprints of the *Rights of Woman* in
1891 and 1892, respectively; and in 1898, Dr Emma Rauschenbusch-
Clough published *A Study of Mary Wollstonecraft and the Rights of Woman*.
With her most famous works in circulation and her conduct no longer
a disgrace to her sex, Wollstonecraft became a writer fit for academic
study and re-appropriation by the accelerating feminist movement.
Fawcett, founder of the National Union of Women's Suffrage, hailed
her as a pioneer of the cause and reminded readers that 'the battle in
which Mary Wollstonecraft took a leading part is still being waged'.[260]
Yet Wollstonecraft's life still took a prime place even in these most
political of discussions:

> Mary Wollstonecraft's great merit, however, lies in this, that … she
> did not sanction any depreciation of the immense importance of the
> domestic duties of women. … she recognized love and the attraction
> between the sexes as a cardinal fact in human nature, and "marriage as

the foundation of almost every social virtue". ... Mary Wollstonecraft, in her writings as well as in her life, with its sorrows and errors, is the essentially womanly woman.[261]

Fawcett refashions Wollstonecraft to suit the agenda of her own brand of feminism, taking liberties that go beyond Paul's whitewashed version. This kind of reinvention continued with each successive generation of feminists.[262]

Still, Godwin's Wollstonecraft, the romantic heroine of sensibility, surfaces even for Fawcett:

> Her sharp wits had been sharpened by every sort of personal misfortune; they enabled her to pierce through all shams and pretences, but they never caused her to lower her high sense of duty. ... her face in the picture in the National Portrait Gallery speaks for her. Southey wrote of her, that ... "her face was the best, infinitely the best".[263]

Pennell, who admired Wollstonecraft's willingness to 'defy public opinion – to step out of the bounds of female reserve', likewise admits:

> Her book gains force when it is realised how entirely her arguments and doctrines are based upon experience. Indeed, without this realisation, without a knowledge of her young life's sorrows and responsibilities, it loses half its interest.[264]

As Barbara Caine argues, 'Godwin made Wollstonecraft a martyr to the cause of personal feeling and emotional honesty' and thus 'gave her a power within nineteenth-century feminism which her published texts alone would not have produced'.[265] The affective responses to Wollstonecraft from *fin-de-siècle* feminists attest to this 'power'.

Wollstonecraft material continued to proliferate in the early twentieth century. The suffragists referenced Wollstonecraft in publications such as Fawcett's *Women's Suffrage: a Short History of a Great Movement* (1912), W. Lyon Blease's *The Emancipation of English Women* (1913) and Evelyn Sharp's periodical articles. Interest in her private life also endured. Roger Ingpen reprinted her correspondence in *Love Letters of Mary Wollstonecraft to Gilbert Imlay* (1908), G. R. Stirling Taylor rehearsed her life in *Wollstonecraft: A Study in Economics and Romance* (1911) and Camilla Jebb's *Mary Wollstonecraft* (1912) featured a series of

extracts considering her writing and personal history. Wollstonecraft
continued to resonate affectively with readers. Todd finds that much
of the Edwardian writing on Wollstonecraft 'testified less to her
notoriety than to her appeal [and was] illuminated more through
emotional insight than through factual research'.[266] Paul's blue-pencil
account of Wollstonecraft allowed late-Victorian readers to embrace
her as morally upright, though later readers were increasingly drawn
to the inconsistencies in her history that surface in Godwin's account
and the construction of Wollstonecraft as a 'flawed' heroine.[267]

Modern scholars have acknowledged the ongoing legacy of
Godwin's *Memoirs*. Shattock accords it a 'near-mythic status' as *the*
biography, like Gaskell's *Life of Charlotte Brontë* (1854), with which every
subsequent Wollstonecraft biographer takes issue. Caine finds that
Wollstonecraft's life, as traced by Godwin, served later generations of
women as an early model of the struggle to accommodate their ideals
to the habits of their everyday lives.[268] However, many critics agree
with Shattock's lament that the *Memoirs* projects the image of 'the
woman, not of a writer'. Like Gaskell, Godwin is seen as 'concerned
with the woman rather than her books'. Yet, as this chapter has shown,
what later readers, novelists and biographers often responded to most
viscerally was the relationship between the woman, her books and the
man who fell in love with both. In this respect, Godwin's biography
is pivotal not only in shaping Wollstonecraft's posthumous reputation
but also in its unique contribution to the genre of life writing itself.

The implications of the *Memoirs* for both Wollstonecraft's legacy
and for biography in general are captured, again, in the writing of
Virginia Woolf. In 'Mary Wollstonecraft', which first appeared in
1929 and was republished in *The Common Reader, Second Series* (1932),
Woolf imagines Wollstonecraft as the equal of the men around her:

> There was also a woman present with very bright eyes and a very eager
> tongue, and the young men, who had middle-class names, like Barlow
> and Holcroft and Godwin, called her simply "Wollstonecraft", as if it
> did not matter whether she were married or unmarried, as if she were
> a young man like themselves.[269]

Woolf also admires her as a 'reformer' with 'Revolution ... in her
blood', who rebelled in her writing as much as in her life, 'against

tyranny, against law, against convention'.²⁷⁰ Woolf's Wollstonecraft experiences the 'agony' of heartbreak, first with Fuseli and later with Imlay, but valiantly recovers her spirits and her independence. Yet Woolf revels, most of all, in the happiness her heroine discovered with Godwin. She extolls their union as a successful experiment that joined passion and principle. As if on cue from Godwin himself, Woolf reads in Wollstonecraft's life romance and revolution.

Not only Woolf's 'Reading Notebooks' but also the version of events in her 'Mary Wollstonecraft' sketch show the overwhelming influence not of Paul or even Wollstonecraft's own work – though she read both – but Godwin's *Memoirs*.²⁷¹ Quoting from Godwin's famous description of 'friendship melting into love', Woolf tenderly retraces their early romance. She explains how Godwin's theories and 'extraordinary views' were modified: 'he had never been in love; now for the first time he was to experience that sensation.'²⁷² She celebrates their domestic felicity and mutual affection and their ongoing aspirations for social and political reform. In the series of lengthy and impassioned rhetorical questions that adds emotional energy to her final paragraph, Woolf marvels at the biographer himself and his unique brand of life writing:

> And what strange upheaval of human life was it that inspired that curious man, who was so queer a mixture of meanness and magnanimity, of coldness and deep feeling – for the memoir of his wife could not have been written without unusual depth of heart – to hold the view that she did right – that he respected Mary for trampling upon the idiotic convention by which women's lives were tied down?²⁷³

Woolf is both puzzled and awed by Godwin's unorthodox biography, which is at once literary, political and deeply personal. Though she expresses grief at Wollstonecraft's early death, she celebrates her legacy, an 'immortality' that she links specifically to Godwin:

> as we read her letters and listen to her arguments and consider her experiments, above all, that most fruitful experiment, her relation with Godwin, and realise the high-handed and hot-blooded manner in which she cut her way to the quick of life, one form of immortality is hers undoubtedly: she is alive and active, she argues and experiments, we hear her voice and trace her influence even now among the living.²⁷⁴

The power of Godwin's *Memoirs*, with its tripartite layering of political meditation, cathartic farewell and real-life love story, is perhaps simple: it keeps Wollstonecraft 'among the living'.

Although the publication of Godwin's controversial biography in 1798 undeniably took a toll on Wollstonecraft's posthumous standing, it also imbued her afterlife with an emotional appeal. Throughout the century, the mythology of Wollstonecraft as a revolutionary romantic heroine held fast, coexisting with a steady (if minority) interest in her political writing. With the introduction of Paul's more palatable account of Wollstonecraft's life, readers could embrace her openly. Yet the proliferation of Wollstonecraft material at the *fin de siècle* revealed a familiar figure: the principled, feeling and beloved protagonist of Godwin's *Memoirs*. Moreover, this interest, which continued into the twentieth century and beyond, was accompanied by a reconsideration of her writing. By the early decades of the twentieth century, her greatest works were being published and studied again, still relevant after 100 years. Therefore, though scandalous biographies may have the potential to undermine authorial agency, they do not necessarily signal the undoing of artistic integrity. Godwin's *Memoirs* stands as an innovative contribution to Romantic life writing, as well as a factor in maintaining – and shaping – the public memory of Wollstonecraft. Mary Robinson's life writing also played a role in her posthumous reputation, though her scandalous history was common knowledge long before the publication of her *Memoirs* (1801). The next chapter will explore how the gaps, rather than the disclosures, in Robinson's *Memoirs* proved most pivotal, evoking a mixture of sympathy, excitement and mystery that gave her an enduring appeal in the nineteenth century and beyond.

## Notes

1 Michelle Levy, 'Women and Print Culture, 1750–1830', in *The History of British Women's Writing, 1750–1830*, ed. Jacqueline M. Labbe (Basingstoke: Palgrave Macmillan, 2012), pp. 38–9; James Raven, 'Historical Introduction: The Novel Comes of Age', in *The English Novel 1770–1829: A Bibliographical Survey of Prose Fiction Published in the British Isles*, ed. Peter Garside, James Raven and Rainer Schöwerling, 2 vols (Oxford: Oxford University Press, 2000), I, pp. 39–48.

2 Vivien Jones, 'Mary Wollstonecraft and the Literature of Advice and Instruction', in *The Cambridge Companion to Mary Wollstonecraft*, ed. Claudia L. Johnson (Cambridge: Cambridge University Press, 2002), p. 120.

3  'Thoughts on the Education of Daughters', *Critical Review*, 63 (April 1787), p. 287; 'Art. 38. Thoughts on the Education of Daughters', *English Review*, 10 (October 1787), p. 315.

4  Jones, 'Mary Wollstonecraft and the Literature of Advice and Instruction', p. 129; William St Clair, *The Reading Nation in the Romantic Period* (Cambridge: Cambridge University Press, 2004), p. 658.

5  'Thoughts on the Education of Daughters', *Critical Review*, 63 (April 1787), p. 287; Pea, 'Art. 26. Mary', *Monthly Review*, 2 (July 1790), p. 352. St Clair suggests *Mary* was still advertised as available in 1794 (*The Reading Nation*, p. 658), though Raven only lists the original 1788 edition ('Historical Introduction', p. 451).

6  Mary Wollstonecraft, *Mary and the Wrongs of Woman*, ed. Gary Kelly (Oxford: Oxford University Press, 1998); 'Mary', *Critical Review*, 66 (July 1788), p. 74.

7  'Mary', *Critical Review*, 66 (July 1788), p. 74; Pea, 'Art. 26. Mary', *Monthly Review*, 2 (July 1790), p. 353.

8  'Original Stories, from Real Life', *Critical Review*, 65 (June 1788), pp. 569–70.

9  [Jabez Hirons], 'Art. 30. Original Stories from Real Life', *Monthly Review*, 79 (September 1788), p. 271.

10  The *Monthly* and *Critical* reviewers made this assumption, perhaps by default. See Jane Hodson, *Language and Revolution in Burke, Wollstonecraft, Paine, and Godwin* (Aldershot: Ashgate, 2007), p. 84.

11  On *The Female Reader* as a 'money-spinner', see Jones, 'Mary Wollstonecraft and the Literature of Advice and Instruction', p. 130.

12  Mary A. Waters explains that this term emerged as a mass audience orientation replaced systems of patronage and coterie circulation. *British Women Writers and the Profession of Literary Criticism, 1789–1832* (Basingstoke: Palgrave Macmillan, 2004), p. 88. On Wollstonecraft's 'hack-work', see Gary Kelly, *Revolutionary Feminism: The Mind and Career of Mary Wollstonecraft* (Basingstoke: Palgrave Macmillan, 1992), pp. 73–4.

13  Gaye Tuchman with Nina E. Fortin, *Edging Women Out: Victorian Novelists, Publishers, and Social Change* (London: Routledge, 1989), p. 177. See also Frank Donoghue, *The Fame Machine: Book Reviewing and Eighteenth-Century Literary Careers* (Stanford, CA: Stanford University Press, 1996), p. 159; Mary Poovey, *The Proper Lady and the Woman Writer: Ideology as Style in the Works of Mary Wollstonecraft, Mary Shelley, and Jane Austen* (Chicago, IL: University of Chicago Press, 1984), pp. 35–8; pp. 46–7.

14  On the ways that women defended authorship as useful or pursued professional authorship without compromising respectability, see Jennie Batchelor, *Women's Work: Labour, Gender, Authorship, 1750–1830* (Manchester: Manchester University Press, 2010), p. 13; p. 22; Betty A. Schellenberg, *The Professionalization of Women Writers in Eighteenth-Century Britain* (Cambridge: Cambridge University Press, 2005), p. 159; pp. 179–80.

15  Mary Astell, Hester Chapone and Hannah More, for example, published conduct books and educational tracts.

16  For more on Wollstonecraft as prefiguring the Victorian 'woman of letters', especially in her periodical writing, see Linda H. Peterson, *Becoming a Woman of Letters: Myths of Authorship and Facts of the Victorian Market* (Princeton, NJ: Princeton University Press, 2009), pp. 4–5.

17  Levy, 'Women and Print Culture', p. 38.

18  Mitzi Myers, 'Mary Wollstonecraft's Literary Reviews', in *The Cambridge Companion to Mary Wollstonecraft*, p. 82; 86. See also Myers, 'Sensibility and the

"Walk of Reason": Mary Wollstonecraft's Literary Reviews as Cultural Critique',
in *Sensibility in Transformation*, ed. Syndy McMillen Conger (London: Associated
University Presses, 1990).

19  Waters, *British Women Writers*, p. 120.

20  *Ibid.*, p. 112.

21  *Ibid.*, p. 112.

22  Fiore Sireci, '"Defects of Temper": Mary Wollstonecraft's Strategies of Self-
Representation', in *Called to Civil Existence: Mary Wollstonecraft's A Vindication of the
Rights of Woman*, ed. Enit Karafili Steiner (Amsterdam: Rodopi, 2014), p. 75.

23  Levy, 'Women and Print Culture', pp. 37–8. Levy mentions Burney but
not Wollstonecraft.

24  In comparison, Burke's *Reflections* was priced at five shillings. Paine's *Rights of Man*
was originally priced at two and a half shillings, but was later reissued for half
a shilling.

25  Paine's *Rights of Man* reportedly sold hundreds of thousands of copies. See St Clair, *The
Reading Nation*, pp. 624–35. On the immediate responses to Mary Wollstonecraft,
*A Vindication of the Rights of Men, in a Letter to the Right Honourable Edmund Burke*, in
*Mary Wollstonecraft: Political Writings*, ed. Janet Todd (London: William Pickering,
1993), see Barbara Taylor, 'Wollstonecraft, Mary (1759–1797)', *Oxford Dictionary
of National Biography* (Oxford: Oxford University Press, 2004), www.oxforddnb.
com/view/article/10893 (accessed 6 October 2014).

26  Marysa Demoor estimates that 94 per cent of women writers confined themselves
to novels, children's books or poetry. *Their Fair Share: Women, Power and Criticism in
the Athenaeum, From Millicent Garrett Fawcett to Katherine Mansfield, 1870–1920*
(Aldershot: Ashgate, 2000), p. 12. St Clair finds: 'to write about war, history, and
voyages to remote lands was to venture into the masculine public sphere about
which [women] could be expected to know little' (*The Reading Nation*, p. 216).
According to St Clair, women writers were also underrepresented in genres of
travel literature, history, natural history and pamphlets (pp. 551–71). See also
Paul Keen, *The Crisis of Literature in the 1790s: Print Culture and the Public Sphere*
(Cambridge: Cambridge University Press, 1999), p. 180.

27  There are notable exceptions, of course, such as Catharine Macaulay.

28  Barbara Taylor, *Mary Wollstonecraft and the Feminist Imagination* (Cambridge:
Cambridge University Press, 2003), pp. 48–51; p. 176.

29  Keen, *The Crisis of Literature*, p. 32. See also Marilyn Butler, 'Introductory Essay', in
*Burke, Paine, Godwin and the Revolution Controversy*, ed. Marilyn Butler (Cambridge:
Cambridge University Press, 1984), p. 2. Thomas Paine's *Rights of Man*, Thomas
Christie's *Letters on the Revolution* and James Mackintosh's *Vindicae Gallicae*, for
example, emerged from Wollstonecraft's circle.

30  Wollstonecraft, *Rights of Men*, p. 17.

31  *Ibid.* p. 5; p. 46.

32  *Ibid.*, p. 53.

33  *Ibid.*, p. 36.

34  *Ibid.*, p. 5.

35  Christine M. Skolnik, 'Wollstonecraft's Dislocation of the Masculine Sublime:
A Vindication', *Rhetorica: A Journal of the History of Rhetoric*, 21:4 (2003), p.
209; Daniel I. O'Neill, *The Burke-Wollstonecraft Debate: Savagery, Civilization,
and Democracy* (University Park, PA: Penn State University Press, 2007), pp.
108–9; Keen, *The Crisis of Literature*, p. 183; Janet Todd, 'Introduction', in *Mary
Wollstonecraft: Political Writings*, p. xii.

36  Wollstonecraft, *Rights of Men*, p. 45.

37  Hodson, *Language and Revolution*, p. 113.

38  On 'gender-bending', see Susan J. Wolfson's, 'Mary Wollstonecraft and the Poets', in *The Cambridge Companion to Mary Wollstonecraft*, pp. 181–2. On anxieties about rhetorical 'cross-dressing', see Keen, *The Crisis of Literature*, p. 198.

39  For more on my approach to literary reviews, see the Introduction.

40  'A Vindication of the Rights of Men', *Critical Review*, 70 (December 1790), p. 694.

41  *Ibid.*, p. 694.

42  *Ibid.*, p. 695.

43  '17. A Vindication of the Rights of Men', *Gentleman's Magazine*, 61:2 (February 1791), p. 151.

44  *Ibid.*, p. 153.

45  *Ibid.*, p. 154.

46  'A Vindication of the Rights of Men', *General Magazine and Impartial Review* (January 1791), p. 26.

47  Pe——e, 'Art. 41. A Vindication of the Rights of Men', *Monthly Review*, 4 (January 1791), p. 97.

48  'Art. XI. A Vindication of the Rights of Men', *English Review*, 17 (January 1791), p. 61.

49  Wollstonecraft, *Rights of Men*, p. 47.

50  Skolnik, 'Wollstonecraft's Dislocation of the Masculine Sublime', p. 209.

51  Taylor, 'Wollstonecraft, Mary (1759–1797)'; Todd, 'Introduction', in *Mary Wollstonecraft*, p. xiv; p. xvi.

52  St Clair, *The Reading Nation*, p. 277; pp. 658–9.

53  For the reception of the French translation, see Isabella Bour, 'A New Wollstonecraft: The Reception of the *Vindication of the Rights of Woman* and of *The Wrongs of Woman* in Revolutionary France', *Journal for Eighteenth-Century Studies*, 36:4 (2013), pp. 575–8. For its publication history in England, Ireland and the United States, see *Mary Wollstonecraft Godwin 1759–1797: A Bibliography of the First and Early Editions with Briefer Notes on Later Editions and Translations*, ed. John Windle, 2nd edn, rev. Karma Pippin (New Castle, DE: Oak Knoll Press, 2000), pp. 15–27.

54  See, for example, 'A Poetical Epistle addressed to Miss Wollstonecraft', *Critical Review*, 14 (May 1795), p. 105; 'Robert and Adela; or, the Rights of Women Best maintained by the Sentiments of Nature', *Monthly Review*, 18 (October 1795), p. 227.

55  Barbara Eaton, *Yes Papa! Mrs Chapone and the Bluestocking Circle* (London: Francis Boutle Publishers, 2012), p. 174; Anne K. Mellor, 'Mary Wollstonecraft's *A Vindication of the Rights of Woman* and the Women Writers of Her Day', in *The Cambridge Companion to Mary Wollstonecraft*, p. 141; p. 156; Taylor, 'Wollstonecraft, Mary (1759–1797)'.

56  Jones, 'Mary Wollstonecraft and the Literature of Advice and Instruction', pp. 137–8.

57  Sireci, '"Defects of Temper"', p. 74; p. 78; p. 82; p. 86.

58  'A Vindication of the Rights of Woman', *Critical Review*, 4 (April 1792), p. 390.

59  [William Enfield], 'Art. XXI. A Vindication of the Rights of Woman', *Monthly Review*, 8 (June 1792), p. 198.

60  Marilyn Butler, *Romantics, Rebels and Reactionaries: English Literature and Its Background 1760–1830* (Oxford: Oxford University Press, 1981), p. 11; Cora Kaplan, 'Wild Nights: Pleasure/Sexuality/Feminism', in *Sea Changes: Essays on Culture and Feminism* (London: Verso, 1986), p. 36; Keen, *The Crisis of Literature*, p. 48.

61  R. M. Janes, 'On the Reception of Mary Wollstonecraft's *A Vindication of the Rights of Woman*', *Journal of the History of Ideas*, 39:2 (April–June 1978), p. 293.

62  Tom Furniss, 'Mary Wollstonecraft's French Revolution', in *The Cambridge Companion to Mary Wollstonecraft*, p. 69.

63  Amy Culley, *British Women's Life Writing, 1760–1840: Friendship, Community, and Collaboration* (Basingstoke: Palgrave Macmillan, 2014), pp. 174–5.

64  'Art. I. An Historical and Moral View of the Origin and Progress of the French Revolution', *Analytical Review*, 20:4 (December 1794), p. 337.

65  'Art. VI. An Historical and Moral View of the Origin and the Progress of the French Revolution', *English Review*, 25 (May 1795), p. 349; 'An Historical and Moral View of the Origin and Progress of the French Revolution', *Critical Review*, 16 (April 1796), p. 391.

66  The Seditious Societies Act of 1799 aimed to stop the circulation of cheap inflammatory material, forced printers to keep records of authors and imprints and imposed penalties for failure to comply. The *Rights of Man* had not been regarded as dangerous until Paine reduced the price to sixpence, making it available to working men. See St Clair, *The Reading Nation*, p. 311; p. 256.

67  Richard Holmes, 'Introduction', in *A Short Residence in Sweden & Memoirs of the Author of 'The Rights of Woman'*, ed. Richard Holmes (London: Penguin, 1987), p. 36.

68  Stuart Curran, 'Charlotte Smith, Mary Wollstonecraft, and the Romance of Real Life', in *The History of British Women's Writing, 1750–1830*, p. 198.

69  Holmes, 'Introduction', in *A Short Residence in Sweden & Memoirs of the Author*, p. 18.

70  *Ibid.*, pp. 39–42; p. 16.

71  Culley, *British Women's Life Writing*, p. 173.

72  Christine Chaney, 'The Intimate Familiar: Essay as Autobiography in Romanticism', in *Romantic Autobiography in England*, ed. Eugene Stelzig (Farnham: Ashgate, 2009), p. 195; p. 201.

73  James Treadwell, *Autobiographical Writing and British Literature, 1783–1834* (Oxford: Oxford University Press, 2005), p. 105.

74  I use this term deliberately, both to echo Godwin's famous comment that it was 'a book calculated to make a man in love with its author' (*Memoirs of the Author of a Vindication of the Rights of Woman*, ed. Pamela Clemit and Gina Luria Walker (Toronto: Broadview Press, 2001), p. 95) and to contest Chaney's claim that 'it was no "calculation" on [Wollstonecraft's] part which prompts this reaction in readers' ('The Intimate Familiar', p. 203).

75  Mary Wollstonecraft, *Letters Written During a Short Residence in Sweden, Norway, and Denmark*, in *A Short Residence in Sweden & Memoirs of the Author*, p. 131.

76  Culley sees this 'invitation to friendship' as an alternative to Rousseau's solitary self-fashioning (*British Women's Life Writing*, pp. 179–80).

77  Wollstonecraft, *Letters*, pp. 152–3.

78  'Art. V. Letters Written during a Short Residence in Sweden, Norway, and Denmark', *English Review*, 27 (April 1796), pp. 316–18.

79  Jane Darcy, *Melancholy and Literary Biography, 1640–1816* (Basingstoke: Palgrave Macmillan, 2013), pp. 129–30. Darcy emphasises Rousseau's influence on Wollstonecraft.

80  Wollstonecraft, *Letters*, p. 128.

81  [William Enfield], 'Art. III. Letters Written during a Short Residence in Sweden, Norway, and Denmark', *Monthly Review* (July 1796), p. 252.

82  O. S., 'Art. II. Letters Written during a Short Residence in Sweden, Norway, and Denmark', *Analytical Review*, 23:3 (March 1796), p. 237.

83  Critics have discussed other aspects of Wollstonecraft's self-construction as feminine. On Wollstonecraft's attention to 'feminine pain', see Mary Spongberg, 'Remembering Wollstonecraft: Feminine Friendship, Female Subjectivity and the "Invention" of the Feminist Heroine', in *Women's Life Writing, 1700–1850: Gender, Genre and Authorship*, ed. Daniel Cook and Amy Cully (Basingstoke: Palgrave Macmillan, 2012), p. 173. On her sympathy for oppressed women, see Culley, *British Women's Life Writing*, pp. 180–1.

84  Curran, 'Charlotte Smith, Mary Wollstonecraft, and the Romance of Real Life', p. 198.

85  Chaney, 'The Intimate Familiar', p. 199.

86  Amelia Alderson, qtd in Holmes, 'Introduction', in *A Short Residence in Sweden & Memoirs of the Author*, p. 37.

87  O. S., 'Art. II. Letters written during a short Residence in Sweden, Norway, and Denmark', *Analytical Review*, 23:3 (March 1796), pp. 229–38 (p. 236).

88  [William Enfield], 'Art. III. Letters Written during a Short Residence in Sweden, Norway, and Denmark', *Monthly Review* (July 1796), p. 251.

89  'Letters Written during a Short Residence in Sweden, Norway, and Denmark', *Critical Review*, 16 (February 1796), p. 209.

90  [William Enfield], 'Art. III. Letters Written during a Short Residence in Sweden, Norway, and Denmark', *Monthly Review* (July 1796), p. 251; p. 257; p. 255.

91  Peter Swaab, 'Romantic Self-Representation: The Example of Mary Wollstonecraft's *Letters in Sweden*', in *Mortal Pages, Literary Lives: Studies in Nineteenth-Century Autobiography*, ed. Philip Shaw and Vincent Newey (Aldershot: Scolar Press, 1996), p. 27.

92  Wollstonecraft, *Letters*, p. 64.

93  *Ibid.*, p. 67.

94  Spongberg does not discuss this passage, but she does emphasise that Wollstonecraft's experience of motherhood ties her to mankind and modifies her political philosophy ('Remembering Wollstonecraft', p. 173). Anna Laetitia Barbauld and Joanna Bailie likewise invest maternal figures with ideological power and aesthetic possibility. See Jerome McGann, *The Poetics of Sensibility: A Revolution in Literary Style* (Oxford: Clarendon Press, 1996), pp. 70–1.

95  Wollstonecraft, *Letters*, p. 158.

96  See Per Nyström, *Mary Wollstonecraft's Scandinavian Journey* (Gothenburg: Acts of the Royal Society of Arts and Sciences of Gothenburg, Humaniora No. 17: 1980).

97  On the effects of Wollstonecraft's omissions, see Holmes, 'Introduction', in *A Short Residence in Sweden & Memoirs of the Author*, especially pp. 35–6; Culley, *British Women's Life Writing*, pp. 177–8; Spongberg, 'Remembering Wollstonecraft', p. 171. Mary Favret suggests that Wollstonecraft wrote for financial reasons. See *Romantic Correspondence: Women, Politics and the Fiction of Letters* (Cambridge: Cambridge University Press), p. 227n4.

98  Holmes, 'Introduction', in *A Short Residence in Sweden & Memoirs of the Author*, p. 19; p. 15; p. 32. See also Swaab, 'Romantic Self-Representation', pp. 17–18.

99  Spongberg speculates along similar lines: 'This lack of candour may have reflected Wollstonecraft's concern regarding her own ambiguous marital status, and its impact upon her reputation and that of her infant daughter' ('Remembering Wollstonecraft', p. 172).

100  [William Enfield], 'Art. III. Letters Written during a Short Residence in Sweden, Norway, and Denmark', *Monthly Review* (July 1796), p. 252.

101  'Art. V. Letters Written during a Short Residence in Sweden, Norway, and Denmark', *English Review*, 27 (April 1796), p. 320.

102  Miriam Brody, *Mary Wollstonecraft: Mother of Women's Rights* (Oxford: Oxford University Press, 2000), p. 130; Emily Sunstein, *A Different Face: The Life of Mary Wollstonecraft* (Boston, MA: Little Brown, 1975), p. 296.

103  Peterson, *Becoming a Woman of Letters*, p. 33.

104  Waters, *British Women Writers*, p. 88.

105  On the market orientation in nineteenth-century periodicals, see Hilary Fraser, Stephanie Green and Judith Johnston, *Gender and the Victorian Periodical* (Cambridge: Cambridge University Press, 2003), p. 48.

106  Spongberg, 'Remembering Wollstonecraft', p. 171. Eugene Stelzig also emphasises autobiography as performance. 'Introduction', in *Romantic Autobiography in England*, p. 9.

107  'Memoirs of the Author of a Vindication of the Rights of Woman', *Critical Review*, 22 (April 1798), p. 415; Y. S., 'Account of a New Work, Entitled, "Memoirs of Mrs. Mary Wollstonecraft Godwin"', *Walker's Hibernian Magazine* (April 1798), p. 291; 'Memoirs of Mrs. Wollstonecraft Godwin, Author of a Vindication of the Rights of Woman', *Scots Magazine*, 60 (May 1798), p. 301.

108  See *Mary Wollstonecraft Godwin 1759–1797*, p. 23; Holmes, 'Introduction', in *A Short Residence in Sweden & Memoirs of the Author*, p. 50. The next reprint in Britain was William Clark Durant's scholarly edition of 1927. An edition was also published in 1927 in New York.

109  Angela Keane discusses Wollstonecraft as a 'courtesan'. See *Women Writers and the English Nation in the 1790s: Romantic Belongings* (Cambridge: Cambridge University Press, 2000), p. 12.

110  [Bissett, Robert], 'Art. V. Memoirs of the Author of the Vindication of the Rights of Woman', *Anti-Jacobin Review*, 1:1 (July 1798), p. 94. Other politically-motivated responses came in verse form. Examples include the conservative curate Richard Polwhele's 68-page mock epic, *The Unsex'd Females: a Poem* (1798), and C. Kirkpatrick Sharpe's 'The Vision of Liberty' (1801).

111  'Memoirs of the Author of a Vindication of the Rights of Woman', *The Critical Review*, 22 (April 1798), p. 414.

112  Mo-y, 'Art. XII. Memoirs of the Author of the Vindication of the Rights of Woman', *Monthly Review*, 27 (November 1798), p. 323.

113  John Evans, 'Remarks on the Religion of the Late Mrs. Wollstonecraft', *Monthly Visitor*, 3 (March 1798), p. 245.

114  'Art. III. Memoirs of the Author of the Vindication of the Rights of Woman', *British Critic*, 12 (September 1798), p. 232.

115  Mo-y, 'Art. XII. Memoirs of the Author of the Vindication of the Rights of Woman', *Monthly Review*, 27 (November 1798), p. 321.

116  Patricia Meyer Spacks, *Privacy: Concealing the Eighteenth-Century Self* (Chicago, IL: University of Chicago Press, 2003), p. 161.

117  Spacks, *Privacy*, p. 150.

118  Lynda M. Thompson, *The 'Scandalous Memoirists': Constantia Phillips, Laetitia Pilkington, and the Shame of 'Publick Fame'* (Manchester: Manchester University Press, 2000), p. 3; Clare Brant, 'Varieties of Women's Writing', in *Women and Literature in Britain, 1700–1800*, ed. Vivien Jones (Cambridge: Cambridge University Press, 2000), p. 292.

119  Treadwell, *Autobiographical Writing and British Literature*, p. 165.

120  Daniel Cook, 'An Authoress to Be Let: Reading Laetitia Pilkington's *Memoirs*', in
     *Women's Life Writing, 1700–1850: Gender, Genre and Authorship*, ed. Daniel Cook and
     Amy Culley (Basingstoke: Palgrave Macmillan, 2012), p. 39.

121  Mary Robinson's *Letter to the Women of England* (1799) and Mary Ann Radcliffe's
     *Female Advocate* (1799) also defended Wollstonecraft in so much as they argued for
     her radical project to be continued. See Andrew McInnes, 'Wollstonecraft's Legion:
     Feminism in Crisis, 1799', *Women's Writing*, 20:4 (2013), pp. 479–95.

122  [Mary Hays], 'Memoirs of Mary Wollstonecraft', in *The Annual Necrology for
     1797–8* (London: Richard Phillips, 1800), p. 412; p. 458. On Hays's depiction
     of Wollstonecraft and her critique of Godwin, see Chapter 4. See also Andrew
     McInnes, *Wollstonecraft's Ghost: The Fate of the Female Philosopher in the Romantic Period*
     (London: Routledge, 2017), p. 57.

123  [Hays], 'Memoirs of Mary Wollstonecraft', p. 458; p. 459.

124  The author of the *Defence* may have been Archibald Hamilton Rowan, an Irish radi-
     cal whom Wollstonecraft met in Paris. See *A Routledge Literary Sourcebook on Mary
     Wollstonecraft's A Vindication of the Rights of Woman*, ed. Adriana Craciun (London:
     Routledge, 2002), p. 52.

125  'The Annual Necrology for 1797–8', *Critical Review*, 28 (March 1800), p. 327.

126  For more on the initial reception of the *Memoirs*, see Janes, 'On the Reception',
     pp. 293–302, Claudia Johnson, 'Introduction', in *The Cambridge Companion to Mary
     Wollstonecraft*, pp. 1–6, and Pamela Clemit and Gina Luria Walker, 'Introduction', in
     *Memoirs of the Author of A Vindication of the Rights of Woman*, pp. 32–6.

127  Harriet Devine Jump, 'Introduction', in *Mary Wollstonecraft and the Critics 1788–
     2001*, ed. Harriet Devine Jump, 2 vols (London and New York, NY: Routledge,
     2003), I, p. 5. See also Harriet Jump, '"One Cry for Justice": Virginia Woolf
     Reads Mary Wollstonecraft', in *The Monstrous Debt: Modalities of Romantic Influence
     in Twentieth-Century Literature*, ed. Damian Walford Davies and Richard Marggraf
     Turley (Detroit, MI: Wayne State University Press, 2006), pp. 43–4.

128  Scholars such as Janet Todd, Barbara Caine, Barbara Taylor and Harriet Jump
     give reception histories that broadly follow this trajectory. See Janet Todd,
     'Introduction', in *A Wollstonecraft Anthology*, ed. Janet Todd (New York: Columbia
     University Press, 1990), pp. 1–22; Janes, 'On the Reception'; Clemit and Walker,
     'Introduction', in *Memoirs of the Author of A Vindication of the Rights of Woman*, for
     detailed accounts of Wollstonecraft's contemporary reception.

129  Joanne Shattock, 'The Construction of the Woman Writer', in *Women and Literature
     in Britain, 1800–1900*, ed. Joanne Shattock (Cambridge: Cambridge University
     Press, 2001), p. 14. Kathryn Gleadle contests this narrative. *Radical Writing on
     Women, 1800–1850: An Anthology* (Basingstoke: Palgrave Macmillan, 2002), p. 1.

130  William Godwin, 'Of History and Romance', in *Political and Philosophical Writings
     of William Godwin*, ed. Mark Philp, 7 vols (London: William Pickering, 1993), V,
     p. 293.

131  *Ibid.*, p. 294.

132  Godwin, *Memoirs*, p. 43.

133  Darcy refers to this reform-minded life writing as 'philosophical biography'
     (*Melancholy and Literary Biography*, p. 107).

134  William Godwin, *The Enquirer: Reflections on Education, Manners, and Literature* (New
     York, NY: August M. Kelley, 1965), p. 287.

135  *Ibid.*, p. 274.

136  Godwin, *Memoirs*, p. 43.

137   Clemit and Walker, 'Introduction', in *Memoirs of the Author of A Vindication of the Rights of Woman*, pp. 18–19.

138   Clarence Tracy, 'Introduction', in *Biography in the Eighteenth Century*, ed. J. D. Browning (London: Garland, 1980), p. 4.

139   Clemit and Walker, 'Introduction', in *Memoirs of the Author of A Vindication of the Rights of Woman*, p. 19.

140   *Ibid.*, p. 17.

141   Godwin, *Memoirs*, pp. 121–2.

142   *Ibid.*, pp. 120–1.

143   McGann, *The Poetics of Sensibility*, p. 46. See also Shattock, 'The Construction of the Woman Writer', p. 14.

144   See Culley for an insightful discussion of Godwin's sympathetic identification with Wollstonecraft and the influence of *Letters* on his *Memoirs* (*British Women's Life Writing*, pp. 183–4).

145   Janice Carlisle, qtd in Peterson, *Traditions of Victorian Women's Autobiography*, p. x.

146   These are terms from Peterson's analysis of the relational mode in the domestic memoir tradition.

147   Godwin, *Memoirs*, p. 217.

148   Favret, *Romantic Correspondence*, p. 128; Catherine N. Parke, 'What Kind of Heroine Is Mary Wollstonecraft?' in *Sensibility in Transformation: Creative Resistance to Sentiment from the Augustans to the Romantics*, ed. Syndy McMillen Conger (London: Associated University Presses, 1990), p. 107; Darcy, *Melancholy and Literary Biography*, p. 117; Shattock, 'The Construction of the Woman Writer', p. 14.

149   I quote Favret (*Romantic Correspondence*, p. 128) here, though Culley makes similar claims (*British Women's Life Writing*, pp. 183–5).

150   Favret, *Romantic Correspondence*, p. 130.

151   Culley has argued that Godwin's *Memoirs* owes a debt to Wollstonecraft's self-presentation in the *Letters*. *British Women's Life Writing*, pp. 183–4.

152   Cora Kaplan, 'Mary Wollstonecraft's Reception and Legacies', in *The Cambridge Companion to Mary Wollstonecraft*, p. 246.

153   Tom Mole, 'Introduction', in *Romanticism and Celebrity Culture, 1750–1850*, ed. Tom Mole (Cambridge: Cambridge University Press, 2009), p. 12.

154   See Favret, *Romantic Correspondence*, p. 132.

155   'Art. II. Memoirs of the Author of a Vindication of the Rights of Woman', *Analytical Review*, 27:3 (March 1798), 235–40 (p. 236); 'Art. III. Memoirs of the Author of the Vindication of the Rights of Woman', *British Critic*, 12 (September 1798), p. 231.

156   'A Defence of the Character and Conduct of the Late Mary Wollstonecraft Godwin', *Anti-Jacobin Review*, 15:60 (June 1803), p. 186.

157   William Godwin, 'Preface', in *Posthumous Works of Mary Wollstonecraft Godwin*, 4 vols (London: J. Johnson, 1798), I, n.p.

158   Harriet Jump, 'Introduction', in *Lives of the Great Romantics III: Godwin, Wollstonecraft & Mary Shelley By Their Contemporaries*, ed. Harriet Jump, 3 vols (London: Pickering & Chatto, 1999), II, p. xviii.

159   See McInnes, *Wollstonecraft's Ghost*.

160   *Ibid.*, p. 16. For more on Wollstonecraft in the fiction of Opie and Shelley, see also Patricia Matthew, 'Biography and Mary Wollstonecraft in *Adeline Mowbray* and *Valperga*', *Women's Writing*, 14:3 (2007), pp. 382–98.

161   Frances Burney, *The Wanderer* (London: Pandora Press, 1988), p. 139.

162   McInnes, *Wollstonecraft's Ghost*, p. 108.

163   *Ibid.*, p. 161.

164  Doody, *Frances Burney*, p. 326.
165  Burney, *The Wanderer*, p. 141. For more on the 'tension between Burney's sympathy for Elinor's Wollstonecraftian ideals and an anxiety about her character and Wollstonecraft's shared transgressions', see McInnes, *Wollstonecraft's Ghost*, p. 107.
166  Percy Bysshe Shelley, *Laon and Cyntha*, in *The Selected Poetry and Prose of Shelley*, ed. Bruce Woodcock (Ware: Wordsworth Poetry Library, 2002), ll, pp. 102–8.
167  Wolfson, 'Mary Wollstonecraft and the Poets', p. 184.
168  Shelley, l, p. 9; l, p. 99.
169  *Ibid.*, ll, pp. 123–4; l, p. 120.
170  St Clair, *The Reading Nation*, pp. 277–8; p. 660. Only one copy of the 1841 edition has been found. St Clair does not list the 1844 edition.
171  *Ibid.* p. 278.
172  Windle, *Bibliography*, p. 17.
173  W. Strange, 'Preface', in *A Vindication of the Rights of Woman*, 3rd edn, revised and re-edited (London: W. Strange, 1844), p. vi. Strange quotes from Godwin, indicating familiarity with the *Memoirs*.
174  St Clair, *The Reading Nation*, p. 28.
175  *Ibid.*, p. 600. St Clair concedes that the 1841 edition 'shows that the *Vindication* was not entirely forgotten by the Chartists' and 'may have been the most widely read edition before the twentieth century'.
176  Taylor, *Mary Wollstonecraft and the Feminist Imagination*, p. 248.
177  Sheila Rowbotham, 'Introduction', in *Sheila Rowbotham Presents Mary Wollstonecraft: A Vindication of the Rights of Woman* (London: Verso, 2010), pp. xxiv–xxv; Gleadle, *Radical Writing on Women*, p. 3.
178  Rowbotham, 'Introduction', in *Sheila Rowbotham Presents Mary Wollstonecraft*, p. xxvii.
179  Gleadle, *Radical Writing on Women*, p. 9.
180  The *Rights of Woman* was republished with greater frequency in early nineteenth-century America than Britain, with reprints in 1833, 1845, 1856, 1890 and 1891. It influenced texts such as Hannah Mather Crocker's *Observations on the Real Rights of Women* (1818), Sarah Grimke's *Letters on the Equality of the Sexes* (1838), Margaret Fuller's *Woman in the Nineteenth Century* (1845) and Elizabeth Cady Stanton's *History of Woman Suffrage* (1881). On the *Rights of Woman* and nineteenth-century American feminism, see Eileen Hunt Botting and Christine Carey, 'Wollstonecraft's Philosophical Impact on Nineteenth-Century Women's Rights Advocates', *American Journal of Political Science*, 48:4 (2004), pp. 707–22.
181  William Thompson, *Appeal of One-Half the Human Race*, ed. Dolores Dooley (Cork: Cork University Press, 1997), p. 47.
182  Dolores Dooley, *Equality in Community: Sexual Equality in the Writings of William Thompson and Anna Doyle Wheeler* (Cork: Cork University Press, 1996), pp. xvi–xviii; p. 126.
183  Alan Ryan, 'Introduction', in *On Liberty and The Subjection of Women*, ed. Alan Ryan (London: Penguin, 2006), p. ix.
184  Wollstonecraft, *Rights of Woman*, p. 70.
185  [Harriet Taylor Mill], 'Enfranchisement of Women', *Westminster Review*, 55:2 (July 1851), p. 308.
186  John Stuart Mill, *The Subjection of Women*, in *On Liberty and The Subjection of Women*, ed. Alan Ryan (London: Penguin, 2006), p. 133.
187  Ryan, 'Introduction', in *On Liberty and The Subjection of Women*, p. xxiii.
188  Wollstonecraft, *Rights of Woman*, p. 293.

189  Molly McLay, 'From Wollstonecraft to Mill: Varied Positions and Influences of the
     European and American Women's Rights Movements', *Constructing the Past*, 7:1
     (2006), pp. 118–19.
190  Gleadle, *Radical Writing on Women*, p. 1.
191  Virginia Sapiro, *A Vindication of Political Virtue:The Political Theory of Mary Wollstonecraft*
     (Chicago, IL: University of Chicago Press, 1992), p. 277.
192  Barbara Caine, *English Feminism: 1780–1980* (Oxford: Oxford University Press,
     1997), p. 6.
193  Taylor, *Mary Wollstonecraft and the Feminist Imagination*, p. 249.
194  Caine, *English Feminism*, p. 6.
195  Attribution of Mozley's article comes from Alexis Antonia and Ellen Jordan,
     'Identifying Anne Mozley's Contributions to the *Christian Remembrancer*: A Compu-
     tational Stylistic Approach', *Victorian Literature and Culture*, 42 (2014), p. 304.
196  Godwin, *Memoirs*, p. 43.
197  Sapiro, *A Vindication of Political Virtue*, pp. 5–6.
198  Jump, *Lives of the Great Romantics III*, p. 269.
199  George Eliot, 'Margaret Fuller and Mary Wollstonecraft', *The Leader* (13 October
     1855), p. 988.
200  Wollstonecraft, qtd in Eliot, 'Margaret Fuller and Mary Wollstonecraft', p. 989.
201  Eliot, 'Margaret Fuller and Mary Wollstonecraft', p. 988.
202  Godwin, *Memoirs*, p. 104; p. 109.
203  Jump, *Lives of the Great Romantics III*, p. 269.
204  Jump, 'Introduction', *Lives of the Great Romantics III*, II, p. xxii.
205  Eliza Lynn Linton, 'Mary Wollstonecraft', in *The English Republic: A Newspaper and
     Review*, ed. W. J. Linton Brantwood (London: Watson, 1854), p. 424.
206  *Ibid.*, p. 424.
207  *Ibid.*, p. 423.
208  [Anne Mozley], 'The Rights of Women', *The Christian Remembrancer*, 30 (July 1855),
     p. 24. On Mozley's contributions to *The Christian Remembrancer*, see Joanne Wilkes,
     *Women Reviewing Women in Nineteenth-Century Britain: The Critical Reception of Jane
     Austen, Charlotte Brontë and George Eliot* (Aldershot: Ashgate, 2010), pp. 86–110.
209  *Ibid.*, p. 25.
210  Nicola Trott, 'Sexing the Critic: Mary Wollstonecraft at the Turn of the Century',
     in *1798: The Year of the Lyrical Ballads*, ed. Richard Cronin (Basingstoke: Palgrave
     Macmillan, 1998), p. 40.
211  See Jump, 'Introduction', *Lives of the Great Romantics III*, II, p. xii; Lyndall Gordon,
     *Mary Wollstonecraft:A New Genus* (London: Little Brown, 2005), p. 385;Trott, 'Sexing
     the Critic', p. 56.
212  Ghislaine McDayter, 'On the Publication of William Godwin's *Memoirs of the
     Author of a Vindication of the Rights of Woman*, 1798', BRANCH, www.branchcolle
     ctive.org/?ps_articles=ghislaine-mcdayter-on-the-publication-of-william-
     godwins-memoirs-of-the-author-of-a-vindication-of-the-rights-of-woman-1798
     (accessed 24 October 2015).
213  Shattock, 'The Construction of the Woman Writer', p. 14.
214  Critics like Alison Booth distinguish between group biographies (also referred to as
     *collective biographies* or *multibiographies*) that 'narrate' women's lives and biographical
     dictionaries and encyclopaedias that 'outline or summarize' these lives. See Alison
     Booth, *How to Make It as a Woman: Collective Biographical History from Victoria to the
     Present* (Chicago, IL and London: University of Chicago Press, 2004), p. 3. However,

I consider these genres together here because both are useful in gauging attitudes toward Wollstonecraft, and because the difference between 'narrat[ing]' and 'outlin[ing]' in these early nineteenth-century texts is often not very pronounced.

215  Alison Booth, 'Collective Biographies of Women: An Annotated Bibliography', *NINES Consortium* (2007), http://womensbios.lib.virginia.edu (accessed 1 May 2013).

216  Mary Hays's *Female Biography* (1803), Donald Fraser's *The Mental Flower Garden* (1807), Mary Roberts's *Select Female Biography* (1821), Mary Belson's *Female Biography* (1822) and T. Sharp and John Starford's *The Heavenly Sisters* (1822) did not include Wollstonecraft.

217  Gleadle, *Radical Writing on Women*, p. 9.

218  Mary Pilkington, *Memoirs of Celebrated Female Characters* (London: Albion Press, 1804), p. 189.

219  *Ibid.*, p. 185.

220  *Eccentric Biography* (London: T. Hurst, 1803), pp. 140–1.

221  *Ibid.*, p. 141.

222  Parke, 'What Kind of Heroine Is Mary Wollstonecraft?' p. 105.

223  Alexander Chalmers, *A New and General Biographical Dictionary* (London: J. Nichols & Son, 1814), p. 55.

224  *Ibid.*, p. 55.

225  Jump, *Lives of the Great Romantics III*, p. 257.

226  Deborah Manley, 'Elwood, Anne Katharine (1796–1873)', in *Oxford Dictionary of National Biography* (Oxford: Oxford University Press, 2004), doi:10.1093/ref:odnb/48643. The volumes by Pilkington and Betham, and the anonymous *Eccentric Biography*, may have fallen out of print by 1843.

227  Anne Katharine Elwood, *Memoirs of the Literary Ladies of England*, 2 vols (London: Henry Colburn, 1843), I, p. v.

228  *Ibid.*, p. 151.

229  Jump, *Lives of the Great Romantics III*, p. 258.

230  Joan W. Scott, 'Fantasy Echo: History and the Construction of Identity', *Critical Inquiry*, 27:2 (2001), pp. 286–7.

231  Elwood, *Memoirs*, I, p. 152.

232  Mary Shelley, 'Life of William Godwin' [1836–1840], qtd in *Lives of the Great Romantics III*, II, p. 250.

233  Harriet Martineau, *Autobiography* [1877], qtd in *Lives of the Great Romantics III*, II, p. 275.

234  Harriet Martineau to Mrs Chapman, July 1840. *Harriet Martineau's Autobiography and Memorials of Harriet Martineau*, ed. Maria Weston Chapman, 2 vols (Boston, MA: James R. Osgood, 1877), http://oll.libertyfund.org/title/2012/140279/2646440

235  Barbara Taylor, 'Mary Wollstonecraft and the Wild Wish of Feminism', *History Workshop*, 33 (1992), p. 203.

236  Jump, '"One Cry for Justice"', p. 44.

237  Godwin, *Memoirs*, p. 78.

238  John Knowles, *The Life and Writing of Henry Fuseli*, 3 vols (London: Colburn and Bentley, 1831), I, pp. 165–6.

239  Charles Kegan Paul, 'Prefatory Memoir', in *Mary Wollstonecraft: Letters to Imlay* (New York, NY: Haskell House Publishers, 1971), p. xxxi; Charles Kegan Paul, *William Godwin: His Friends and Contemporaries*, 2 vols (London: Henry S. King, 1876), pp. 207–8.

240  Paul, *William Godwin*, p. 207; Paul, 'Prefatory Memoir', pp. xxxi–xxxii.

241  Paul, 'Prefatory Memoir', p. xxxii.

242  *Ibid.*, p. v; p. vi; Paul, *William Godwin*, p. 214.

243  Paul, 'Prefatory Memoir, p. v.

244  Shattock, 'The Construction of the Woman Writer', p. 17.

245  Leslie Stephen, 'William Godwin', *Fortnightly Review*, 20 (October 1876), p. 445.

246  *Ibid.*, p. 444.

247  *Ibid.*, p. 446.

248  Mathilde Blind, 'Mary Wollstonecraft', *New Quarterly Magazine*, 10 (July 1878), p. 392; p. 396.

249  *Ibid.*, p. 398.

250  *Ibid.*, p. 290.

251  Margaret Oliphant, *The Literary History of England in the End of the Eighteenth and Beginning of the Nineteenth Century*, 3 vols (London: Macmillan, 1882), II, p. 249.

252  *Ibid.*, p. 251.

253  *Ibid.*, p. 251; p. 252.

254  *Ibid.*, pp. 252–3.

255  *Ibid.*, pp. 1–2.

256  Elizabeth Robins Pennell, *Mary Wollstonecraft Godwin* (London: W. H. Allen, 1885), p. 1.

257  *Ibid.*, p. 90.

258  *Ibid.*, p. 90.

259  Alison Chapman, 'Achieving fame and canonicity', in *The Cambridge Companion to Victorian Women's Writing*, ed. Linda H. Peterson (Cambridge: Cambridge University Press, 2015), p. 82. Julia Ward Howe wrote on Margaret Fuller, Mathilde Blind on George Eliot, Emma Raymond Pitman on Elizabeth Fry, Lucy Madox Rossetti on Mary Shelley and Mary Yonge on Hannah More.

260  Millicent Garrett Fawcett, 'Introduction to the New Edition', in *A Vindication of the Rights of Woman* (London: Unwin, 1891), p. 15.

261  *Ibid.*, p. 22.

262  Taylor, *Mary Wollstonecraft and the Feminist Imagination*, p. 9.

263  Millicent Garrett Fawcett, *Women's Suffrage: A Short History of a Great Movement* (London: T. C. & E. C. Jack, 1911), p. 6.

264  Elizabeth Robins Pennell, 'Prefatory Note', in *A Vindication of the Rights of Woman* (London: Walter Scott, 1892), p. vii.

265  Caine, *English Feminism*, p. 43.

266  Janet M. Todd, *Mary Wollstonecraft: An Annotated Bibliography* (New York, NY: Garland, 1976), p. xv.

267  On the flawed heroes in other biographies of the period, see Darcy, *Melancholy and Literary Biography*.

268  Caine, *English Feminism*, pp. 7–8.

269  Virginia Woolf, 'Four Figures', in *The Second Common Reader*, ed. Andrew McNeillie (London: Harcourt, 1986), pp. 156–7.

270  *Ibid.*, p. 158.

271  Jump, '"One Cry for Justice"', p. 41. Woolf follows Godwin's version of the Fuseli episode and of Wollstonecraft's suicide attempts.

272  Woolf, 'Four Figures', p. 161; p. 162.

273  *Ibid.*, p. 161.

274  *Ibid.*, p. 163.

# Chapter 3

# 'Beyond the power of utterance': Reading the gaps in Mary Robinson's *Memoirs* (1801)

IN 1780, THE STUNNING actress and poet Mary Darby Robinson (1758–1800) sparked a media frenzy known as the 'Perdita' affair when she began a high-profile amour with the teenaged Prince of Wales, later King George IV. Robinson spent her adult life transforming her public position from sex object to writing subject. Her *Memoirs of the Late Mrs. Robinson, Written by Herself* (1801), edited by her daughter Maria Elizabeth and published the year after her death, has been read as an 'Apology' for her life and a vindication of her character. In this tale of transgression and suffering, Robinson establishes herself as a gothic heroine of sensibility and a victim of circumstance. Yet the jarring shifts in tone, conspicuous gaps in the narration of events and structural inconsistencies of the *Memoirs* have caused readers – contemporary and modern – to question its veracity and its literary integrity. However, this chapter suggests that the formal and rhetorical gaps in the *Memoirs* comprise a strategy of self-representation that allowed Robinson to straddle the contradictory identities of the victimised heroine of sensibility and the titillating actress. The *Memoirs* was reprinted ten times in the nineteenth century and spurred responses in reviews, essays, novels, illustrated fiction, poems and biographies. Through analysis of the text itself; comparison with a similar but much less well-known 'scandal memoir', *The Life of Mrs Gooch* (1792); and an examination of Robinson's nineteenth-century afterlife, this chapter argues that it may be the so-called failures of Robinson's *Memoirs* – its interruptions, omissions and contradictions – that made it so effective in evoking the sympathy and curiosity of readers for decades to come. Robinson could not obliterate the scandal of her youth, but she was able to shape reactions to it and to secure for herself an afterlife as a literary celebrity.

## Critical appraisals of Robinson's *Memoirs*

The *Memoirs* has long perplexed readers. On the one hand, it appears to be a 'vindication', a last effort to rescue Robinson's reputation by countering the image of the avaricious, licentious, vain courtesan with that of the sensitive, good-hearted victim of circumstance and of her own 'Romantic' susceptibilities.[1] Echoing Robinson's own description, critics have seen the *Memoirs* as a 'corrective to unauthorized memoirs'[2] and a 'redemptive project'[3] intended 'to rehabilitate her reputation'.[4] Robinson's use of tropes from gothic fiction, both to emphasise her sensibility and suffering and to evoke sympathy, has also been noted.[5] Finally, the account of childhood and young adulthood in the 1770s and 1780s is repeatedly interrupted by the forty-year-old Robinson writing in 1800, who reminds the reader of her age, infirmity and sorrow. These present-day interludes act as a kind of foreshadowing that furthers our sense of Robinson as the doomed heroine of her own 'melancholy story'.[6]

Yet several discursive and structural features of Robinson's narrative have complicated this reading. The pathetic tale of transgression and sorrow is undercut by jarring shifts in tone. The narrative swings from the plaintive strains of the long-suffering heroine to the 'electricity' and excitement of the aspiring actress, to the minute observations of 'dress, parties, adulation' in pleasure gardens, in tea-rooms and at table.[7] Moreover, the *Memoirs* seems to narrate events selectively, leaving out large portions of Robinson's life (such as her sixteen-year post-Prince relationship with Banastre Tarleton, which is relegated to a footnote), and breaking off completely at the most infamous moment: her decision to join the Prince of Wales in his private apartments. The narration, when it resumes, switches to a 'Continuation by a Friend'. This third-person account then gives way a few pages later to a long-lost letter supposedly written by Robinson in 1783 and 'found' by her editor, which conveniently begins just where the preceding section has left off. This letter, however, only details events up to the year 1781, after which the 'Friend' resumes narration. The remainder of Volume Two is taken up with poems composed by or dedicated to Robinson. Volumes Three and Four of the original edition of 1801 are devoted to Robinson's unpublished writing. Only two years later, the publisher Richard Phillips issued a two-volume edition, which became the standard for the text that was reprinted in the nineteenth century. Contemporary responses to the *Memoirs* will be discussed later, but for now it is important to mention that these irregularities, omissions and disruptions were registered from the start and have fuelled long-standing debates about the veracity of the text, Robinson's level of involvement in producing it and her motivations in writing it.

These inconsistencies threaten the coherent narrative of a unitary, unique self that is the underlying norm or gold standard of autobiography.[8] Many modern critics have treated the gaps and contradictions in Robinson's *Memoirs* as flaws that undermine the veneer of artlessness and ingenuity. Eleanor Ty has discussed the omissions in the narrative as censorship (enacted by both Robinson and her daughter Maria Elizabeth, as editor), and therefore as evidence of her 'problems establishing and maintaining herself', her 'struggle with her subjectivity' and her difficulty assuming 'a position outside of these preconceived notions of what a woman should be'.[9] Cheryl Wanko likewise deems Robinson's disruption of the text at its critical moment of sexual transgression the result of the 'shame of admitting this dalliance publicly' and her 'inability to sustain her textual role of misguided youth and ignorance'.[10] Even Hester Davenport, whose analysis of the *Memoirs* manuscript indicates that Robinson most likely did *not* abandon her narrative at its climax but introduced the third-person narration of the 'Continuation' and subsequent letter as a 'distancing strategy', maintains that Robinson 'seems a little confused about her objectives in the *Memoirs*'.[11] For Davenport, the lacunae, fluctuations in tone and 'pretence' of the fragmented narrative leave us with 'two aspects of her nature' that are irreconcilable: 'the gay and the grave, the confident socialite and the sensitive melancholic'.[12]

Some scholars have approached the dual, or even multiple, selves that Robinson projects, both in the *Memoirs* and elsewhere, as part of a more coherent representational strategy.[13] Judith Pascoe argues that in Robinson's many pseudonyms, she imports theatrical modes of self-representation that constitute a fluid, unorthodox idea of self.[14] Pascoe reads the shifts in narration and structural breaks in the *Memoirs* as a conscious 'distancing strategy' to heighten the 'theatricality of the moment'.[15] Similarly, Anne Mellor considers Robinson's contradictory self-images as part of 'what we now call a "postmodern subjectivity," a concept of the self as entirely fluid, unstable, and performative'.[16] Unlike Pascoe, though, Mellor takes at face value the 'pretence' that Robinson abandoned her autobiographical project mid-narrative, though she too regards the *Memoirs* as 'a self-conscious artistic creation'.[17]

Building on the work of Pascoe in particular, Laura Engel also situates Robinson's multiple identities within a highly crafted strategy of self-fashioning. Engel argues that Robinson is neither confused nor self-censorious but 'deeply aware' of the challenges in writing a sympathetic autobiography given her stage career and her equally public romantic affairs.[18] Engel reads Robinson's literal and figurative 'costume changes' in the *Memoirs* as a means of creating suspense and mystery while also eliciting sympathy:

> When she finds herself in a difficult or suspicious moment, she reappears in a different outfit, leaving the phantom of her guilty self in the wings. Robinson writes her memoir as a celebrity ghost. Capitalizing on the Gothic potential of her own history, she attempts to juxtapose sympathy with seduction in order to create a narrative that captures her reader's attention, desire and compassion.[19]

Moreover, Engel argues, in casting herself as 'a simultaneously tragic and seductive heroine' who is 'available and elusive', Robinson does not 'solely ai[m] at redemption of her self-image but also at seduction and self-promotion'.[20] For Engel, though, Robinson's strategy is only 'partially' successful: 'in the same way that she vanished from her memoir, she gradually disappeared from public view'.[21] In what follows, I build on the work of Engel and Pascoe by examining a kind of 'Gothic disappearing act'[22] that operates not in the plot or narration of the *Memoirs* but at the level of language itself. By examining this little-noticed pattern of silence in the text, situating Robinson's memoir alongside other scandal memoirs (like that of her contemporary Elizabeth Gooch) and moving on to discuss a series of nineteenth-century responses to Robinson, I suggest that her self-fashioning may have been not only more 'self-conscious' but also more successful than critics have allowed.

## Self-professed silences

Throughout the *Memoirs*, moments of emotional intensity are described paradoxically as 'undescribable' or 'beyond the power of utterance'.[23] In more than twenty such affective peaks, Robinson indicates an inability – or an unwillingness – to reveal herself completely, and she draws attention to the breaches in her narrative. In repeatedly and overtly signposting these gaps, however, Robinson tells us that she is not telling us everything, hinting at a complex mode of self-presentation that pervades the *Memoirs*. These self-professed silences fall into different categories. Sometimes, they signal a linguistic incapacity that results from feelings that overwhelm language. At others, they bespeak a refusal (rather than a lack of ability) to describe her feelings, leaving implicit a range of unacceptable sentiments that must be conveyed obliquely to the reader because direct communication is textually or morally inappropriate. At other times, still, they are noticeable visible breaks in the narration that enact silence through an absence of verbal text. In all instances, announcing her silences is a move which, like the 'costume changes' discussed by Engel, has complex and sometimes contradictory effects, accentuating sensibility, validating authenticity, securing feminine privacy and kindling both sympathy and curiosity.

Robinson often highlights her linguistic incapacity in order to emphasise the feelings she experiences amidst the trials and disappointments of life as a young wife and soon-to-be mother. Though heavily pregnant and newly aware of both the insolvency and the infidelity of her husband, the teenaged Robinson nevertheless agrees to leave her family in London because 'the propriety of wedded life commanded the sacrifice'.[24] She explains her mixed emotions:

> With tender regret, with agonizing presentiments, I took leave of my mother and my brother. Such a parting would but *mock the powers of language!* My delicate situation, my youth, my affection for my best of mothers; all conspired to augment my sorrow.[25]

Her exclamation here underlines the intensity of her feelings. Later in the narrative, when she recounts the 'afflicting humiliations' of accompanying her husband to debtors' prison, she uses the same trope to reinforce her admirable marital conduct and pathetic circumstances:

> *Were I to describe* one half of what I suffered, during fifteen months captivity, the world would consider it as the invention of a novel ... my duty as a wife was exemplary, my chastity inviolate; he knows that neither poverty nor obscurity, neither the tauntings of the world nor his neglect, could tempt me even to the smallest error ... my attentions were exclusively dedicated to him and to my infant.[26]

These are not just hyperbolic or 'histrionic'[27] turns of phrase that stress her pitiable circumstances, for they also imply other, perhaps unspeakable, emotions. The unfairness of her situation, in both of these episodes, might have justified anger or resentment against her husband, but Robinson names only the emotions commensurate with the victimised status of the exemplary but hard-done-by wife.[28] In restricting her disclosures, Robinson displays a genteel femininity. She avoids unduly criticising her husband or expressing unladylike sentiments that might undermine the decorum expected of a middle-class woman.[29] The *Memoirs* manuscript reveals her painstaking choice of words in framing her husband's conduct not as 'impropriety', which is crossed out, but 'unkindness', which moves the emphasis back into the realm of emotions.[30] By focusing on her own feelings, Robinson's trope of self-professed silence enables her to maximise her appeal for sympathy.

Robinson's juxtaposition of sensory details and self-professed silence also allows her to build intimacy and trust with her reader.

When her daughter Maria Elizabeth is born, the description abounds
with tactile and kinetic specifics that make it feel believable:

> *I cannot describe the sensations of my soul* at the moment when I pressed
> the little darling to my bosom, my maternal bosom; when I kissed its
> hands, its cheeks, its forehead, as it nestled closely to my heart, and
> seemed to claim that affection which has never failed to warm it.[31]

Despite the concrete detail that Robinson provides about external
sensations, the internal 'sensations of [her] soul' evade her pen.
Robinson's reticence to put her newfound maternal affections
into words also accords, as in the earlier example, with a decorous
bourgeois femininity that reserves certain aspects of domestic life
as private or even sacred.[32] A few pages later, when the infant Maria
Elizabeth is saved from 'convulsive spasms', she explains her relief:
'What I felt may be pictured to a fond *mother's* fancy, but my pen
would fail in attempting to describe it'.[33] Again, Robinson signals not
only the force of her feelings but also that such feelings could only be
understood by the reader who can 'picture' them based on her own
(maternal) experience. The 'fail[ure]' of Robinson's pen here becomes
a rhetorical means of making her credible and sympathetic in the eyes
of the reader, just as the physicality of the earlier scene works together
with the silence about her internal response to it to underscore its
emotional intensity and its reliability.

Robinson likewise uses these self-professed silences to showcase
her 'Romantic' sensibility. When the newly married Mary Robinson
returns to Bristol, she has just learned of her husband's lies about his
professional status, birth and fortune. Increasingly 'wretched' and
'dejected', she seeks out a 'sweet and melancholy' solace in visiting
her childhood haunts. Foremost among these is the gothic church of
St Augustine.[34] As she listens to the mournful melodies of the morning
service, her sentiments are so profound that they escape expression:

> *Language cannot describe* the sort of sensation which I felt, when I
> heard the well-known, long-remembered organ flinging its loud peal
> through the Gothic structure. I hastened to the cloisters. The nursery
> windows were dim, and shattered; the house was sinking to decay.
> The mouldering walk was gloomy, and my spirits were *depressed beyond*

*description*: – I stood alone, rapt in meditation: "Here," said I, "did my
infant feet pace to and fro"; here, did I climb the long stone bench, and
swiftly measure it, at the peril of my safety.[35]

As several critics have noted, Robinson fashions herself here in the
image of a heroine of sensibility in order to illustrate her emotional
and aesthetic responsiveness.[36] This scene and its language recall
not only the protagonists of Radcliffe's gothic fiction – such as *A Sicilian
Romance*'s Julia Mazzini, who also finds shelter and tranquillity in 'the
obscure recesses of St. Augustin'[37] – but also the women of Robinson's
own novels.[38] Sharon Setzer has linked Robinson's self-portrait here
to Wordsworthian poetics, calling this episode one of 'three distinct
Bristol spots of time' which underline her consistency of character
and thus evidence her endeavour to 'create a more traditionally
"Romantic" subjectivity'.[39] Amy Culley finds that 'Robinson's self-
representation seems to be influenced by the image of Wollstonecraft
as the Romantic artist, abandoned lover, solitary wanderer, and
devoted mother in *A Short Residence in Sweden, Norway and Denmark*
(1796)'.[40] Like both Wordsworth and Wollstonecraft, Robinson
traces, in this scene, a typically 'Romantic' response pattern that moves
from solitary aesthetic appreciation, to transcendent 'meditation', to
memory, and finally ends with an emotional outpouring in 'a tear'
of grief for the long-departed friend 'Evelyn'.[41] A similar trajectory
might be identified in the work of many other Romantic writers such
as Coleridge, Keats, Shelley and Landon.

Moreover, in layering the remarks of the middle-aged writer
over the teenage self, who in turn nostalgically remembers her early
years (detailed in the opening paragraphs of the *Memoirs*), Robinson
suggests that the selves of her childhood, adolescence and adulthood
are consistent in 'temper' of soul. She posits this as her true self, and
in showing it to us she means 'not to write my own eulogy' but to
'succeed in my vindication'.[42] She is distressed that she has been taken
for a shallow and dissolute woman, lamenting that the world has
'mistaken the character of [her] mind' and echoing this a page later:
'how little has the misjudging world known of what has passed in
my mind'.[43] Her 'vindication' is predicated on persuading us that her
real 'character' is not what people have thought but what she reveals

in these pages. And what she reveals here chimes with many traits and values of a cultural trend that we now call 'Romanticism', but perhaps most of all with 'the Romantic ideal of the human soul that has, through painful experience, come to know itself and to be able to share itself with others'.[44]

At the same time, there is a muted tension here between being misunderstood and failing to make herself understood. In order to come across as sympathetic, Robinson needs to demonstrate her character as virtuous but victimised. She endeavours, as Sharon Setzer has discussed, to 'replace a two-dimensional public image with a three-dimensional character possessing thoughts and feelings'.[45] Yet Robinson does not straightforwardly open her heart to us, for she repeatedly lays stress on the fact that she is *not* revealing everything. Indeed, Robinson's bids for sympathy and for trust are marked by a self-professed failure of expression. This rhetorical device can be seen as a performance or manipulation of authenticity enacted through language.[46] Eleanor Ty has suggested that although 'Robinson purports to be telling the truth, she is constrained not only by her feelings about what is acceptable to polite society, but also by language itself'.[47] Yet Ty's statement might usefully be formulated in the reverse. It is not that Robinson's truth-telling is constrained by her use of language, but rather that the constraints of language, which Robinson continually and explicitly invokes, persuade us that she *is* 'telling the truth', even as she insists on the incompleteness of her account.

Establishing this truthfulness is especially important for Robinson, whose *Memoirs* is competing with so many unauthorised versions of her life. However, even far less scandalous self-biographers would be likely to feel some pressure to verify their accounts. This is because autobiography, increasingly prevalent and popular in the period, was nevertheless seen as both unstable and 'suspicious: it raises questions about motivations, purposes, and, inevitably, about authenticity'.[48] Autobiography has not only to 'textualis[e] the private space of character' but also to justify its impulse to make this 'private space' public.[49] Maria Elizabeth's 'Advertisement' defends this impulse primarily on the basis of her filial duty – 'the *solemn injunction* of a dying parent' – and on the 'vindication' of her mother's '*real* character'.[50] Mary Robinson, of course, also claims self-vindication as a legitimating impulse for writing. Yet it is no coincidence that Robinson fashions herself in the image of emergent Romantic literary and aesthetic values, or that she employs a sophisticated rhetorical pattern to underline and to play out aspects of her (sincere, sensitive, sympathetic, admirably 'feminine') character. Robinson appears to realise that the character of the autobiographical text and its subject are interlinked, and that she can utilise literary style to authenticate both.[51] In other words, she can validate the moral and literary integrity of her narrative, and thus of herself, through the cultivation of a unique poetics of self-expression. By the late eighteenth century, autobiography was starting to be regarded as a literary, rather than a historical, practice, and individual expression was becoming a cornerstone of 'Romantic' verse.[52] Robinson's self-professed silences can be seen as an innovation in life writing in the Romantic period.

## Robinson and the scandal memoir tradition

At the same time, Robinson's *Memoirs* cannot escape links to a largely 'lowbrow' subgenre of eighteenth-century women's life writing that contains the so-called scandalous memoirists, or 'appeal memoirists', as well as actresses and other celebrities.[53] This tradition includes texts such as *The Memoirs of Laetitia Pilkington* (1748), *An Apology for the Conduct of Mrs. Teresia Constantia Phillips* (1748–79), *The Narrative of the Life of Charlotte Charke* (1755), *The Memoirs of Mrs. Sophia Baddeley* (1787) and *The Life of Mrs. Gooch* (1792). Although critics often suggest that Robinson avoids association with scandal memoirs or that she is more circumspect than other scandalous memoirists,[54] Robinson's *Memoirs* displays the structure, rationale and thematic preoccupations that appear in many of these earlier texts. And even if Robinson adopts the conventions of the genre selectively, the republication of her *Memoirs* with Charke's *Narrative of the Life of Mrs. Charlotte Charke* in Volume Seven of Hunt and Clark's *Autobiography* series (1826–87) indicates that she was nonetheless associated with the genre. She certainly follows the trajectory of the 'appeal memoir' as outlined by Caroline Breashears, by detailing a period of initial innocence, the difficulties that follow a transitional event (her marriage), her subsequent 'misstep' (adultery), its fallout and finally her attempt to make a new life for herself.[55] Like other appeal memoirists, Robinson frames her story as a 'public tribunal' to effect 'restoration of reputation and status, and/or vindication against injustice', and in contrast to writers of whore biographies or earlier scandal chronicles, Robinson's narrative admits faults but is not essentially confessional.[56] Robinson also borrows from the mid-eighteenth-century lexicon of sensibility to participate in the rescripting of sexual transgression from sinful to sentimental.[57] She attempts to challenge the link between virtue and chastity and adopts the defensive critical strategy visible in the life writing of her fellow female performers, which involves showing the decency and relatability of her private life.[58]

Robinson's style and strategy seem, in particular, to resemble the 1792 memoir of Elizabeth Sarah Gooch, nee Villa-Real (1756–after 1806), which is distinguished by its sensitive narrative and sentimental appeals for sympathy. The *Life of Mrs. Gooch* details Elizabeth's marriage to William Gooch, a fortune hunter who later accuses her of adultery and then abandons her in France, where she takes up a series of lovers and is imprisoned for debt before returning to England to become an actress and a writer. According to Dianne Dugaw, Gooch employs 'sentimental modes of Gothic fiction and Romanticism' to show how she 'withstands her suffering with the moral high-mindedness and pathos of a heroine of sensibility'.[59] Like Robinson at the cloisters of St Augustine's abbey, Gooch goes to the 'ruins of Fountaine's Abbey' where her 'soul finds food for contemplation', and Gooch likewise stresses that her 'extreme sensibility has ever been the bane of [her] peace'.[60] Several other features work to heighten the portrayal of this sensibility in much the same way that they do in Robinson's *Memoirs*: the use of rhetorical questions such as 'What *can* I do?', impassioned interjections like 'alas!' and 'Fatal sacrifice!' and moments of direct address or positioning of the reader, such as 'Conceive, if it be possible, the agonies I felt' or 'Put yourselves in idea, for a few moments, in *my* situation'.[61] Gooch even underlines the depth of her feelings in two key moments by expressing that she was 'too much affected to speak' and that 'it is impossible to describe, nay, it is impossible to conceive, what I suffered'.[62] These stylistic similarities suggest an overlap in strategies of self-representation, though it is difficult to ascertain whether Robinson read and borrowed from Gooch's *Memoir*. What is certain is that there *was* a line of influence in the opposite direction. Gooch, along with fellow courtesan memoirists Sophia Baddeley and Julia Johnstone, is known to have admired Robinson's writing.[63] The similarity may therefore arise because Gooch is emulating the style of Robinson's earlier writing, such as her poetry. These speculations notwithstanding, it is clear that Robinson's *Memoirs* has more in common with the subgenre of 'scandalous memoirs' than many critics have allowed, both in terms of structure, and at least in some instances, style.

However, Robinson parts ways with even the highly sentimentalised appeal memoir of Elizabeth Gooch in several respects. Like many scandalous memoirists, Gooch lists her reasons for writing early in the text: the 'first (for I must speak the truth, and it is a forcible one) is NECESSITY' and the 'second is in compliance with that justice that I owe to myself as an oppressed individual'.[64] Robinson, by contrast, links her *Memoirs* with restitution of reputation but never with financial restitution. This difference in emphasis allows Robinson, even more than Gooch, to emphasise her Romantic sensibilities and to nudge her narrative towards the position of literature, away from the sub-literary association with scandal memoirs.

The effects of this shift in emphasis can be seen when we examine comparable moments from the two texts. Gooch, at the end of her narrative, summarises her situation in emotive language:

> Ingratitude, ill-treatment, and fraud – my constitution ruined – my peace of mind destroyed – and debts encompassing me on every side. … My first attachment will be my last … may these pages catch his eye, and when I may be buried in my long-wished-for grave, may he (if it be possible he lives!) give a tear to my hard fate![65]

Robinson's synopsis, which comes about two-thirds of the way through the text, seems at first glance remarkably similar in tone:

> I transcribe this passage on the twenty-ninth of March, 1800. I feel my health decaying, my spirit broken. I look back without regret that so

many of my days are numbered; and, were it in my power to choose, I
would not wish to measure them again: – but whither am I wandering?
I will resume my melancholy story.[66]

Both passages conjure abject images of mistreated, forlorn women
who look back on their lives with only the slight consolation that death
is approaching. Yet there are key differences here. By not mentioning
her 'debts' (though by 1800 she certainly had her share), and by
splicing her deathbed summary midway through the text, Robinson
accentuates the sense that she is compelled to write for reasons that are
aesthetic and emotional rather than financial. Though the *Memoirs* may
well have been written for money, perhaps even as a legacy to support
Maria Elizabeth,[67] neither Robinson nor her daughter mentions it in
this light. Gooch, on the other hand, composed *Life* when she was
destitute, and makes her financial plea openly, thus linking her narrative
to an aspect of this pulpy brand of life writing that Robinson is keen
to avoid.[68] Moreover, the fact that Gooch lived another fourteen years
after the publication of her *Life* makes the gesture to her 'long-wished-
for grave' feel like an artificial ploy for sympathy, or worse, for sales.
In contrast, the timing of Robinson's fatalistic comment, which was
written only months before her death in December of 1800, lends her
*Memoirs* a further stamp of authenticity.

Furthermore, Robinson seems less concerned than these earlier
memoirists with the 'arraignment of others, and the gathering of
evidence'.[69] Evidentiary documents are not included in the manner of
earlier eighteenth-century memoirs, and she avoids satire and humour
altogether. According to Lynda Thompson, mid-century scandalous
memoirists such as Phillips and Pilkington tended to come off as
'independent, strident, witty, ready to attack, yet willing to admit
their own flaws'.[70] In Robinson's *Memoirs*, however, negative emotions
such as anger, resentment and indignation are selectively displayed
and rarely aimed directly at her husband or her lover, the two figures
who might seem to warrant them most. She appears charitable in
her judgement of the former: 'I do not condemn Mr Robinson; I but
too well know that we cannot command our affections. I only lament
that he did not observe some decency in his infidelities'.[71] She tends
to 'lament' rather than 'condemn' throughout the *Memoirs*, stressing

the tenor of feelings rather than the ethics of actions.[72] Furthermore, though often grouped with other courtesan memoirists such as Gooch and Phillips, Robinson confesses less and titillates more than these precursors. According to Dugaw, scandalous memoirs are often 'grounded in sexual liaisons and householding with various men' but appear 'notably "unsexy" in the details'.[73] Robinson never discusses such arrangements (though she is purported by modern biographers to have had them) but appears remarkably 'sexy', especially at the climax of her narrative, as will be discussed later. Robinson, as we shall continue to see, is careful in both what she confesses and what she conceals.

## Silence, speech and social critique

Robinson comes closest to the 'strident' denunciations of the earlier appeal memoirists in the scenes that stage her refusal of would-be seducers. As Laura Runge has noted, these episodes feature a recurring 'pattern of gallantry and coercion' through which Robinson exposes 'the nature of masculine power and its economic stranglehold over women' and indicts the way that 'female dependence on male protection' becomes a 'commodity that can be bartered'.[74] The manifestation of male power becomes increasingly dangerous in Robinson's interactions with George Robert ('Fighting') Fitzgerald, Lord Lyttelton and George Brereton, respectively,[75] as they attempt to use flattery, secrets, bribery and/ or violence to manipulate Robinson into capitulating to their advances. Lord Lyttelton, for example, informs Robinson of her husband's 'connection with a woman of abandoned character', and then tries to exploit her disappointment and indignation by offering to put his 'fortune' and 'powers' at her disposal.[76] Fitzgerald, whose pistol marks the violence of which he is capable, attempts to abduct Robinson in his chaise. Brereton detains her husband, giving Robinson the ultimatum that her husband must 'pay' his debts, 'fight' or 'go to prison' unless she will 'behave more kindly'.[77] Dramatic dialogue, heightened emotion and last-minute escapes from violence and sexual assault lend theatricality to these encounters in which the men resemble the villainous rakes of contemporary fiction.

Robinson's rhetorical expressions of linguistic failure contribute to this effect, underlining her status as a virtuous heroine. In the Lyttelton incident, for example, Robinson explains: 'My sensations, my sufferings were undescribable … Language cannot describe what I suffered'.[78] Robinson likewise appears 'terrified beyond all description' with Fitzgerald and 'distressed beyond the power of utterance' with Brereton.[79] As in some of the sections discussed previously, Robinson uses this trope to emphasise her distress, humiliation and outrage in these emotive set pieces.

However, in the last and most extreme of these seduction scenes, Robinson marshals a combination of silence and speech to dramatise her resistance of Brereton. As Robinson's desperation grows, she finally retorts with a threat of her own:

> I now lost all command of myself, and, with the most severe invective, condemned the infamy of his conduct. 'I *will* return to Bath', said I, 'but it shall be to expose *your* dishonourable, your barbarous machinations … I will proclaim to the world that the common acts of seduction are not sufficiently depraved for the mind of a libertine and a gamester'. I uttered these words in so loud a tone of voice that he changed colour, and desired me to be discreet and patient.[80]

Robinson succeeds here, according to Runge, because she understands how to play the 'games of public exposure and private reputation'.[81] Yet despite her valiant resistance and Brereton's subsequent decision to release her husband, Robinson soon becomes mute: 'I trembled, and was incapable of speaking'.[82] Though effective, Robinson figures her defensive tools – her 'invective', threat to 'proclaim' Brereton's actions and 'loud' voice[83] – as a loss of 'command', or in other words, a loss of feminine self-restraint. Robinson only turns to these masculine tools as a last resort, and her return to silent 'trembl[ing]' marks her re-entry into the realm of acceptable feminine behaviour. What is significant here, however, is not that voice and silence are gendered qualities but that Robinson reveals that she is capable of both, when the situation – or the narrative – requires. Like the gothic motifs which, according to Engel, allow Robinson to move between the personae of 'terrorized heroine' and 'accessible and desirable sexual object',[84] the trope of silence links to her protean capabilities. Though earlier writers like Charke have been seen to sabotage the authenticity of their feminine personae with the display of masculine attributes, Robinson weaves them together in the *Memoirs* through a sophisticated thematic and rhetorical representation of silence.[85]

At times, the silences in Robinson's narrative signal more unambiguously that she is refusing to describe rather than simply unable to do so. Discussing her acting debut and the London society to which she is introduced as a result, Robinson bemoans the 'perils attendant on a dramatic life'.[86] In addition to their long-standing association with prostitution, of course, actresses, who courted media attention and profited from self-display, were seen to lack proper feminine modesty and moral virtue.[87] Robinson is therefore careful to distance herself from the stereotype of the eighteenth-century actress, so often conflated with the courtesan. Still, stressing her virtuous navigation of these sexual 'perils' is often more than a self-vindicating display of her chastity and fidelity. In one particular instance, she cites the stream of wealthy men who offer to make her their mistress:

> *Were I to mention the names* of those who held forth the temptations of fortune at this moment of public peril, I might create some reproaches in many families of the fashionable world. *Among others* who offered most liberally to purchase my indiscretion was the late Duke of Rutland: a settlement of six hundred pounds per annum was proposed, as the means of estranging me entirely from my husband. I refused the offer. ... *I shall not enter into a minute detail* of temptations which assailed my fortitude.[88]

Though Robinson's coy conditional phrase at the start of this passage makes clear that she is withholding information, she reveals just enough 'detail' to convince us of her reliability. This 'detail' comes in the form of Charles Manners, fourth Duke of Rutland (1754–87), a notorious gambler, drinker and womaniser who is credited with writing a pamphlet in defence of modern adultery while at Cambridge.[89] Rutland, with these reprehensible credentials, seems to stand in for the 'names' that go unmentioned. At the same time, the suppression of the 'others' serves to spark curiosity and perhaps indignation.

Embedded here is a social critique of gender and class power dynamics and the flawed social and economic institutions that foster them. In explaining the seductive 'perils' of a stage career, Robinson implies that the designation of 'volatile and dissipated' pertains not to herself but to these moneyed male predators who attempt to take advantage of vulnerable women as a matter of course. The language of commodification runs throughout the paragraph. It suggests the 'temptations' (repeated three times) are monetary, as indicated by phrases such as 'purchase my indiscretion', 'offer' and 'patronage' (repeated twice). In the two subsequent paragraphs, Robinson splices the particulars of her husband's profligacy and adultery with her efforts to support her family 'honourably' through her acting 'salary'.[90] Robinson's precarious financial independence is thus situated between two poles of masculine depravity. On the one hand, there is 'the increasing neglect' of her improvident husband, who lives off Robinson's earnings and passes 'all his hours that he could *steal*' in the company of his Covent-garden mistresses; on the other, the parade of rakish aristocrats who put a price on Robinson's 'indiscretion'.[91] Robinson demonstrates the injustice of a patriarchal society that offers women few alternatives to financial dependence on negligent or predatory men.

This objection tallies with those made in earlier appeal memoirs, which likewise arraign the injustice of marriage as well as other political, legal and economic institutions.[92] Mid-century life-writers like Pilkington and Phillips were pioneering in their refusal to remain silent, and their willingness to 'put private or personal experience to service in order to make a more general protest about women's unjust treatment'.[93] Robinson, however, wields silence strategically in order to accentuate her critique, to draw sympathy or to pique interest. In this way, like her precursors, she plays to readers' appetite for tales of private life.[94] But her canny self-representation, which toggles between communication and concealment and calls attention to its own omissions, feeds what Gill Perry calls the 'fantasy of "public intimacy"' and 'seduce[s] the reader into believing that he or she is being given access to the "real" or private person'.[95] Robinson establishes a bond with her readers, who are encouraged to feel that they know her and yet are left wishing to know more.

### Unspeakable emotions

In its climactic episodes (those involving the Prince of Wales), the *Memoirs* also has structural gaps. The narration of Robinson's affair with the Prince is fragmented, appearing in three different sections of the *Memoirs*: the 'Narrative', the early pages of the 'Continuation' and the 'letter' supposedly written in 1783. The 'Narrative' closes with their epistolary courtship, the Prince's proposal to meet in person and Robinson's fears about taking this step. In the 'Continuation', the 'Friend' retraces these fears and elaborates on Robinson's internal 'conflicts' and 'passions' before explaining the arrangements for her upcoming 'interview' with the royal suitor.[96] The 1783 letter begins with this 'interview' and goes on to tell of their subsequent relationship, its termination and the emotional aftermath. The 'Friend' then resumes again, lingering over Robinson's sorrow before summarising the events from 1781 up until her death in 1800. The stop-start structure, with its visible textual breaks and shifts in narration, and the overlapping events of the 'Narrative', 'Continuation' and letter make this sequence feel disjointed. This feeling of unevenness is exacerbated by the disproportionate focus on Robinson's turbulent emotions – her reservations and regrets in particular – at the expense of her more positive feelings in the company of the Prince. As a result, the sexual frisson is often elided, and any enjoyment Robinson found in the year-long affair is heavily compressed. The architecture of the narrative thus foregrounds affective over sexual experience and stresses pain over pleasure. These emphases accord well with burgeoning Romantic values that 'prize emotional over the rational, finding heroes and heroines … in the members of the social body who suffer most'.[97] Though the narrative is, broadly speaking, chronological and coherent (especially if we accept the conceit of the 'found' letter), these qualities are masked by a structure which gives the impression of a patchwork of 'found' texts. The obvious ruptures in the narrative disguise not only its structural integrity but also its more subtle imbalances in emphasis.

Robinson accentuates the heartbreak and disillusionment that she experiences when the Prince leaves her. As several critics have noted, Robinson rewrites her transgressive relations with the Prince

of Wales as a story of 'star-crossed lovers' in order to make herself
more sympathetic.[98] By presenting herself as a victim of a doomed
attachment, Robinson can continue in the role of the English Sappho,
one of her most powerful poetic personae.[99] The Prince's decision
to end the affair heralds the most painful episode of the *Memoirs*.
Robinson appears 'amazed, afflicted, *beyond the power of utterance*',
and she states: 'My agonies were now *undescribable*'.[100] Soon after,
Robinson's 1783 letter ends and the narration is resumed, for the
second time, by the 'Friend.' First linguistically and then textually,
Robinson asserts that she cannot or will not express fully the 'agonies'
of her heart. In fact, Robinson has already described her 'foreboding',
'dreadful' situation, 'distress', 'complete despair' and 'oppression'.[101]
However, many other emotions do not appear: anger at the men in
her life, outrage at society for offering her such limited opportunities
to support herself, humiliation at being jilted publicly, frustration,
resentment, hatred. By alluding to these unspeakable emotions as
'undescribable', Robinson leaves the reader to imagine this emotional
prism and to commiserate with her.

This strategy enables Robinson to strengthen the affective bond
with the reader. As Jonathan Lamb has argued, 'it is not through our
senses that sympathy works, but through the imagination'.[102] Robinson
curtails description and signals explicitly that she is doing so, forcing
us to undergo this imaginative process of engagement. The ruptures
and shifts in the narrative frustrate our expectations of the memoir
form, which may be doubly effective in adding an element of surprise.
Lamb suggests that surprise heightens the 'passionate spontaneity of
sympathy' and that 'sympathy thrives in situations of comparative
powerlessness in which the function and tendency of social roles is
no longer directly apparent'.[103] Here the memoirist ceases disclosure,
stops writing and seems to disappear from the text entirely, inviting
the reader to fill in the 'undescribable' gaps.

Robinson, then, is not merely, as Anne Mellor suggests, a
'tortured heroine of suffering who *speaks* to a sympathetic listener',[104]
but one who suggests, implies or gestures, leaving this 'listener' – or
reader – to infer the rest. This strategy of self-representation follows
partial confession with concealment in order to win compassion.

The combination of revelation and refusal, what the German sociologist Georg Simmel terms 'semi-concealment', has been linked by Gill Perry to the complicated relationship of the eighteenth-century actress and her audiences, both on and off stage.[105] Semi-concealment involves presentation and disguise in such a sequence that the whole is visualised more readily. According to Perry, it also involves 'ornamentation', for we 'conceal that which is adorned and thus draw attention to it'.[106] Joanna Baillie's 1798 'Introductory Discourse' likewise theorises that 'the most powerful moments in theatre, moments of the greatest empathetic connection between audience and characters, are those that reveal intentionally concealed passion'.[107] The references to 'undescribable' emotion may function in the *Memoirs* as a kind of verbal 'ornamentation' akin to the hand gesture, facial expression or bodily movement of an actor on stage. In these moments, Robinson adapts theatrical modes into a verbal refrain that can similarly 'reveal intentionally concealed passion' and thus connect with her readers emotionally. It is not that Robinson censors her negative emotions so much as that she finds innovative ways of expressing them.

Robinson models this strategy early in the *Memoirs* when she details the separation of her own parents. When her mother learns of the 'alienation of my father's affections', Robinson explains: '*Language would but feebly describe* the varying emotions which struggled in her bosom ... My mother's agitation was *undescribable*'.[108] Robinson describes the breakup as a 'death blow' to her mother, bringing 'anguish' and 'decided misery', but again she leaves more masculine feelings like bitterness, frustration and jealousy unspecified.[109] Without delineating all her mother's 'varying emotions' individually, Robinson conveys her understanding of them and invites ours. Critics like Engel have emphasised Robinson's sympathetic identification with her father, who becomes a double for herself and 'her attempts to gain sympathy for her own position as a married woman taken in by a "fatal attachment"'.[110] However, the early commiseration with her mother similarly foreshadows the reaction she will expect of readers when she is forsaken by the Prince. The rhetorical trope of the 'undescribable' links these instances of feminine 'anguish'. In both, she keeps critical commentary to a minimum and indelicate emotions like anger or animosity at the level of subtext. Like a performance on stage, Robinson's recourses to the 'undescribable' become complex 'loci of shared emotion'.[111] She reinforces her image as a sympathetic heroine and yet suggests to the reader's imagination a darker set of sentiments that remain unspoken.

## Sexual transgression

Robinson had long practised this strategic management of privacy and public revelation, which was central to Romantic celebrity culture.[112] By the late eighteenth century, actresses including Robinson, Sarah Siddons, Dora Jordan and many others had attained unprecedented levels of publicity in newspapers, magazines, books, images and even merchandise.[113] If they were savvy, performers could begin to shape their reputations through what Robyn Asleson calls a 'strategic deployment of private life'.[114] Robinson, in particular, was well known for participating in her own media 'spectacle' and for reappropriating versions of herself in her adept use of poetic 'avatars'.[115] As discussed earlier, Robinson's *Memoirs* employs the 'star-crossed lovers' trajectory, which allows her to keep the focus on emotional motivations and ramifications and to reinforce her image as an eighteenth-century Sappho, the tragically spurned lover who channels affective overflow into writing. The Sapphic persona involves more than unrequited love, blending the sorrowful and the erotic.[116] Engel, in particular, emphasises how Robinson straddles incongruous qualities, appearing, for example, 'suffering and triumphant', 'available and elusive' and 'vulnerable and seductive'.[117] According to Gill Perry, the lasting 'fascination' and 'personal magnetism' of female performers lies specifically in this 'power of embodying, apparently without effort, contradictory qualities simultaneously'.[118] Part of Robinson's popularity and endurance as a celebrity rests on her ability to encompass these contradictory combinations.

One of the biggest sources of tension in Robinson's persona (apparent both in her poetry and her life writing) remains her insistence on her status as a victimised heroine of sensibility and her renown as a glamorous and worldly actress-turned-courtesan.

Nowhere is this contradiction more obvious than at the crescendo of the *Memoirs*, her notorious liaison with the Prince of Wales. This episode inaugurates her public 'fall' from chastity and concomitant rise to mega-celebrity. It also marks one of the most salient structural anomalies of the *Memoirs*, as it coincides with the first textual break and the most noticeable narrative gap. Robinson's omission of sexual content is not itself surprising. As we have seen, she distances herself from certain conventions of scandalous memoirs, and it makes sense that she would likewise have avoided the quasi-pornographic revelations typical of biographies of actresses such as Anne Catley and Elizabeth Billington.[119] When the emotionally and sexually charged, not to mention highly overdetermined, moment – the one the reader has been waiting for – arrives, Robinson's narration ceases entirely, and language is replaced by a series of twenty-three asterisks spread over three lines. A brief note follows: '*The Narrative of Mrs Robinson closes here*'.[120] On the next page begins the 'Continuation By a Friend', a third-person narrator-editor who transitions into more general reflections. What is perhaps more surprising, but easy to overlook, is that the abrupt termination of the narrative and the circumlocutions of the 'Friend' who continues it are not so much hidden as highlighted by the insertion of the asterisks.

Though often ignored or dismissed as an 'accidental', the use of this typographical feature is most likely *not* an accident but a graphic innovation borrowed from eighteenth-century fiction. Writers such as Jonathan Swift, Laurence Sterne and Samuel Richardson experimented with 'printer's ornaments', visual markers such as flowers, dots, dashes and asterisks, which can stand in for or supplement verbal text. The asterisk, in particular, is used by Sterne in *Tristram Shandy* (1759–67) to replace lewd content. At the same time that Sterne appears to censor out the immodest, however, he in fact not only draws attention to it but also implicates the reader in doing so, for the reader has to fill in the gaps.[121]

It is often assumed that women did not engage in this kind of typographical play because, unlike their male counterparts, they often used intermediaries and did not have the same direct access to the printing house or contact with the booksellers.[122] Yet the life writing of

Mary Robinson and her contemporary Elizabeth Gooch may indicate otherwise. As discussed above, in her self-vindicating memoir *The Life of Mrs. Gooch* (1792), actress and novelist Elizabeth Gooch defends her conduct, in part, by constructing herself as a sentimental heroine with a virtuous heart who becomes a victim of circumstance. In a poignant moment early in the narrative, she emphasises her sensibility by reflecting on the process of writing and bemoaning the torrent of painful emotions it precipitates:

> Why cannot I write this page with composure? ... why, at this long, distant period, do my eyes swim in tears, and blot what I am writing – But I must not, I dare not revert to my own feelings – would that they were buried in a long, long oblivion![123]

Directly after this outburst follow three small asterisks, and on the next page, forty further asterisks replace the first four lines of text. The asterisks enact not only a visual interruption of the writing, the effect of the overwhelming emotion described in the previous paragraph, but also symbolise the disintegration of her mental 'composure'. The asterisks signal psychological authenticity and heightened emotion and work to evoke the reader's sympathy.

Like Gooch's *Life*, Robinson's *Memoirs* also uses asterisks at its turning point. The asterisks underline the depth of Robinson's feelings, convey her genteel sensibility (she modestly throws a veil over her past shame) and help to elicit compassion. Yet in this instance, they also have a titillating effect. Robinson's unwillingness to speak her emotions or to detail her transgressions leaves the reader to infer the thoughts, sensations and actions that are concealed by the twenty-three asterisks. The asterisks highlight the illicit and erotic aspects of Robinson's story, which, in refusing to name, she invites us to imagine. This usage of asterisks, in conjunction with the textual break, may function as another type of 'semi-concealment', providing a formal counterpart to the rhetorical trope of the 'undescribable' discussed earlier. Again, a so-called 'failure' in the text may be viewed as a productive innovation that helps Robinson to balance sympathetic identification and erotic titillation.

It is not possible to know how much input Robinson had in these kinds of printing decisions. Certainly, writers such as Swift, Sterne and Richardson exerted control beyond the manuscript phase and intervened in decisions about the printing of their books.[124] The asterisks in the memoirs of Gooch and Robinson seem to engage readers in ways that recall the graphic innovations of eighteenth-century fiction. However, to experiment with typography would require direct access to the printing house or bookseller. Typically, the eighteenth-century author is at one remove from the printing (which was contracted out by a bookselling publisher), unless the publisher *was* the author, in which case the intervention could be much more direct.[125] For Gooch, who published the book herself in her lifetime, it is likely that she dealt with the printer directly.[126] She may not only have approved the proofs but may even have made suggestions.

Robinson's *Memoirs*, by contrast, was published posthumously by Richard Phillips, with the aid of Maria Elizabeth as editor.[127] Robinson therefore could not have wielded direct control over the printing. It may have been the work of the entrepreneurial Phillips, who was experimenting with new formats as part of his strategy to dominate the growing market for life writing.[128] Robinson's first publisher, John Bell, had also been a pioneer in book design and production, known for the sumptuousness of his publications and for attempting to capture the sensuous aspects of Robinson's verse through unique printing features.[129] Robinson's proclivity for ornamental, innovative poetic forms gave Bell 'opportunities for elaborate printing features, such as conspicuous indentations … plus a bewildering array of italics and small capitals'.[130] Her work for Stuart's *Morning Post* would also have given her knowledge of newspaper layout and its varied typographical effects. Robinson had employed Hookham and Carpenter earlier in her career and therefore would have had direct input in the printing of her fourth novel *Hubert de Sevrac* (1797).[131] Moreover, according to Cheryl Wanko, it was not uncommon for thespian life writing to draw inspiration from the 'unusual narrative experiments of the day – mimicking *Tristram Shandy* or Fielding's narratives'.[132] Robinson may even have indicated to her daughter how she wanted the *Memoirs* to appear, but of course there is no evidence for this. However, regardless of who made the decision, the *outcome* is certain. The use of printer's ornaments in Robinson's *Memoirs* shows that life writing could import graphic techniques from fiction to contribute to the construction of sympathetic *and* erotic heroine-protagonists.

Like the 'undescribable' moments in the *Memoirs*, the asterisks function as another type of 'semi-concealment' but one that is textual rather than verbal. The asterisks shield the action from view, even though writer and reader know perfectly well what action is taking place. Christopher Flint has discussed similar 'typographical effects' in Sterne's fiction: 'these little textual moments paradoxically enjoin ... active participation ... at the same time that they bar the reader from fully reading the text' and therefore push us into 'a double posture' whereby we both inhabit and yet remain at a distance from the narrated events.[133] Flint also stresses the self-consciousness and the playfulness of these moments. The asterisks in Robinson's *Memoirs* have the similarly paradoxical effect of heightening not only what they purportedly conceal but also the pretence of the concealment itself. This coy double-dealing involves the seductive contradiction between revelation and disguise so common to eighteenth-century theatrical roles and costumes. Robinson seems practically to be winking at the reader even as she draws the curtain on her own narration.

This flirtation with the reader actually begins on the page before the asterisks with Robinson's reference to her success in one of her well-known breeches parts. Again, Robinson is ostensibly demonstrating her propriety and decorum. She recounts her refusal to 'meet his Royal Highness at his apartments, in the disguise of male attire' and makes a point of eschewing the 'indelicacy of such a step'.[134] She differentiates between her on-stage and off-stage behaviour. Yet by specifying her sensational performance as 'the Irish Widow' in Garrick's play of the same name, she conjures a titillating image of herself in male dress.[135] As Gill Perry has shown, 'cross-dressing reinforced the actress's body as seductive and provocative' as 'legs, ankles and calves were exposed in tighter clothing'.[136] With her trim figure, Robinson had maximised her sex appeal in breeches roles that involved revealing garments as well as thrilling instabilities in sexual identity and morality.[137] *The Irish Widow*, a two-act comedy with 'a measure of lasciviousness', features one particularly 'prurient' scene in which the 'widow starts to undo her garters, drawing the audience's attention to her legs'.[138]

By stressing this provocative performance and then the 'distressing agitation' of the Prince and the 'violent' passion of Lord Malden, Robinson reminds us obliquely of her sexual attractiveness. She also hints at the nature of the content obscured by the asterisks on the following page.

The break in the narrative and the asterisks which adorn it may support a delicate balancing act that could not be managed with words alone. With her insightful emphasis on 'reading the visual in narrative and the narrative in visual', Laura Engel has explained how Robinson's use of clothing and Gothic tropes enables her

> to foreground the seductive desirable qualities of her persona and to subsequently disappear when those qualities signify the possibility of immorality ... by highlighting and obscuring her "real" body ... Robinson creates her own celebrity allure.[139]

The use of printer's ornaments here may contribute to her 'celebrity allure' in a similarly 'visual' way. As James Treadwell has suggested, 'neither pleasure nor instruction can be derived, apparently, from an autobiographical practice which is openly, confessedly immoral'.[140] Yet part of Robinson's appeal lies in her sexual transgressions, and she knows all too well of the public appetite for revelations about the private lives of actresses. The cheeky pseudo-break in the narrative wordlessly announces *and* undermines a suppression of salacious content. It constitutes the kind of self-conscious paratextual apparatus that Treadwell identifies as the most important feature of Romantic-period autobiographical texts.[141] According to Treadwell, 'we can read Romantic autobiographical writing not as texts of the self, of privacy, consciousness, or inwardness, but as discourses on textuality, on publication, interaction, and legibility'.[142] Thus it may not be, as Engel suggests, that Robinson has to 'disappear' at the transgressive climax of the text because she *runs out* of 'Gothic' and 'literary categories to rescue her reputation'.[143] Perhaps her disappearance behind the asterisks means that Robinson indeed abandons 'literary' strategies for those of a typographical, textual nature.

This strategy would make sense given the formal innovations of Robinson's poetry at the end of her career. Daniel Robinson has demonstrated how Robinson devised new meters and verse forms in which the poetic and the erotic could work together.[144] He has also explored how Robinson's usage of 'textual but not verbal features' and her attention to 'texts, paratexts, contexts, and intertexts' influenced the reception of her poetry, connecting her formal virtuosity to a bid for a lasting literary fame.[145] It is important to clarify what fame means in this context. For Daniel Robinson, fame connotes a serious, enduring literary immortality and differs from celebrity, which is more ephemeral and therefore inferior.[146] He makes the distinction not because he believes that Robinson could really opt for one over the other but because he wants to stress that she understands the 'fine line between her celebrity and ignominy'.[147] Not simply a self-promoter exploiting her infamous history, Robinson, he suggests, aspires to 'professional legitimacy, recognition, and fame'.[148] His point tallies with Engel's claim that Robinson's *Memoirs* aims at 'redemption of her self-image but also at seduction and self-promotion'.[149] Both Laura Engel and Daniel Robinson see Mary Robinson striving for effects that are longer lasting and more complex than many critics have allowed. Some of these effects, I am suggesting, are facilitated by the unorthodox form, conspicuous gaps and perplexing contradictions of the *Memoirs*. These features, though often taken as flaws, allow her, as we have seen, to strike a balance between sympathy and curiosity and to reveal herself while maintaining the privacy and mystery so important to the cultivation of enduring interest. This balancing act may seem precarious or ungainly to modern scholars, but it resonated with nineteenth-century readers.

## Publication and early reception

Robinson's renown lasted long beyond her death in 1800 and spanned, at least, the duration of the long nineteenth century. During this time, her *Memoirs* never went out of print. Richard Phillips first brought out the *Memoirs of the late Mrs. Robinson, written by herself, with some posthumous pieces*, in four volumes in 1801. At least two American editions followed in the next year, in New York and Philadelphia, respectively.[150] The *Memoirs* was also translated into French in 1802.[151] Phillips then released a two-volume edition in London in 1803, which became the basis for subsequent nineteenth-century imprints, of which there were at least ten.[152] This two-volume edition excluded Robinson's lengthier unpublished verse and prose pieces but included the narrative of the *Memoirs*, the 'Continuation by a friend' (in the middle of which is inserted the 1783 letter), a handful of Robinson's shorter poems, a description of their composition and a comprehensive list of her works.[153] Phillips was also responsible for publishing the first two posthumous collections of her verse, *The Wild Wreath* (1804) and *The Poetical Works of the Late Mrs. Robinson* (1806).[154] Still, by omitting the two volumes of the *Memoirs* devoted exclusively to Robinson's verse and prose in his 1803 edition, Phillips seems both to have responded and contributed to the demand for Robinson's life writing at the expense of her other work.[155] The *Memoirs* was widely read and reviewed, and there seems to have been sustained enthusiasm for further editions.

The *Memoirs* soon became the defining source on Robinson's life. Though not necessarily fully trusted, it was nearly always referenced in biographical accounts of Robinson's life and often in those of the Prince of Wales (afterwards George IV). The enduring appetite for fictional and non-fictional retellings of Robinson's story was fed by essays, entries in multibiographies, illustrated stories, novels and poems, which in turn prompted further reviews, responses in the periodical press and fiction. Though disparate in form and quality, this material deserves attention for what it reveals about Robinson's posthumous reputation and the influence of her *Memoirs* in shaping it. According to Sharon Setzer, 'For more than two hundred years, Robinson's *Memoirs* has met with a largely sympathetic audience, though few readers find her entirely blameless or truthful.'[156] Examination of this nineteenth-century material helps to substantiate and extend Setzer's claim, shedding light on how and why Robinson's *Memoirs* continues to capture readers' imaginations and to cultivate responses at once curious and critical, 'sympathetic' and sceptical, enamoured and dismissive. Moreover, it indicates that the inconsistencies in tone, story, and character; the gaps; and the hybrid form of the *Memoirs* help to facilitate the enduring interest in Robinson, in part because they evoke (and can sustain) such conflicting reactions.

The early periodical reviews mingle sympathy for Robinson's misfortunes with a robust critique of the *Memoirs* for its omissions and discrepancies. The prevailing opinion is that Robinson remains, like King Lear, '"more sinned against than sinning"', a sentiment repeated frequently in later nineteenth-century responses to Robinson.[157] Reviewers often praise admirable qualities such as her 'rich and powerful imagination', 'rectitude and vivacity of moral feeling' and 'natural taste', and her misfortunes are acknowledged as mitigating her errors.[158] The *Monthly Visitor*, for example, 'lament[s] her early, hasty ... rash marriage', and the *Critical Review* bemoans the fact that 'the lot of beauty is often unfortunate'.[159] However, nearly all of the initial reviewers raise doubts about the truthfulness of Robinson's account. The *British Critic* is the most disparaging, comparing the *Memoirs* to cheap commodity fiction:

> We treated the performance of this well-known female, when alive, with a certain complacency inspired by her misfortunes, and justified by the degree of talents she possessed. These Memoirs have nothing to do with the one, and exhibit no proof of the other. ... The whole is little better than a catch-penny.[160]

In more subdued tones, the *Monthly Review* finds the '*Apologist* ... invading the office of the biographer', pronounces that 'though this be the truth, it may not be the *whole truth*' and laments that the narrative 'abruptly breaks off in the most interesting part'.[161] For the *Monthly* reviewer, Robinson's studied narrative tries to vindicate her name by appealing to our emotions: 'she labours to touch the feelings and to melt the heart of the reader.' The book exhibits, in fact, 'all the air of a novel'. The *Critical* reviewer likewise calls it 'a varnished tale' and politely hints at the (unflattering) nature of the events omitted: 'We are old enough to remember this period, and to be able to add to the tale; but what she ... chooses to conceal, we shall not enlarge on.'[162] The reviewers communicate a degree of feeling for Robinson but acknowledge the ways in which the *Memoirs* has been shaped and selectively edited in order to elicit this response.

Alongside the criticism of Robinson's whitewashed narrative and the sanctimonious comments on her transgressions, however, a more vulgar curiosity also surfaces. The *Critical Review* complains of the 'short and unsatisfactory' end to the memoir and the fact that 'much is left to conjecture: much might be filled from the scandalous chronicle of the times'.[163] Still, this reviewer concludes that these 'entertaining' volumes will interest both 'those who have seen and known Mrs. Robinson' and

'those who have only heard of her', even if the *Memoirs* ultimately leaves
readers 'wish[ing] to know more'.[164] Robinson is so famous that the
reviewer does not mention the possibility of a reader not knowing her,
a reminder that her *Memoirs* is expected to add to a reader's knowledge
of her, not initiate it. For the *Critical* reviewer, even though the gaps in
the narrative are easy to spot and to fill in with 'scandalous' content, the
narrative as a whole remains absorbing. The *Memoirs* has a paradoxical
effect: readers may be able to 'conjecture' what belongs in those gaps,
but they are still left wanting more. Robinson's simultaneous publicity
and elusiveness recall an emerging eighteenth-century configuration of
celebrity distinguished, according to Leo Braudy, by the intertwining
of the 'fame of ostentation and the fame of evasion'.[165] The *British
Critic* lets slip another, similar contradiction:

> The editor pretends [the *Memoirs*] were published from motives of filial
> piety; in our opinion, the greater proof of filial piety would have been to
> have suppressed these volumes altogether. The *Memoirs* of the lady tell
> very little, and cease at the moment they begin to excite curiosity.[166]

This reviewer seems outraged at the revelations of the *Memoirs* and at
the same time frustrated at its failure to satisfy his 'curiosity'. On the
one hand, the reviewers seem sanctimoniously to excuse Robinson
for her selective transcription of events, declaring they will help to
'conceal' or 'draw a veil over' transgressions (which are both too
indecent and too well known to need spelling out). On the other
hand, though, the reviewers can barely contain their excitement,
curiosity and frustration at what remains undisclosed. There appears
to be tension between a tendency towards genteel moralising and a
more prurient curiosity. This tension mirrors that of the *Memoirs* itself,
which, as we have seen, manages to tug at our heart strings while also
appealing to our less noble impulses.

## Fictionalisations

Other tensions surface in the fictional rewritings of Robinson's
*Memoirs* which appeared in the early nineteenth century, including
Sarah Green's *The Private History of the Court of England* (1808), *The
Royal Legend: A Tale* (anonymous 1808) and Pierce Egan's *The Mistress of*

*Royalty* (1814). These were not the first texts to dramatise Robinson's royal affair. Epistolary novels like *The Effusions of Love* (Anon, c. 1780) and *The Budget of Love* (Anon, c. 1781), satirical pamphlets like *Poetic Epistle from Florizel to Perdita* (Anon, 1781) and pornographic fictions such as *Letters from Perdita to a Certain Israelite* (1781), *The Rambler's Magazine* (1783–88) and *The Memoirs of Perdita* (1784) had, decades earlier, translated the dalliance of the Prince of Wales and the stunning actress into saleable narratives. Featuring frame stories of 'fortuitous discovery'[167] and a campy mixture of sentiment and satire, *Effusions* and *The Budget of Love* claim to comprise the real letters between Florizel and Perdita and to deliver the details of a love story from courtship and consummation to betrayal and dissolution. Though obviously 'close approximations' rather than 'the real thing', these mass-produced fictions offer a tantalising glimpse into the private lives of the rich and famous.[168] The more sexually explicit texts of the 1780s operate on a similar pretence, though the distance from reality is heightened by far-fetched scenes in which lewdness and vice are used to attack political credibility as much as personal reputation.[169] Robinson's own *Memoirs* implicitly responds to – and rewrites – this material. The narrative reflects, in part, the 'tonal instability' and 'generic complexity' that Kristin Samuelian identifies in these 1780s narratives, which promote both 'objectification and covert identification'.[170]

At first glance, it seems that the nineteenth-century fictional renditions of 'the Perdita affair' simply rehash these earlier works. Plagiarism certainly runs rampant in this cache. The epistolary novels borrow from periodical articles and cartoons, the pornographic novels from each other and from the earlier sources, Egan's *Mistress of Royalty* from *Effusions*. Egan revives the fake pastoralism of *Effusions* and *The Budget of Love* by purporting to present the 'loves of antiquity' via the correspondence of Florizel and Perdita. Similarly, *The Private History* and *The Royal Legend* parade as historical accounts of a pseudo-medieval past. Like their predecessors, all three novels use easily recognisable personae to stand in for the Prince of Wales and Mary Robinson as well as a range of supporting characters, adopting the premise and some of the conventions of the earlier satirical novels.

However, unlike the eighteenth-century renderings, these later fictionalisations of the affair bear traces of Robinson's *Memoirs* in their scope, form, characterisation, content, tone and language. The former tend to focus on the royal romance, whereas the latter incorporate details of Robinson's upbringing, her life outside of her relationship with the Prince and her fate after their affair ends. Even *Mistress of Royalty*, which resembles the earlier works most closely, does not end when the Prince breaks off their affair. Instead, Egan details Robinson's travels to the continent, her relationship with Tarleton and her literary career. Egan replays the bawdy elements of the *Effusions*, for example, when Perdita flirts with her lover: 'I have received your present of the buckles … methinks I see a thousand Florizels sparkle in every brilliant knob.'[171] Yet later, Egan's tone seems closer to Robinson's own as she becomes 'the victim to her excessive sensibility'.[172] Her 'splendid talents' and the 'real merit' of her verse, tragedy and prose are praised so effusively that, as in the earlier epistolary novels, it is not always clear whether the tone is genuine or satirical.[173]

Still, the page-long epitaph that concludes the novel offers a seemingly genuine 'memorial' to its heroine, whose individual trajectory has now superseded her liaison with the Prince of Wales.[174] Egan distils the moral of Robinson's story:

The
CHARACTER of PERDITA,
might have been the admiration of ages, had not
the want of
CHASTITY
disfigured her fair form; and from the omission of
this inestimable quality in her composition,
HER LIFE
Became *checquered, restless, and unhappy!* [...]
**FEMALES**
in emulating her talents, avoid her errors; and
profit by her unhappiness;
that throughout all the unforeseen events which
may occur to you in life,
you may not be deprived of the consolation of reflecting,
that you are not destitute
of the very BASIS of all female excellence,
CHASTITY.[175]

Egan, who boasted of writing, printing and composing the type for his novel, introduces a range of typographical effects here. Positioning the words in the centre of the page so that they resemble a poem or a tombstone inscription and using a mixture of capitalisation, italics, boldface, punctuation and variable font sizes, Egan not only extracts a maxim from Robinson's life story but conveys a degree of personal investment in her story as well. Again, the moralising here may appear so over the top as to verge on irony, but the painstaking arrangement of the page bespeaks an editorial pathos absent from the eighteenth-century fictionalisations of Robinson's life.

Egan's characterisation of and personal response to Robinson also suggest a familiarity with her *Memoirs* that is visible throughout these novels, all of which either echo or quote Robinson directly. In *The Private History of the Court of England* (1808), Sarah Green's language is particularly reminiscent of Robinson's in her treatment of Thomas Robinson (who barely makes an appearance in the eighteenth-century novels). Green describes his 'thousand little delicate attentions' during courtship; Robinson, his 'little interesting attentions'.[176] Green frames Mary Robinson's reaction to her suitor as the 'grateful affection of a sister', paraphrasing Robinson's description of the 'zeal of a brother' stamping 'gratitude upon [her] heart'.[177] Even more strikingly, though, Green amplifies Robinson's embedded critique of the dynamics of male power discussed earlier. As Fiona Price suggests, Green's 'exposure of the exigencies which force women into sexually compromising situations helps her to place blame on the male upper ranks' and to critique the 'sexual double standard'.[178] She portrays Thomas Robinson as 'a husband, whose conduct was of the blackest die [sic]', a man who not only tries to redeem his debts by 'bartering' his wife's body for money but actually informs her: '"You are my property"'.[179] By respinning Thomas Robinson's negligence as outright villainy (primarily through the addition of melodramatic dialogue) and detailing Robinson's opposition to the propositions of noblemen, Green adopts – and extends – Robinson's own strategies for proving herself an essentially virtuous woman. Green even suggests that Robinson falls for the Prince not only because he wins her heart through 'every seductive art and persuasion' but also because

'maternal love' urges her to secure 'safe provision for her child'.[180]
Green, like Robinson, implies that fallen women can be good mothers.
Though 'formed for virtue', the fair protagonist is 'assailed by manly
beauty, grace, and power', and Green advocates 'lenity' to Robinson
(whose story occupies only the first few chapters in the novel).[181]
She reserves her true criticism for the Prince, who symbolises the
moral failings of the ruling class. Like later biographers, she figures his
treatment of Robinson as the first step in a long descent into vice and
depravity. Robinson, on the other hand, emerges as she does from her
own *Memoirs*: the unfortunate, sensitive, flawed but principally good-
hearted heroine of sensibility. Green's summary could almost come
from Robinson's own pen:

> When alluring vice draws the strings of the heart that is formed to be
> the seat of virtue, when no resource remains to soothe the reproacher,
> conscience – happiness flies affrighted, and melancholy, resignation,
> and repentance ... support the forlorn transgressor.[182]

Though the anonymous *Royal Legend* (1808) is far less sympathetic to
Robinson than the novels of Egan and Green, it also shows evidence of
being influenced by the *Memoirs* in both its form and narrative strategy.
This novel parodies the *Memoirs* by rewriting the love affair of 'Perdita'
and the Prince as a pseudo-gothic romance. Robinson's use of asterisks
is replayed to maximum satirical effect. Just as in the *Memoirs*, here too
asterisks replace language at the critical moment of Perdita's sexual fall:
when she decides to join the Prince in his chamber. However, instead of
thirty asterisks, there are almost 100. The novel's exaggerated replication
of the asterisks points to Robinson's hypocrisy and pretended modesty
and suggests that the breaks in her prose and the fractured structure
of the *Memoirs* are nothing more than the bald tricks of a courtesan
attempting to shore up respectability when her life merits anything but.

The critique continues, inverting the roles so that a few pages later,
we see the Prince nervously approaching Perdita's apartment. At this
crucial moment, again, we have another fifty asterisks, interrupted by
an editorial note claiming that many pages were destroyed. Shortly
afterward, the Prince is lost in the 'delirium' of possessing his lovely
but 'wily mistress'.[183] Thus is Robinson portrayed as a selfish and

calculating seductress who ensnares the Prince to secure wealth, status and splendour. The novel contradicts her self-portrait as a tortured heroine of sensibility or a love-struck innocent. It provides a cynical reading of Robinson's *Memoirs* which is revealed to be as affected and mercenary as Robinson herself.

The novel continues this burlesque of the *Memoirs* through its appraisal of the Prince, who is shown to be as immoral as his innamorata. The third-person omniscient narrator informs us that from the Prince's very first encounter with Perdita, his imagination has already started to 'trample on the laws of honour and virtue, mark her for his prey, and fix on her, though a wife and a mother, as the object of sating his dawning unruly passions'.[184] Yet despite undermining Robinson's account of the Prince, the novel copies her *Memoirs* verbatim, recounting his 'attentive' ways, 'the graces of his person, the irresistible sweetness of his smile, the tender tones of his melodious yet manly voice'.[185] The novel interrogates this whitewashed portrait of the Prince, giving a window onto his selfish motives and vicious ways and gesturing towards the ways in which Robinson mistook or misrepresented him in her narrative. Though these critiques of Robinson and the Prince are nothing new, the form (replaying the asterisks used by Robinson) and the language (also copied from Robinson) are. The incorporation of Robinson's techniques – even if used against her – reveals how pervasively her *Memoirs* affected her posthumous portrayal, even by her detractors.

*The Royal Legend* bears even more profound traces of Robinson's influence. The Perdita story makes up just one of several episodes in the novel, which primarily follows the Prince's life. If Green's *Private History* tracks the Prince's deterioration into debauchery, *The Royal Legend* provides its counter-narrative, a hopeful story of redemption in which the Prince ultimately learns from his mistakes and develops into a worthy heir to the English throne. Samuelian argues:

> The act of remembering recorded within the text of *The Royal Legend* is cathartic and exculpatory. When his life story is retold via a recovered text, the Prince is already halfway to reformation ... *The Royal Legend* mixes its political satire with other modes, not puffery or pornography this time but gothic and sentimental romance.[186]

As a conversion narrative with a sentimental hero, *The Royal Legend* is a direct descendent of Robinson's own *Memoirs*. Late in *The Royal Legend*, as compassion and self-realisation are dawning in the protagonist, he muses wistfully that 'if he were a father, if he had been united to a woman of worth and virtue ... how happy he would have been! – how he would have cherished her and his dear babe!'[187] The cast of his reflections recalls Robinson's: 'how would my soul have idolized such a *husband*! Alas! how often ... have I formed the wish that being were *mine alone*!'[188] Just as the anonymous author of *The Royal Legend* exploits Robinson's typography for its comic potential, he also appropriates the character arc of the sentimental hero(ine) for its affective impact. If Robinson's transgressions can be mitigated by her suffering and repentance, so too can the Prince's. Even the unforgiving fictionalisations of Robinson, it would seem, are influenced by her *Memoirs*, whether it be in structure, content, style or tone.

## Affective responses to the *Memoirs*

Many non-fictional accounts of Robinson's life that emerged later in the nineteenth century also show the impact of the *Memoirs* in conveying an affecting picture of its author. Both the *Temple Bar's* biographical essay 'Our Old Actors: Perdita: A Romance' (1877) and Mary Craven's chapter on Robinson in her group biography *Famous Beauties of Two Reigns* (1906) seem convinced by Robinson's self-construction as the heroine of sensibility and the doomed victim of unrequited love, and they find it easy to explain away the inconsistencies of her narrative.[189] The *Temple Bar* compares her *Memoirs* to 'a novel of the last century', with an opening passage 'as weird and mysterious as anything Mrs. Radcliffe could have invented', and yet pronounces: 'There is little doubt, however, but that the record is, in the main, true – that she was far more sinned against than sinning'.[190] Echoing the King Lear reference that appeared in the early reviews, the *Temple Bar* writer puts a generous construction on Robinson's fanciful narration in part because he accepts Robinson's description of herself, despite its seeming contradictions. In accordance with the *Memoirs*, Thomas Robinson appears here as 'nothing but an adventurer'.[191] The Prince receives even harsher treatment:

The whole affair was probably a deliberate plan from beginning to end. These moonlight walks and nocturnal meetings had thrown a halo of poetry about the connection, and were the surest means of subduing her romantic and sentimental temperament … Whether the prince ever had any more attachment for her than for his other unconscious victims it would be difficult to assert, but he decidedly made her a scapegoat of his interests.[192]

This article invokes a version of Robinson drawn by the *Memoirs*: the naive 'romantic' who falls in love with the Prince and who 'cannot find in her heart one thought of resentment against him'.[193] The *Temple Bar* reads beyond Robinson's muted comments on the Prince, finding her to be even more a victim than she herself allows.

Three decades later, Mary Craven likewise credits Robinson's story of 'star-crossed lovers': 'There is no doubt as to the reality of her affection for the prince; she was absolutely disinterested'.[194] Craven easily imagines that the 'always impulsively good-natured'[195] Robinson could have cherished a lifelong 'obsession' for the Prince, never having 'realised what a contemptible object he became' and 'obstinately refus[ing] to displace from her imagination the Florizel of that moonlight evening'.[196] According to modern critic Kristin Samuelian, Robinson's *Memoirs* takes a view on her royal affair and on the Prince's treatment of her which, by 1800, 'she must have known was implausibly naïve', and which would be difficult, after 1801, to read 'without irony'.[197] Still, Craven reads it 'without irony', generously favouring Robinson's version of events. Craven also writes off Robinson's lengthy descriptions of her figure, fine attire and attendance at social events as 'artistic caprices of dress' and 'harmless vanity'.[198]

Edward Robins's chapter on Robinson in his collective biography *Twelve Great Actresses* (1900) also retraces the lines of the lovelorn victim of sensibility. From the start of the chapter, Robinson appears much as she does in her own narrative, as a 'melancholy' and 'dreamy' girl with 'large haunting eyes, and attractive features of a thoughtful almost sad expression'.[199] Borrowing the *Memoirs*'s tone of overdetermination and despondency, Robins shows Robinson 'slowly but inevitably … hurrying towards disaster', and 'behav[ing] like a heroine' though 'destined' for 'real troubles'.[200] Like Craven and the *Temple Bar* contributor, though, Robins goes much further than Robinson in his indictment of the supporting cast in her life. To Robins, it seems obvious that the young actress never stood a chance of fair treatment at the hands of the 'empty, selfish George IV', who 'gambled, drank, spent money as if it had been dirt' and exhibited 'contempt for womanly purity'.[201] Though Robins 'has no desire to condone the fault of Mary Robinson', he calls the Prince to account and stresses the other factors that conspired against her:

> We must not forget that she suffered, from the first, from bad surroundings. At the outset she had a selfish father and a foolish, weak mother; then, in the prime of her rare beauty, when noblemen paid her devoted court, she had no better protector than a husband who was only fit to live in debtor's prisons or sponging-houses. And think of the laxity of the 'high' society wherein she moved.[202]

Robins elucidates the ways in which Robinson was 'doomed', and they are nothing to do with destiny. They comprise disadvantages that might face any young woman of the late eighteenth century with no fortune, negligent (or naïve) parents, an unscrupulous husband and few opportunities for respectable work. He ends this section with a direct address to the reader: 'Remember all that, you who would cast an indignant stone at Mrs. Robinson.'[203] Though Robins duplicates the imagery, tone and characterisation of the *Memoirs*, his emotive portrayal of Robinson is complemented by a practical analysis of her social and economic circumstances. He joins other nineteenth-century writers like Craven and the *Temple Bar* essayist, whose sympathy for Robinson leads them to read into and beyond her own account of her life, redirecting blame, criticism and anger at those who deserve it more than she does.

Robinson also frequently appears as a pathetic figure whose misfortune and suffering are sufficient expiation for her transgressions. Robinson is repeatedly referred to with a patronising affection; she is called, for example, 'poor child!',[204] 'poor Perdita',[205] 'poor woman'[206] or even 'poor trembling thing'.[207] According to Craven, '"Perdita" had much to excuse her faults. She was neurotic, highly strung, and, possessing the fatal artistic temperament, she was always more or less the sport of Fate'.[208] In a description that could apply to any number of writers, past and present, Craven links Robinson with a type recognisable even to us today: the tortured Romantic artist. The *Temple Bar* likewise cites Robinson as a one-time star – 'the rage' and '*the* celebrity' – who fell out of fashion and fortune.[209] Her 'youth, beauty, her sad story, and above all her notoriety, undoubtedly greatly contributed to her success', lending her a 'melancholy celebrity'.[210] Robinson's 'star-crossed' fame prompts the *Temple Bar* to make exclamations of pity for one whose 'years of suffering' deserve, ultimately, not judgement but sympathy.

Yet pity for Robinson often coexists, oddly, with a sense of exhilaration and wonder about her life. Though many texts express sympathy for Robinson in tones that suggest both moral and temporal distance, they also seem to enjoy reliving her exciting stage career, romantic affairs and literary success. In her multibiography *Memoirs of Celebrated Female Characters* (1804), Pilkington justifies including a lengthy *Memoirs* extract detailing the royal courtship expressly 'for the entertainment of my readers', and she peppers the passage that follows with exclamation points to emphasise the thrills and the disappointments of the affair.[211] She is careful, however, to avoid seeming too excited or too sympathetic: 'Whilst we commiserate the situation of this too fascinating young female, we must not forget that it was occasioned by her deviation from the path of rectitude into the road of vice'.[212] Craven, too, plays up the 'fairy-tale' quality of Robinson's life.[213] Craven's language is sensational as she explains how the 'irresistible' Robinson 'became the fashion', was 'intoxicated with her success' and manifested '*joie de vivre*', speculating that Robinson was 'no doubt quite happy' during her liaison with the Prince.[214] And yet Craven, like Pilkington, does not want to seem too taken with Robinson. Craven offers condolences for her 'pitiful' fate and extensive 'suffering': 'As for her faults, she has passed to a higher judgement than ours. "Say, ye severest / What would you have done?"'[215] Expressions of pity may point to genuine feeling for Robinson's 'pathetic' self-portrait but may also function as a defensive technique to avoid seeming too absorbed, intrigued or thrilled. Again, this double-edged response recalls Robinson's own self-presentation, which utilised a range of linguistic and formal tactics to come off, simultaneously, as sympathetic, seductive and mysterious.

Furthermore, many of the nineteenth-century redactions of Robinson's story present Robinson's two selves, the unfortunate victim of sensibility and the accomplished woman of stage and society, as reconcilable. Dutton Cook titles his ten-page mini-biography of Robinson, which appears in two parts in the May and June issues of *Once a Week* in 1865, 'Poor Perdita', immediately calling to mind her status as figure of pathos and misfortune.[216] Nonetheless, in a paraphrase of the *Memoirs*, he narrates her acting debut in pacey, upbeat prose:

> Mr. Garrick sits in the orchestra to witness the performance of the new actress. She is so nervous she can hardly stand .... Presently she fronts the footlights: a very beautiful young woman in pale pink satin trimmed with lace and spangled with silver, with white feathers in her hair .... The curtain falls amidst a clamour of approbation. The new *Juliet* is a thorough success. During the following month the lady essayed her second character: *Statira*.[217]

Cook's shift into present tense for part of this passage allows him to convey immediacy and excitement to his mid-Victorian readers. Robinson's pride in her 'monumental suit' and 'clamorous approbation' does not nullify 'the various emotions of hope and fear' which are 'impossible to describe'.[218] In Cook's retelling, the scene feels both gripping and true to life. Cook connects Robinson's success with her protean abilities:

> The actress had made great way in public favour .... She was very lovely, dressed beautifully, could be arch and sparkling, or tender and pathetic. The good-natured audience demanded no more – they gave her their hands and hearts without further question, thundering their applause.[219]

The actress seems, paradoxically, in complete harmony with the heroine of sensibility. The description of Robinson's 'public favour' as an actress could apply just as well to her *Memoirs*, a textured self-portrait in which the reader sees she is performing but feels, likewise, that behind the performance lies a sincere, feeling subject.

## Scepticism

Nonetheless, scepticism about Robinson's truthfulness runs along-side even this substantial affective investment in the *Memoirs*. Dutton Cook finds the *Memoirs* 'palpably decorated and disposed with an eye to effect', 'apologetic and exculpatory in character' and 'conveniently fragmentary', and alludes to it wryly as 'not the most impartial of histories'.[220] In this two-part mini-biography, 'The prince is urgent; the lady deliberates; and … just at this time, too, the husband becomes more and more conveniently perfidious'.[221] An *Athenaeum* reviewer later concurs that 'the memoirs of Mary Robinson are an apology' that attempts to 'account decently for her frailty, since no violence was used and she went, trembling with love and loyalty'.[222] The word 'trembling' suggests not only Robinson's melodramatic performance of her vindication in the *Memoirs* but also the sexual undertones of her narrative. The *Athenaeum* columnist emphasises this double meaning by comparing Robinson to *Don Juan*'s Donna Julia, as a variation on that 'familiar phrase of Byron, protesting that she could not think of consenting she consented'.[223] Yet Cook's conclusion does not criticise the 'romanticist's tone' but celebrates the opportunities it affords:

> Now, when a lady tells her story, and purposely leaves blanks in it, it is clearly permissible to supply those blanks, if not with suppositions and suspicions, at any rate with such evidence at all bearing on the subject as can be secured from other quarters.[224]

As Cook's comments suggest, a memoir that is 'conveniently fragmentary', 'adroitly shaped' and full of 'blanks' leaves interesting work for future readers or writers.[225] The lexicon here is more legal than literary, as the reader (or later writer) is figured as a judge who cross-checks the narrative with extant facts but also relies on his imagination and intuition as well.

A similar quasi-judicial engagement with Robinson's *Memoirs* appears in Robert Huish's *Memoirs of George the Fourth* (1830), which was published amidst the flurry of royal biographies prompted by the death of George IV in 1830. Huish frames the Prince's whole affair with Robinson as the first event in a long series that damaged the future king's public image, stamping him 'with the character of the adulterer' and 'creating suspicions' and 'dissatisfaction which were never afterwards entirely obliterated'.[226] Appropriating the language of the courtroom, much like Cook, Huish finds it 'a case of the most studied, the most deliberate seduction' and he cannot 'acquit his Royal Highness' of 'unfeeling conduct'.[227] The 'advocates' of the King, he says, 'contended that the connexion was improper … [and] criminal … But to such defense it was replied that the Prince had *sought*, flattered, caressed, and won the heart of Mrs. Robinson'.[228] Word choices like 'case', 'advocates', 'criminal', 'defense' and 'acquit' contribute to the impression of a trial . The *Memoirs* requires an active reader who will engage in judgement, imagination and feeling. Life writing provides documentary evidence in an ongoing tribunal by which we judge the events of the past and in turn write our own verdicts.

However, Robinson's narrative 'testimony' is authenticated not by its contents but by its voice. For Huish, Robinson's writing itself 'bears on the face of it unquestionable marks of sincerity and genuineness' as its 'language and sentiments are such as a person of a sensible and well cultivated mind, but of strong feelings, would in all probably [sic] use'.[229] The perplexing gaps and glitches in the narrative are counterbalanced by the 'sincerity' and 'veracity' of the voice that articulates them. The language itself could not have been written by one who did not experience the 'strong feelings' depicted. The credibility of the *Memoirs* hangs on Robinson's literary skill in textualising her authenticity. Treadwell has suggested that in this period, 'literary style defines at once the character of the text and of the author', replacing the 'Johnsonian criterion of usefulness' with 'self-expression' as the defining feature of Romantic autobiography.[230] Here, Huish's emotional connection with the narrating persona trumps all other considerations, validating the *Memoirs* in spite of the misgivings about its probity.

Still, Huish does acknowledge the gaps and irregularities in the *Memoirs*. Though he professes to 'feel no hesitation in using her own materials' in his biography of George IV, his laboured justification for doing so indicates otherwise.[231] He notes that 'inconsistencies' and 'anachronisms' have thrown 'discredit' on Robinson's memoir.[232] He cannot, for example, accept Robinson's claim that during their evening strolls together, the Prince used to burst into song. At a time when their meetings were held under the strictest dictates of secrecy, Huish finds it impossible to imagine the Prince risking exposure by singing publicly. Huish also suspects that Robinson withholds information. He notes a 'studied and mysterious concealment of the motive', referring to Robinson's claim that she did not understand why the Prince broke off their relationship.[233] This 'mysterious concealment' seems also to link to other lacunae in the text. Her tendency to skip over events and relay only part of her thoughts and actions lends her memoir an air of mystery. Huish even reflects that 'we see only the puppets, but not the secret machinery by which they are moved', hinting at undisclosed motivations and raising the idea of life writing itself as a performance. Like Cook's remarks on the 'blanks' in life writing, Huish's allusion to the 'mysterious' aspects of the *Memoirs* may mean, again, that its concealments and incongruities are a draw rather than a flaw. The air of mystery sparks interest and gives readers an opportunity to figure out, for themselves, the 'secret machinery' of the 'puppets' in the show.

This mystery seems also to have fuelled further fictionalisations of Robinson's life, which offer their writers unique scope for making sense of Robinson and interpreting her *Memoirs* afresh. In *Perdita: A Romance in Biography* (1908), Stanley Makower explains fiction as his choice of genre because it can 'preserve a larger truth than could be conveyed in a purely historical narrative'.[234] Makower aims to give an entertaining but, more importantly, an authentic portrayal of Robinson's life, one which will deliver new insight into this intriguing figure. To this end, the novel has an almost scholarly paratextual apparatus, with a bibliography, index and 'notes' section and comprehensive lists of her stage roles and her publications. The gaps and ambiguities that hover around Robinson's life make it an attractive one for revisiting. Makower begins and ends *Perdita* by ruminating on a portrait of Robinson and the questions it raises about her psychology and her circumstances. His comments, however, could also relate to his own enterprise:

It is a face with a story; and when the pleasures of idly wondering who she was, where she lived and what she did, yields [sic] to the pursuit of practical inquiry, we find the gates of research wide open to a domain of mingled reality and romance in which enchantment and disenchantment tread upon each other's heels.[235]

Makower's journey as fictobiographer comprises conjecture, investigation, interpretation, emotion and a bit of magic. His well-researched novel will tell Robinson's 'story' and, like the painting, perhaps, evoke 'wonder, admiration, curiosity'.[236] Makower considers these visual and verbal texts important in their 'power to fix for ever the character and the incarnate existence of a personality buried ... deep in the debris of what is called history'.[237] Makower lists the *Memoirs* in his bibliography but does not discuss it elsewhere. Still, he borrows heavily from Robinson's characterisation and chronology (though he does alter details and add dialogue), providing what the *Athenaeum* reviewer calls an 'analysis of her character'.[238] The *Athenaeum* praises the novel generally but laments that in Makower's 'analysis', he 'relied rather too much upon the so-called "Memoirs" of the somewhat mythical Hibernian' and 'idealized his heroine'.[239] Robinson's *Memoirs* are connected with a 'mythical' afterlife – incredible, perhaps, but exciting and emotive – that Makower has endorsed. His fictional adaptation of Robinson's life reminds us that the ambiguities and so-called imperfections in life writing can make up part of its appeal for later historians, biographers, novelists and, of course, readers.

A similar interest in analysing Robinson's psychology and dramatising her life also emerges in Elizabeth Barrington's *The Exquisite Perdita*, a story which was serialised, with illustrations, in *Nash's and Pall Mall Magazine* in 1925–26 and reissued in book form in London in 1926.[240] Barrington's popularity as a historical novelist rests, in the words of the *English Review*, on her 'power of visualizing the past combined with a decided talent for dialogue and command of literary expression'.[241] Her compelling recapitulation of Robinson's life uses free indirect discourse to illuminate the thinking of various characters. She also inserts period detail and fleshes out Robinson's contemporaries (some of whom are not mentioned in the *Memoirs*) and their social mores. With the aid of Dean Cornwell's sensuous illustrations, Barrington brings Robinson to life as a sighing young beauty whose 'large eyes so full of pleading' and 'quick, agitated sensibility' make it impossible for Sheridan to look at her 'without imagining her quivering in his arms, all melting smiles and tears and tender shame'.[242] Barrington makes clear that the appeal of 'Perdita' is at once affective and erotic: the sensitive melancholic and the fascinating actress are inextricably linked.

Barrington's narrative also demonstrates a masterful engagement with Robinson's *Memoirs*. Barrington opens with a discerning analysis of her source text:

> She told a small part of her own story to the world, quitting the subject when it became delicate, and it would need telling had she given the whole, for how is it possible that a woman should autobiographise? … The poor Perdita cannot but court sympathy and support in every glance of her eyes, every curve of her body, her fluttering hands and drooped lashes … . She tells what she will of her own story so fluently that you shall not have leisure to note the hiatus here, the contradiction there … . No, her story is a confidence, not an affidavit. And even were it one, more is needed. … . You will not surprise her off stage in her own brief story. It will be much if I can so catch her for a moment in mine.[243]

Barrington compares the *Memoirs* to a seductive performance in which Robinson 'stage[s]' her femininity, sensibility, and charms through her 'fluent' storytelling. The reader may be so enthralled that she does not notice the 'hiatus[es]' and 'contradiction[s]'. Barrington's *Exquisite Perdita* will, necessarily, supplement Robinson's memoir, illuminating the 'complex' character that remains hidden behind the 'studied simplicity'.[244]

To this end, Barrington both borrows and departs from Robinson. In emotionally intense moments, Barrington recycles Robinson's trope of self-professed silence. When Mary Robinson discovers her husband's infidelity with Miss Wilmot, Barrington writes: 'To describe his mortification would be impossible'.[245] Similarly, as Robinson's stage debut approaches, 'her terrors were beyond all words'.[246] *The Exquisite Perdita* draws praise from the *English Review* for its 'masterly study of sentimentality', a 'study', perhaps, of Robinson's writing.[247]

At the same time, the narrator periodically steps outside the story to contrast her own narrative with Robinson's. Amidst an early scene where Robinson angrily refuses to follow the commands of her faithless husband, this canny narrator pauses to address the reader:

> You could never suppose this was the drooping sylph of her memoirs, she did it so defiant, and with an expression quite unbecoming the lady all tears and martyrdoms she there depicts for us in such moving terms.[248]

Barrington's narratorial aside highlights the discrepancy between her novel and the story relayed in the *Memoirs*. The scene is not so much an embellishment, though, as an insight into the unseen Robinson. Perhaps this is what Makower means in observing that fiction can carry 'a larger truth than … a purely historical narrative'.[249] Barrington, too, reminds the reader that *The Exquisite Perdita* is both an adaptation and a critique of its source text.

## A literary reputation?

The biographical and fictional material on Robinson discussed above suggests that her fame lasted well into the twentieth century.[250] Robinson does not seem to have 'disappeared from public view' after 1800, nor does it seem that her reputation limited her popularity after her death.[251] Rather, it appears that her multi-faceted reputation lent her a 'staying power' typical of eighteenth-century actresses, one that 'depended more on a brand of personal magnetism than simple beauty'.[252] This reputation, as we have seen, owes much to her *Memoirs*. As Gill Perry has discussed, thespian life writing was crucial in 'produc[ing] a market of reputations, fuelling a public obsession with performers and their lives that can be seen as marking the beginning of a modern celebrity culture'.[253] It seems that Robinson's *Memoirs* contributed heavily to shaping and sustaining her celebrity afterlife.

Yet it is clear that Robinson's nineteenth-century reputation was not exclusively literary. Robinson was sometimes categorised as an actress or a beauty rather than as a writer.[254] Indeed, Robinson's fame as an actress, a royal mistress and a publicly 'fallen' woman preceded any renown as an author. Many commentators, during her lifetime and afterward, ascribed the popularity and sales of her writing to 'curiosity' or 'notoriety' rather than any intrinsic merit.[255] Her writing, especially her poetry, was often read as an unmediated outpouring of emotion and a 'consolation' for her grief.[256] Most accounts of her life, even the fictional ones, mention, but do not focus on, her literary output.[257] For many, like Robins, despite Robinson's 'literary aspirations', it is 'through the story of Perdita, and not through the stories of her imagination, that Mary Robinson would become an interesting figure to posterity'.[258] Joseph Knight's 1897 *Oxford Dictionary of National Biography* entry, in spite of its comprehensive list of her prose, poetry and drama, distils the dismissive view of her oeuvre: 'though her verse has a certain measure of facility, it appears, to modern tastes, jejune, affected, and inept'.[259]

Nonetheless, Knight's judgement seems not to have been the only or the final appraisal of her literary status. Several nineteenth-century women writers, in particular, manifest a personal affinity and a literary respect for Robinson. Romantic poet Charlotte Dacre includes the lyric, 'To the Shade of Mary Robinson' in her collection *Hours of Solitude* (1805), published four years after Robinson's *Memoirs*.[260] As Ashley Cross has argued, 'the poem articulates Dacre's identification with Robinson as a woman writer' and 'attempts to create a poetic relationship that transcends the boundaries of mortality'.[261] Addressing Robinson's ghost, the speaker expresses regret for Robinson's death and for her treatment by the 'cruel world'.[262] In her elegiac tone, she suggests a sensibility akin to Robinson's, affirming that she has 'an heart form'd to love thee – /An heart which responsive had beat to thine own'.[263] It is difficult not to read this as a direct reply to Robinson's downcast comments on female friendship in the *Memoirs*:

> I have never felt the affection for my own sex which perhaps some women feel … I have almost uniformly found my own sex my most inveterate enemies; I have experienced little kindness from them; though my bosom has often ached with the pang inflicted by their envy, slander and malevolence.[264]

According to Dacre, even after death, Robinson manages to 'triumph victorious, / Thy fame sounding loud in thine *enemies'* ears!'[265] This 'fame' seems related to her 'virtues' and is therefore likely a 'literary' fame that lives on and is re-affirmed here in verse. Dacre's empathy is matched by her respect for Robinson, who inspires 'my wonder, my pride, and my tears'.[266]

A more perplexing authorial identification with Robinson can be found in the *Memoir of Maria Edgeworth* (1867), which includes a passing reference to her. Frances Edgeworth gives the following anecdote: 'Shortly after the publication of *Belinda* in 1801 Maria Edgeworth ... decided to surprise her aunt and test her response to the novel, by pretending it was a new work by some other writer, possibly a posthumous work by Mary Robinson'.[267] This comparison does not immediately indicate Edgeworth's opinion of her contemporary. Robinson may be chosen as the 'test' author because of the quality of her novels or the lack thereof. She may also be chosen for other reasons: her knowledge of London social circles, her scandalous status, the tendency towards social critique evinced in her late fiction, her topicality (1801 was the year of her *Memoirs*). At the very least, though, it is clear that Robinson is regarded as not simply a social but also a literary celebrity.

Authorial kinship was also felt for Robinson by Victorian writer Violet Fane, the pseudonym of Mary, Baroness Currie (1843–1905). Her personal library contained an original subscription copy of Mary Robinson's *Poems* (1791), which she had rebound and inscribed with her pen name and personal insignia. Three other books are known to feature this same personalised design of the green binding and the gold violet: Lady Currie's own *Collected Verses* (1880) and the two volumes of her collected *Poems* (1892).[268] However, the bound copy of Robinson's *Poems* is the only one that bears the inscription of 'Violet Fane' on the front and back covers. Lady Currie's personalised copy of Robinson's *Poems* suggests that she felt a strong connection with her eighteenth-century predecessor, and the similarities in their private lives are striking. Both writers were known for their loveless marriages, affairs and scandalous reputations. Moreover, Lady Currie, like Robinson before her, was nicknamed 'Sappho' by her contemporaries, and the thinly veiled satire of her marriage, *Edwin and Angelina* (1878), may be a gesture towards Robinson's 1796 novel *Angelina*. This copy of

Robinson's *Poems* indicates both literary admiration and sympathetic identification.

A further and more public mark of respect and interest for Robinson as a literary figure can be found in the version of Robinson's autobiography published in 1930 and titled *Memoirs of the Late Mrs Robinson Written By Herself, in Four Volumes with a New Introduction.* The reversion to the original 1801 title, which omits reference to 'Perdita', suggests a correction to Molloy's 1894 edition, and the choice of the four-volume edition as the source text works to legitimate and promote her writing. The new introduction cites several biographical sources on Robinson, including *Public Characters* (1800), Pilkington's *Female Characters* (1804) and A. M. Broadley's *Chats on Autographs* (1910). The editor seems particularly intrigued by Broadley's account of the 'holograph copy' of the *Memoirs*, 'written nearly entirely on the covering sheets of old letters upon which one reads the signatures of such important and fashionable personages', and finds it 'curious too to think of her writing the story of her troubles on the very scraps of paper concerned in them'.[269] He wonders about the unique manuscript form and the apparent self-consciousness of her writing process.

In addition, unlike the prefatory material in earlier versions of the *Memoirs*, this introduction focuses more on Robinson's verse than on her life. An extended discussion of Robinson's poetic exchanges with Samuel Taylor Coleridge details not only his admiration but also his imitation of her. Poems written by Coleridge and Robinson are extracted and discussed. Despite some fanciful commentary on 'the Ancient Mariner and Perdita' as the 'dreamer' and the 'charmer' and unsubstantiated speculation that 'Coleridge had fallen in love with Perdita', this introduction repositions Robinson as a Romantic poet.[270] Strictly speaking, an edition published in 1930 does not qualify as a 'long'-nineteenth-century text, yet it has been included here because it signals that Robinson's legacy remained literary, at least in part, even before her resuscitation in the late twentieth century.

Robinson's reputation differs from the literary renown of Burney or Wollstonecraft, but she was better known – and differently remembered – than other royal mistresses.[271] She retained her literary celebrity alongside her reputation as a beauty, actress and royal mistress. I am not ascribing to Mary Robinson the pure 'Petrarchan' fame discussed by Daniel Robinson or the 'immortality effect' described Andrew Bennett.[272] Nor am I contesting the commonplace that Robinson's literary recognition dramatically shifted in the late twentieth century.[273] I am emphasising only that Robinson seems to have enjoyed a composite posthumous reputation which 'incorporate[s] fame' as well as 'a cult of personality … at least partly dependant on the relationship with an audience'.[274] Leo Braudy explains:

> Fame is metamorphic. It arises from the interplay between the common and the unique in human nature, the past and what we make of it. … But to be talked about is to be part of a story, and to be part of a story is to be at the mercy of storytellers – the media and their audience. The famous person is thus not so much a person as a story about a person.[275]

Since the publication of her *Memoirs* in 1801, Mary Robinson has become the most significant of these 'storytellers', exerting a lasting power in shaping her posthumous reputation and even, perhaps, the ways in which a woman's 'story' could be told.

## Conclusion

Robinson's *Memoirs* enjoyed a robust afterlife in the long nineteenth century. Though her inconsistencies in content, tone and structure have been deemed flaws, we have seen how she uses rhetorical and structural silences strategically to balance opposing qualities. Linguistically and formally, Robinson reveals just enough of herself to affect and titillate and conceals just enough to remain both virtuous and coy. These contradictions appear irreconcilable, raising as many questions as they answer. Robinson's *Memoirs* therefore seems not so much to haunt as to invite the depictions of her life that appear in nineteenth-century biographies, essays, reviews, poetry and fiction. Since the early reviews, nineteenth-century commentators have noticed the irregularities in the *Memoirs* and have called it all manner of names: a fiction, a 'catch-penny', a 'stage' performance, a testimony, a lie, a confidence. They have disputed its veracity and wondered about its author. They have judged but also sympathised with her. They have remarked on and rewritten her narrative, over and over again. These later responses and redactions, sympathetic, sceptical and disparaging in turn, have been shown to carry reactions that mirror her own perplexing and paradoxical self-portrayal. Cheryl Wanko maintains that Robinson 'could only salvage [her character] so much', and Laura Engel that her 'attempts to rescue her damaged reputation were thwarted'.[276] These claims are true in the sense that Robinson could not erase her scandalous history or escape the public knowledge of her sexual transgression(s).

Nevertheless, the nineteenth-century texts considered in this chapter indicate some of the ways that Robinson's *Memoirs* influenced the texture of her afterlife. As a case study, Robinson's *Memoirs* and its afterlife suggest that a reputation is not something merely to be 'damaged' or 'salvaged' but something to be shaped. Women have long been appraised according to what Katharine Kittredge calls 'the good woman/bad woman dichotomy',[277] and yet one of Robinson's most troubling and appealing features is that she embodies such oppositions. She tells us what she is not telling us, and she visually highlights what she conceals. Behind the coquettish actress is the heroine of sensibility and behind the heroine of sensibility, the coquettish actress. We feel we know her intimately and yet, as Hester Davenport observes, it is difficult 'to pin down the image that Robinson was projecting of herself'.[278] This difficulty may suggest neither a confusion nor a deficiency but a literary innovation that manages to 'resist the dominant cultural constructions' and 'substitute alternatives'.[279] Robinson's *Memoirs* wields a nuanced strategy of self-representation that contributed to her nineteenth-century afterlife and to her enduring status as a literary celebrity. Moreover, it prevents what Katharine Kittredge terms 'the most insidious effects of a woman's being identified as a representative of the female antitype': the erasure of identity.[280] Robinson's *Memoirs* affirmed her identity and became the backbone of her posthumous legacy. Mary Hays, too, struggled with the implications of life writing for her public standing and experimented with different forms to find a suitable channel for expressing her personal and political beliefs. It is to her life and work that we now turn.

# Notes

1 Mary Robinson, *Memoirs of the Late Mrs. Robinson, Written by Herself*, ed. M. J. Levy (London: Peter Owen, 1994), p. 46.
2 Sharon Setzer, 'Introduction', in *A Letter to the Women of England and the Natural Daughter* (Toronto: Broadview, 2003), p. 10.
3 Judith Pascoe, 'Introduction', in *Mary Robinson: Selected Poems*, ed. Judith Pascoe (Toronto: Broadview, 2000), p. 47.
4 William D. Brewer, 'General Introduction', in *The Works of Mary Robinson*, ed. William D. Brewer, 8 vols (London: Pickering & Chatto, 2009), I, p. xv. For similar assertions, see Laura Engel, *Fashioning Celebrity: Eighteenth-Century Actresses and Strategies for Image Making* (Columbus, OH: Ohio State University Press, 2011), p. 13 and Sharon Setzer, 'Introduction [to Mary Robinson]', in *Women's Theatrical Memoirs, Part I*, ed. Sharon Setzer, 5 vols (London: Pickering & Chatto, 2007), I, p. 2.
5 See, for example: Anne K. Mellor, 'Mary Robinson and the Scripts of Female Sexuality', in *Representations of the Self from the Renaissance to Romanticism*, ed. Patrick Coleman, Jayne Lewis and Jill Kowalik (Cambridge: Cambridge University Press, 2000), p. 250; Sharon Setzer, 'The Gothic Structure of Mary Robinson's *Memoirs*', in *Romantic Autobiography in England*, ed. Eugene Stelzig (Farnham: Ashgate, 2009), p. 34; James Treadwell, *Autobiographical Writing and British Literature, 1783–1834* (Oxford: Oxford University Press, 2005), p. 41; p. 71; Setzer, 'Introduction', in *A Letter*, p. 10.
6 Robinson, *Memoirs*, p. 91. For more on this line of interpretation, see Setzer, 'The Gothic Structure', p. 34; p. 39; Lisa M. Wilson, 'From Actress to Authoress: Mary Robinson's Pseudonymous Celebrity', in *The Public's Open to Us All: Essays on Women and Performance in Eighteenth-Century England* (Newcastle: Cambridge Scholars Publishing, 2009), p. 159.
7 Robinson, *Memoirs*, p. 55; p. 85.
8 James Olney, *Metaphors of the Self: The Meaning of Autobiography* (Princeton, NJ: Princeton University Press, 1972), qtd in Mary Jean Corbett, *Representing Femininity: Middle-Class Subjectivity in Victorian and Edwardian Women's Autobiographies* (Oxford: Oxford University Press, 1992), p. 5. Philippe Lejeune's definition of autobiography is often cited as the benchmark: a 'retrospective prose narrative produced by a real person concerning his own existence, focusing on his individual life, in particular on the development of his personality'. See 'The Autobiographical Contract', in *French Literary Theory Today: A Reader*, ed. Tzvetan Todorov (Cambridge: Cambridge University Press, 1982), p. 193. Felicity Nussbaum, in contrast, questions the existence of an essential self and sees autobiography as 'repetitive serial representations of particular moments held together by the narrative "I"'. See *The Autobiographical Subject: Gender and Ideology in Eighteenth-Century England* (Baltimore, MD: Johns Hopkins University Press, 1989), p. 18. For more on Romantic-period definitions of and debates about 'self biography', see James Treadwell, *Autobiographical Writing and British Literature*, and Eugene Stelzig, 'Introduction', in *Romantic Autobiography in England*.
9 Eleanor Ty, 'Engendering a Female Subject: Mary Robinson's (Re)presentations of the Self', *English Studies in Canada*, 21:4 (1995), p. 412; p. 414.
10 Cheryl Wanko, *Roles of Authority: Thespian Biography and Celebrity in Eighteenth-Century Britain* (Lubbock, TX: Texas Tech University Press, 2003), p. 211.
11 Hester Davenport, 'Introduction', in *The Works of Mary Robinson*, VII, p. xx; p. xxiv. Davenport is not the first critic to regard the letter as a 'distancing strategy'. See, for

example, Judith Pascoe, *Romantic Theatricality: Gender, Poetry, and Spectatorship* (Ithaca, NY: Cornell University Press, 1997), p. 117.

12  Davenport, 'Introduction', p. xx; p. xxiv. See also Wilson, 'From Actress to Authoress', pp. 159–60.

13  Pascoe, *Romantic Theatricality*, p. 26; Daniel Robinson, *The Poetry of Mary Robinson: Form and Fame* (Basingstoke: Palgrave Macmillan, 2011), pp. 20–1.

14  Judith Pascoe, 'Mary Robinson and the Literary Marketplace', in *Romantic Women Writers: Voices and Countervoices*, ed. Paula R. Feldman and Theresa M. Kelley (Hanover: University Press of New England, 1995), pp. 261–2; Pascoe, *Romantic Theatricality*, p. 3.

15  Pascoe, *Romantic Theatricality*, p. 117.

16  Mellor, 'Mary Robinson and the Scripts of Female Sexuality', p. 252; p. 254.

17  *Ibid.*, pp. 250–2; p. 250.

18  Engel, *Fashioning Celebrity*, p. 81.

19  *Ibid.*, p. 61; p. 81.

20  *Ibid.*, p. 22; pp. 62–3.

21  *Ibid.*, p. 96; p. 95.

22  *Ibid.*, p. 123.

23  Robinson, *Memoirs*, p. 95; p. 97.

24  *Ibid.*, p. 67.

25  *Ibid.*, p. 67, my italics.

26  *Ibid.*, p. 84, my italics.

27  Setzer, 'General Introduction', in *Women's Theatrical Memoirs*, I, p. xv.

28  Davenport, 'Introduction', VII, p. xxiv.

29  On the similar expectations of Victorian female autobiographers, see Corbett, *Representing Femininity*, p. 94.

30  'Memoirs of Mrs. Mary Robinson', in *The Works of Mary Robinson*, VII, p. 257.

31  Robinson, *Memoirs*, p. 70, my italics.

32  Women's spiritual autobiographies, for example, often kept details of marriage and family lives private. See Corbett, *Representing Femininity*, p. 73. On Robinson's *Memoirs* and its links to spiritual autobiography, see Amy Culley, *British Women's Life Writing, 1760–1840: Friendship, Community, and Collaboration* (Basingstoke: Palgrave Macmillan, 2014), p. 104.

33  Robinson, *Memoirs*, p. 75, italics in original.

34  *Ibid.*, p. 43; p. 45; p. 47.

35  *Ibid.*, p. 47, my italics.

36  Setzer, 'The Gothic Structure', p. 30; Mellor, 'Mary Robinson and the Scripts of Female Sexuality', p. 250; Setzer, 'Introduction', in *A Letter*, pp. 10–11; Engel, *Fashioning Celebrity*, p. 81; Culley, *British Women's Life Writing*, pp. 106–7.

37  Ann Radcliffe, *A Sicilian Romance*, ed. Alison Milbank (Oxford: Oxford University Press, 2008), p. 116.

38  See, for example, Robinson's description of Elvira in *Vancenza*: 'agitation chained her tongue. She *looked* a thousand unutterable things' (*The Works of Mary Robinson*, II, p. 325), and of Julia in *The Widow*: 'My grief was beyond the power of utterance!' (*The Works of Mary Robinson*, II, p. 394).

39  Setzer, 'The Gothic Structure', p. 34; p. 35. See also Michael Gamer and Terry F. Robinson, 'Mary Robinson and the Dramatic Art of the Comeback', *Studies in Romanticism*, 48:2 (2009), pp. 241–2, and Culley, *British Women's Life Writing*, p. 106.

40  Culley, *British Women's Life Writing*, p. 106.

41  Robinson, *Memoirs*, p. 47.

42  *Ibid.*, p. 46.

43  *Ibid.*, p. 46; p. 47.

44  Elizabeth Campbell Denlinger, *Before Victoria: Extraordinary Women of the British Romantic Era* (New York, NY: Columbia University Press, 2005), p. 21.

45  Sharon Setzer, 'Introduction [to Mary Robinson]', in *Women's Theatrical Memoirs*, p. 2.

46  On the 'artificiality of authenticity', see Pascoe, *Romantic Theatricality*, p. 3. Engel likewise stresses the importance of the appearance of authenticity for female celebrity. See *Fashioning Celebrity*, p. 5.

47  Ty, 'Engendering a Female Subject', p. 408.

48  Treadwell, *Autobiographical Writing and British Literature*, p. 14. According to Treadwell, the term *autobiography* was coined in 1797 (p. ix).

49  *Ibid.*, p. 13.

50  Robinson, *Memoirs*, p. xv.

51  See Treadwell, *Autobiographical Writing and British Literature*, especially pp. 14–16.

52  On D'Israeli's evaluation of autobiography in contrast to Johnson's, see Treadwell, *Autobiographical Writing and British Literature*, p. 14.

53  Caroline Breashears differentiates between an 'appeal memoir' like Robinson's and other subgenres such as secret histories, scandal novels and whore biographies. 'The Female Appeal Memoir: Genre and Female Literary Tradition in Eighteenth-Century England', *Modern Philology*, 107:4 (2010), pp. 607–31. Though I see the utility of these distinctions, for ease of reference, I use the terms *appeal memoir* and *scandalous memoir* interchangeably.

54  See Diego Saglia, 'Commerce, Luxury, and Identity in Mary Robinson's "Memoirs"', *Studies in English Literature*, 49:3 (2009), p. 722; Setzer, 'Introduction [to Mary Robinson]', in *Women's Theatrical Memoirs*, p. 2; Engel, *Fashioning Celebrity*, p. 16.

55  Breashears, 'The Female Appeal Memoir', p. 618.

56  *Ibid.*, p. 613; p. 628.

57  Culley, *British Women's Life Writing*, p. 80.

58  *Ibid.*, p. 85. See also Gill Perry, 'Ambiguity and Desire: Metaphors of Sexuality in Late Eighteenth-Century Representations of the Actress', in *Notorious Muse: The Actress in British Art and Culture 1776–1812*, ed. Robyn Asleson (New Haven, CT: Yale University Press: 2003), p. 63.

59  Dianne Dugaw, 'General Introduction', in *Memoirs of Scandalous Women*, ed. Dianne Dugaw, 5 vols (London: Pickering & Chatto, 2011), I, p. xviii.

60  Elizabeth Gooch, *The Life of Mrs. Gooch*, in *Memoirs of Scandalous Women*, ed. Dianne Dugaw, 5 vols (London: Pickering & Chatto, 2011), IV, p. 31; p. 76.

61  *Ibid.*, p. 8; pp. 40–1; p. 99; p. 155; p. 483.

62  *Ibid.*, p. 36; p. 386.

63  Culley, *British Women's Life Writing*, p. 85.

64  Gooch, *The Life of Mrs. Gooch*, pp. 16–17.

65  *Ibid.*, p. 490.

66  Robinson, *Memoirs*, p. 91.

67  Linda H. Peterson, 'Becoming an Author: Mary Robinson's *Memoirs* and the Origins of the Woman Artist's Autobiography', in *Re-Visioning Romanticism: British Women Writers, 1776–1837*, ed. Carol Shiner Wilson and Joel Haefner (Philadelphia, PA: University of Pennsylvania Press, 1994), p. 48.

68  On the links between thespian biography and 'lucre', see Wanko, *Roles of Authority*, p. 12.

69  Breashears, 'The Appeal Memoir', p. 613; p. 617.

70  Lynda M. Thompson, The 'Scandalous Memoirists': Constantia Phillips, Laetitia Pilkington and the Shame of 'Publick Fame' (Manchester: Manchester University Press, 2000), p. x.

71  Robinson, Memoirs, p. 91.

72  Ibid., p. 91.

73  Dugaw, 'General Introduction', pp. xvii–xviii.

74  Laura L. Runge, 'Mary Robinson's Memoirs and the Anti-Adultery Campaign', Modern Philology, 101:4 (2004), pp. 574–5; p. 580; p. 581.

75  Ibid., p. 580.

76  Robinson, Memoirs, p. 58.

77  Ibid., p. 96.

78  Ibid., p. 58.

79  Ibid., p. 63; p. 97.

80  Ibid., p. 96, italics in original.

81  Runge, 'Mary Robinson's Memoirs and the Anti-Adultery Campaign', p. 581.

82  Robinson, Memoirs, p. 97.

83  On similar 'bids for masculine power' in Charke's Apology, see Wanko, Roles of Authority, p. 83.

84  Engel, Fashioning Celebrity, p. 62.

85  On Charke, see Wanko, Roles of Authority, p. 85.

86  Robinson, Memoirs, p. 93.

87  See Perry, 'Ambiguity and Desire', pp. 57–80; p. 57. See also Robyn Asleson, 'Introduction', in Notorious Muse, p. 1; Sandra Richards, The Rise of the English Actress (Basingstoke: Palgrave Macmillan, 1993), p. 70; Perry, 'Ambiguity and Desire', p. 57; Gill Perry, with Joseph Roach and Shearer West, The First Actresses: Nell Gwyn to Sarah Siddons (Ann Arbor, MI: University of Michigan Press, 2011), p. 24.

88  Robinson, Memoirs, pp. 93–4, my italics.

89  Roland Thorne, 'Manners, Charles (1754–1787)', Oxford Dictionary of National Biography (Oxford: Oxford University Press, 2004), www.oxforddnb.com/view/article/17950

90  Robinson, Memoirs, p. 94.

91  Ibid., p. 93; p. 94, my italics. The sizeable sum offered by the Duke of Rutland may be mentioned here because it exceeds the annuity eventually settled on her by the Prince of Wales.

92  For more on the social critiques proffered by scandal memoirs, see Dugaw, 'General Introduction', p. xii; Breashears, 'The Female Appeal Memoir', p. 630; p. 625; Susan Goulding, 'Claiming the "Sacred Mantle": The Memoirs of Laetitia Pilkington', in Lewd and Notorious: Female Transgression in the Eighteenth Century, ed. Katharine Kittredge (Ann Arbor, MI: University of Michigan Press, 2003), p. 53; Thompson, The 'Scandalous Memoirists', p. 6.

93  Thompson, The 'Scandalous Memoirists', p. 9.

94  Ibid., p. 10; Perry et al., The First Actresses, p. 13. On earlier eighteenth-century interest in private, especially sexual, lives, see also Nussbaum, The Autobiographical Subject, pp. 186–7.

95  Perry et al., The First Actresses, p. 31.

96  Robinson, Memoirs, p. 109; p. 110.

97  Denlinger, Before Victoria, p. 4.

98  The phrase comes from Mellor ('Mary Robinson and the Scripts of Female Sexuality', p. 244), though other critics have also discussed Robinson's need to

rewrite her transgressive love affair. See, for example, Engel, *Fashioning Celebrity*, p. 7, and Setzer, 'Introduction [to Mary Robinson]', in *Women's Theatrical Memoirs*, p. 2.

99  On Robinson's deployment of her personal life in her Sapphic identity, see Robinson, *The Poetry of Mary Robinson*, p. 126.

100  Robinson, *Memoirs*, p. 115, my italics; p. 116, my italics.

101  *Ibid.*, p. 116; p. 118; p. 119.

102  Jonathan Lamb, *The Evolution of Sympathy in the Long Eighteenth Century* (London: Pickering & Chatto, 2009), p. 7.

103  *Ibid.*, p. 1.

104  Mellor, 'Mary Robinson and the Scripts of Female Sexuality', p. 250.

105  Gill Perry, *Spectacular Flirtations: Viewing the Actress in British Art and Theatre 1768– 1820* (New Haven, CT: Yale University Press, 2007), p. 11.

106  *Ibid.*, p. 14.

107  Dawn M. Vernooy-Epp, 'Introduction [to *Vancenza*]', in *The Works of Mary Robinson*, II, p. 228.

108  Robinson, *Memoirs*, pp. 27–8, my italics.

109  *Ibid.*, p. 27; p. 28.

110  Engel, *Fashioning Celebrity*, p. 85.

111  Wanko, *Roles of Authority*, p. 15. For a discussion of a similarly dual capacity in Robinson's pseudonyms, see Pascoe, 'Mary Robinson and the Literary Marketplace', p. 263.

112  Several critics have referred to the late eighteenth century as the start of modern celebrity culture. See Leo Braudy, *The Frenzy of Renown: Fame & Its History* (Oxford: Oxford University Press, 1986); Denlinger, *Before Victoria*, pp. 8–9; Perry et al., *The First Actresses*, p. 12; Tom Mole, 'Introduction', in *Romanticism and Celebrity Culture, 1750–1850*, ed. Tom Mole (Cambridge: Cambridge University Press, 2009), pp. 2–3.

113  Denlinger, *Before Victoria*, pp. 8–9. On trends in accessories and clothing inspired by Robinson, see Gamer and Robinson, 'Mary Robinson and the Dramatic Art of the Comeback', p. 223.

114  Asleson, 'Introduction', p. 4.

115  Perry, *Spectacular Flirtations*, p. 54. See also Robinson, *The Poetry of Mary Robinson*, p. 34.

116  Robinson, *The Poetry of Mary Robinson*, p. 126. See also Pascoe, *Romantic Theatricality*, p. 25, and Mellor, 'Mary Robinson and the Scripts of Female Sexuality', p. 250.

117  Engel, *Fashioning Celebrity*, p. 22; p. 62; p. 89.

118  Perry et al., *The First Actresses*, p. 74.

119  Kimberly Crouch, 'The Public Life of Actresses: Prostitutes or Ladies?' in *Gender in Eighteenth-Century England: Roles, Representations, and Responsibilities*, ed. Hannah Barker and Elaine Chalus (London: Longman, 1997), p. 62.

120  Mary Robinson, *Memoirs of the Late Mrs. Robinson, Written by Herself*, 4 vols (London: Richard Phillips, 1801), II, p. 52, italics in original.

121  Christopher Flint, *The Appearance of Print in Eighteenth-Century Fiction* (Cambridge: Cambridge University Press, 2011), pp. 112–13.

122  Christopher Flint, 'The Eighteenth-Century Novel and Print Culture', in *A Companion to the Eighteenth-Century English Novel and Culture*, ed. Paula R. Backscheider and Catherine Ingrassia (Oxford: Blackwell, 2005), p. 360.

123  Gooch, *The Life of Mrs. Gooch*, p. 77.

124 See Flint, *The Appearance of Print*, and Janine Barchas, *Graphic Design, Print Culture, and the Eighteenth-Century Novel* (Cambridge: Cambridge University Press, 2003).

125 My thanks go to James Raven for explaining this process to me.

126 Several eighteenth-century women, including Laetitia Pilkington, Teresia Constantia Phillips, Anne Bellamy, Elizabeth Gooch, Margaret Coghlan and Margaret Leeson, self-published appeal memoirs. See Breashears, 'The Appeal Memoir', p. 611n16.

127 Hester Davenport has speculated that another person, perhaps Samuel Jackson Pratt, co-edited the *Memoirs* with Maria Elizabeth and took an active role in editing, revising and preparing the manuscript for the printer ('Introduction', p. xxi). If so, this use of printer's ornaments could have been Pratt's innovation or something he carried forward from an earlier manuscript.

128 Gina Luria Walker, 'General Introduction', in *Memoirs of Women Writers, Part II*, ed. Gina Luria Walker, 3 vols (London: Pickering & Chatto, 2013), V, p. xii.

129 Pascoe, *Romantic Theatricality*, p. 70; Robinson, *The Poetry of Mary Robinson*, p. 201.

130 Robinson, *The Poetry of Mary Robinson*, p. 71.

131 For details of Robinson's interactions with Hookham and Carpenter, see Rita J. Kurtz and Jennifer L. Womer, 'The Novel as Political Marker: Women Writers and their Female Audiences in the Hookham and Carpenter Archives, 1791–1798', *Cardiff Corvey*, 13 (2004), p. 49.

132 Wanko, *Roles of Authority*, p. 19.

133 Flint, *The Appearance of Print*, p. 151.

134 Robinson, *Memoirs*, p. 106.

135 *Ibid.*, p. 106.

136 Perry, 'Ambiguity and Desire', p. 72. For more on breeches roles, see Crouch, 'The Public life of Actresses', p. 65, and Perry, *Spectacular Flirtations*, p. 9.

137 On Robinson's roles as Viola and Fidelia, see Robinson, *The Poetry of Mary Robinson*, p. 4. On her role as Nancy in *The Camp*, see Wendy C. Nielson, *Women Warriors in Romantic Drama* (Newark, NJ: University of Delaware Press, 2013), p. 119. See also Perry, *Spectacular Flirtations*, pp. 9–10.

138 Nielson, *Women Warriors*, p. 119.

139 Engel, *Fashioning Celebrity*, p. 23.

140 Treadwell, *Autobiographical Writing and British Literature*, p. 20.

141 *Ibid.*, pp. 112–13.

142 *Ibid.*, pp. 120–1.

143 Engel, *Fashioning Celebrity*, p. 95.

144 Robinson, *The Poetry of Mary Robinson*, p. 201.

145 *Ibid.*, pp. 5–6; p. 18; p. 71.

146 *Ibid.*, pp. 6–7.

147 *Ibid.*, pp. 5–6.

148 *Ibid.*, p. 6.

149 Engel, *Fashioning Celebrity*, p. 62.

150 The first of these was published by Swords, Mesier and Davis in New York. Although scholars like Byrne list this edition as appearing in 1802, the *American Literary Review* lists a two-volume duodecimo edition in 1801. See *American Literary Review*, 1 (1801), p. 503. The second American edition was published by Bradford in Philadelphia in 1802.

151 The French edition was published in Paris and titled *Mémoires de Mistriss Robinson* [sic].

152 According to Eleanor Ty, the *Memoirs* was published and reprinted at least ten times in the nineteenth century. In addition to the four early imprints, I have located six further editions, all of which comprise one volume only. It was republished in 1826

(and again in 1830) as Volume VII of Hunt and Clark's *Autobiography* series, which also included Charlotte Charke's *Narrative of the Life of Mrs. Charlotte Charke* (1755). J. Fitzgerald Molloy edited *Memoirs of Mary Robinson 'Perdita'*, which was published in London by Gibbings in 1894 and 1895 and was reprinted in Philadelphia by Lippincott. *The Queens of Society*, by Grace and Phillip Wharton, the pseudonyms of Katherine Thomson (1797–1862) and her son Henry Thomson, appeared in 1861 (with reprints in 1867, 1890 and 1900). It included many women writers and aristocratic ladies but did not include Robinson. However, *Beaux and Belles of England: Mrs. Mary Robinson Written by Herself with the Lives of the Duchesses of Gordon and Devonshire*, by Grace and Phillip Wharton, appeared in 1900 in London (Groiler Society), and it brought together Robinson's *Memoirs* and the 'Editor's Preface' by Molloy with two shorter subsequent chapters on the Duchesses of Gordon and Devonshire taken from *The Queens of Society*. *Beaux and Belles of England* saw at least two further reprints after the initial 1900 edition. Richard Cobden-Sanderson then issued *Memoirs of the Late Mrs. Robinson Written by Herself* (1930), which reverted to the title and text of the original 1801 edition published by Phillips.

153  Full contents of the first two volumes include: a picture of Robinson, a frontispiece, an 'Advertisement' written by Maria Elizabeth, the narrative of the Memoirs and finally the 'Continuation by a friend' (in the middle of which is inserted the 1783 letter), plus some of Robinson's poems, a description of how they were composed and a comprehensive, four-page list of all her works. Volumes three and four include 'The Sylphid' poems, *Jasper, A Fragment*, 'The Savage of Aveyron', 'The Progress of Liberty' and 'Tributary Lines addressed to Mrs. Robinson, by different friends, with her answers'.

154  *The Wild Wreath* (1804) featured Robinson's works alongside those of poets such as Samuel Taylor Coleridge, Robert Southey, Matthew Gregory Lewis, Erasmus Darwin and Joanna Baillie. *The Poetical Works of the Late Mrs. Robinson, Including Many Pieces Never Before Published* (1806), which saw further editions in 1824 and 1826, included only Robinson's poetry. Maria Elizabeth edited both.

155  There were a handful of nineteenth-century editions of her other works, including a sixth reprint of *Vancenza* (1792) in 1810, an edition of *Julie St. Lawrence* (1797) in 1812 in Germany and a London reprint of *Sappho and Phaon* (1796) in 1813.

156  Setzer, 'Introduction [to Mary Robinson]', in *Women's Theatrical Memoirs*, p. 3.

157  Moo-y, 'Art. II. *Memoirs of the Late Mrs. Robinson*', *Monthly Review*, 36 (December 1801), p. 345.

158  'Memoirs of the Late Mrs. Robinson', *Monthly Visitor* (March 1801), p. 231.

159  *Ibid.*, p. 228; 'Art. IX.-Memoirs of the Late Mrs. Robinson', *Critical Review*, 33 (November 1801), p. 295.

160  'Art. 62. Memoirs of the Late Mrs. Robinson', *British Critic*, 18 (August 1801), pp. 217–18.

161  Moo-y, 'Art. II. *Memoirs of the Late Mrs. Robinson*', *Monthly Review*, 36 (December 1801), p. 345.

162  'Art. IX.-Memoirs of the Late Mrs. Robinson', *Critical Review*, 33 (November 1801), p. 295.

163  *Ibid.*, p. 298.

164  *Ibid.*, p. 301.

165  Braudy, *The Frenzy of Renown*, p. 392.

166  'Art. 62. Memoirs of the Late Mrs. Robinson', *British Critic*, 18 (August 1801), p. 218.

167  Kristin Flieger Samuelian, *Royal Romances: Sex, Scandal, and Monarchy in Print, 1780– 1821* (Basingstoke: Palgrave Macmillan, 2010), p. 30.

168 *Ibid.*, p. 26.

169 On the political subtext of these depictions, see Samuelian, *Royal Romances*, especially pp. 52–3.

170 Samuelian, *Royal Romances*, p. 32.

171 Pierce Egan, *The Mistress of Royalty; or, the Loves of Florizel and Perdita, Portrayed in the Amatory Epistles, Between an Illustrious Personage, and a Distinguished Female; with an Interesting Sketch of Florizel and Perdita* (London: Egan, 1814), p. 32.

172 Robinson, *Memoirs*, p. 118.

173 Egan, *The Mistress of Royalty*, p. 126; p. 137.

174 Robinson, *Memoirs*, p. 144.

175 Egan, *The Mistress of Royalty*, pp. 142–4, italics in original.

176 Sarah Green, *The Private History of the Court of England*, ed. Fiona Price (London: Pickering & Chatto, 2011), p. 21; Robinson, *Memoirs*, p. 39.

177 Green, *The Private History*, p. 21; Robinson, *Memoirs*, p. 39.

178 Fiona Price, 'Introduction', in *The Private History of the Court of England*, p. xv; p. xvi.

179 Green, *The Private History*, p. 10; p. 30.

180 *Ibid.*, p. 12.

181 *Ibid.*, p. 10; p. 52.

182 *Ibid.*, pp. 63–4.

183 Anonymous, *The Royal Legend: A Tale* (London: Ballintine and Law, 1808), p. 75.

184 *Ibid.*, p. 42.

185 *Ibid.*, p. 71. For comparison, see Robinson, *Memoirs*, p. 111.

186 Samuelian, *Royal Romances*, pp. 88–9.

187 Anonymous, *The Royal Legend*, p. 186.

188 Robinson, *Memoirs*, p. 112, italics in original.

189 I follow Alison Booth in using the terms *group biography*, *multibiography* and *collective biography* interchangeably. See Alison Booth, *How to Make It as a Woman: Collective Biographical History from Victoria to the Present* (Chicago, IL and London: University of Chicago Press, 2004), p. 3.

190 'Our Old Actors. "Perdita." A Romance', *Temple Bar*, 51 (December 1877), p. 536.

191 *Ibid.*, p. 540.

192 *Ibid.*, p. 547.

193 *Ibid.*, p. 547.

194 Mary Craven, *Famous Beauties of Two Reigns* (London: Eveliegh Nash, 1906), pp. 221–2.

195 *Ibid.*, p. 227.

196 *Ibid.*, pp. 230–1.

197 Samuelian, *Royal Romances*, p. 62; p. 65.

198 Craven, *Famous Beauties*, p. 218.

199 Edward Robins, *Twelve Great Actresses* (New York, NY and London: G. P. Putnam's Sons, 1900), p. 236.

200 *Ibid.*, p. 245; p. 234; p. 239.

201 *Ibid.*, p. 250; p. 254.

202 *Ibid.*, p. 254.

203 *Ibid.*, p. 254.

204 Craven, *Famous Beauties*, p. 214; Robins, *Twelve Great Actresses*, p. 236.

205 'Our Old Actors. "Perdita." A Romance', *Temple Bar*, 51 (December 1877), p. 545; Dutton Cook, 'Poor Perdita: Part I', *Once a Week*, 12 (27 May 1865), p. 625; E.

Barrington, 'The Exquisite Perdita: Part I, Chapter I', *Nash's and Pall Mall Magazine*, 76:392 (December 1925), p. 22.

206 Dutton Cook, 'Poor Perdita: Part II', *Once a Week*, 12:310 (3 June 1865), p. 651.

207 E. Barrington, 'The Exquisite Perdita: The Story Begins', *Nash's and Pall Mall Magazine*, 76:393 (January 1926), p. 118.

208 Craven, *Famous Beauties*, p. 211.

209 'Our Old Actors', p. 542, italics in original.

210 *Ibid.*, p. 542; p. 546.

211 Mary Pilkington, *Memoirs of Celebrated Female Characters* (London: Albion Press, 1804), p. 293.

212 *Ibid.*, p. 294.

213 Craven, *Famous Beauties*, p. 218.

214 *Ibid.*, p. 218.

215 *Ibid.*, p. 230; p. 232.

216 This biographical essay appeared in two issues, as follows: Dutton Cook, 'Poor Perdita: Part I', *Once a Week*, 12 (27 May 1865), pp. 625–30; Dutton Cook, 'Poor Perdita: Part II', *Once a Week*, 12 (3 June 1865), pp. 648–53.

217 Cook, 'Poor Perdita: Part I', p. 628.

218 Robinson, *Memoirs*, p. 87; p. 88.

219 Cook, 'Poor Perdita: Part I', pp. 628–9.

220 Cook, 'Poor Perdita: Part II', p. 653; Cook, 'Poor Perdita: Part I', p. 627.

221 Cook, 'Poor Perdita: Part I', p. 630.

222 'Memoirs of Mary Robinson, "Perdita"', *Athenaeum*, 3587 (25 July 1896), p. 138.

223 *Ibid.*, p. 138. Lord Byron's lines are: 'A little still she strove, and much repented, / And whispering "I will ne'er consent" – consented'. See *Don Juan*, I, ll. 935–6.

224 Cook, 'Poor Perdita: Part II', p. 653.

225 *Ibid.*, p. 650; p. 653.

226 Robert Huish, *Memoirs of George the Fourth* (London: T. Kelly, 1830), p. 76.

227 *Ibid.*, p. 73.

228 *Ibid.*, pp. 76–7.

229 *Ibid.*, pp. 67–8.

230 *Ibid.*, p. 16.

231 Huish, *Memoirs of George the Fourth*, p. 57.

232 *Ibid.*, p. 106.

233 *Ibid.*, p. 70.

234 Stanley V. Makower, *Perdita: A Romance in Biography* (London: Hutchinson & Co., 1908), p. 343.

235 *Ibid.*, p. 3.

236 *Ibid.*, p. 340.

237 *Ibid.*, p. 340.

238 'Perdita, a Romance in Biography', *Athenaeum*, 4194 (14 March 1908), p. 316.

239 *Ibid.*, p. 316.

240 Barrington is one of several pseudonyms used by Elizabeth Louisa 'Lily' Moresby (1862–1931). See Alan Twigg, 'Beck, Lily Adams (1862–1931)', *ABC Bookworld*, BC Bookworld (2015), www.abcbookworld.com/view_author.php?id=7186

241 'The Exquisite Perdita', *The English Review* (January 1927), p. 124.

242 Barrington, 'The Exquisite Perdita', *Nash's and Pall Mall Magazine* (January 1926), p. 117; p. 120.

243 Barrington, 'The Exquisite Perdita', *Nash's and Pall Mall Magazine* (December 1925), pp. 22–3.

244 *Ibid.*, p. 23.

245 *Ibid.*, p. 92.

246 Barrington, 'The Exquisite Perdita' (January 1926), p. 119.

247 'The Exquisite Perdita', *The English Review* (January 1927), p. 124.

248 Barrington, 'The Exquisite Perdita' (January 1926), p. 92.

249 Makower, *Perdita*, p. 343.

250 Several other biographies and fictobiographies were published in the twentieth and twenty-first centuries which lie outside the scope of this study, including Marguerite Steen, *The Lost One* (1937); Robert Bass, *The Green Dragoon* (1957); Jean Plaidy, *Perdita's Prince* (1969); Paula Byrne, *Perdita* (2004); Hester Davenport, *The Prince's Mistress* (2004); Sarah Gristwood, *Perdita: Royal Mistress, Writer, Romantic*.

251 Engel, *Fashioning Celebrity*, p. 95; Mary Mark Ockerbloom, 'Mary Darby Robinson (1758–1800)', *A Celebration of Women Writers*, http://digital.library.upenn.edu/women/robinson/biography.html

252 Richards, *The Rise of the English Actress*, p. 71.

253 Perry *et al.*, *The First Actresses*, p. 27.

254 Robinson was not always considered in actress multibiographies, however. She did not appear in Mrs C. Baron Wilson's *Our Actresses*, 2 vols (London: Smith, Elder and Co, 1844), for example.

255 See Cook, 'Poor Perdita: Part I' and 'Poor Perdita: Part II', and Joseph Knight, 'Robinson, Mary (1758–1800)', *Oxford Dictionary of National Biography* (Oxford: Oxford University Press, 2004), www.oxforddnb.com/view/olddnb/23857

255 See, for example, Craven, *Famous Beauties*, p. 228; Pilkington, *Celebrated Female Characters*, p. 295.

257 For a rare example of a source that neglects her writing entirely, see H. E. Lloyd, *Memoirs of the Life and Reign of George IV* (London: Treuttel and Würtz, 1830).

258 Robins, *Twelve Great Actresses*, p. 258.

259 Knight, 'Robinson, Mary (1758–1800)'.

260 Novelist and poet Charlotte Dacre, who was born Charlotte King and who also wrote under the pseudonym Rosa Matilda, was the daughter of John King, born Jacob Rey.

261 Ashley Cross, *Mary Robinson and the Genesis of Romanticism: Literary Dialogues and Debts, 1784–1821* (Abingdon: Routledge, 2017), p. 201; p. 204.

262 Charlotte Dacre, 'To the Shade of Mary Robinson', *Hours of Solitude* (London: Hughes, 1805), l. 13.

263 *Ibid.*, ll. 9–10.

264 Robinson, *Memoirs*, p. 82.

265 Dacre, 'To the Shade of Mary Robinson', ll. 27–8.

266 *Ibid.*, l. 26.

267 Frances Edgeworth, *Memoir of Maria Edgeworth*, in *The Novels and Selected Works of Maria Edgeworth*, ed. Siobhan Kilfeather, 12 vols (London: Pickering & Chatto, 2003), II, p. vii.

268 I am grateful to Ceylan Kosker for sharing this information with me.

269 'Notices of the Authoress', *Memoirs of the Late Mrs Robinson Written By Herself, A New Edition* (London: Cobden-Sanderson, 1930), p. xv; p. xiv.

270 *Ibid.*, p. xi.

271  For comparison, see E. Beresford Chancellor, *The Lives of the Rakes, Volume VI: The Regency Rakes* (London: Philip Allan, 1925), pp. 44–5; Martin J. Levy, *The Mistresses of King George IV* (London: Peter Owen, 1996), p. vii.

272  Robinson, *The Poetry of Mary Robinson*, p. 3; Andrew Bennett, *Romantic Poets and the Culture of Posterity* (Cambridge: Cambridge University Press, 1999), p. 2.

273  On Robinson's late-twentieth-century 'recovery', see, for example, Setzer, 'Introduction [to Mary Robinson]', in *Women's Theatrical Memoirs*, p. 4.

274  Perry *et al.*, *The First Actresses*, p. 133.

275  Braudy, *The Frenzy of Renown*, pp. 591–2.

276  Wanko, *Roles of Authority*, p. 210; Engel, *Fashioning Celebrity*, p. 96.

277  Katharine Kittredge, 'Introduction', in *Lewd and Notorious: Female Transgression in the Eighteenth Century*, ed. Katharine Kittredge (Ann Arbor, MI: University of Michigan Press, 2003), p. 7.

278  Davenport, 'Introduction', p. xxiv.

279  Nussbaum, *The Autobiographical Subject*, p. xiv.

280  Kittredge, 'Introduction', p. 7.

# Chapter 4

# 'By a happy genius, I overcame all these troubles': Mary Hays and the struggle for self-representation

FROM THE START OF her career, Mary Hays (1759–1843) struggled with the problem of writing as a woman. In her early works, her pious, feminine authorial persona garnered praised even as its originality was questioned. The publication of her titillating autobiographical epistolary fiction, *Memoirs of Emma Courtney* (1796), rebranded her as a scandalous radical and positioned her as a target for the conservative backlash sweeping Britain in the wake of war with France. Her reputation suffered further after scathing parodies of Hays swapped sexual allure for ridicule, characterising her as a follower and a literary laughing stock. Too womanly, too scandalous or too ridiculous, Hays seemed unable to find a voice that was both authentic and acceptable. Scholars have suggested that, by 1800, Hays had lost control of her reputation, abandoned her former radicalism and transitioned into didactic literature in order to support herself. However, the writing and reception of Hays's work and in particular her ambitious *Female Biography* (1803), the first comprehensive English-language biographical dictionary written for and about women, suggest otherwise. With its innovative form and progressive content, *Female Biography* furthered the feminist, pedagogical and political principles she had long espoused and accommodated an oblique self-defence as well. By situating Hays within the context of Dissenting religious and literary subcultures as well as 1790s radicalism, and looking not only at *Emma Courtney* but also at other works like *Female Biography*, this chapter argues that Hays found an innovative mode of writing through which she defended her reputation; promoted long-held ideas about the representation, education and advancement of women; and shaped the genre of life writing for decades to come. The chapter ends by tracing Hays's largely unacknowledged legacy in the work of her niece, Matilda Mary Hays (1820–97). Though Hays did not achieve the fame of Burney, Wollstonecraft or Robinson, she nevertheless had a significant impact on life writing by and about women in the nineteenth century.

## Crafting a persona

Mary Hays constructed a pious and feminine early-career persona in her first publication, a pamphlet titled *Cursory Remarks on an Enquiry into the Expediency and Propriety of Public or Social Worship* (1791), which responded to Dissenting scholar Gilbert Wakefield's critique of communal worship. In this text, Hays drew on scripture as well as personal experience to defend the necessity of group worship, especially for women, who would not otherwise gain access to public intellectual life. Though she argues against Wakefield, she defers to his 'understanding and genius' before humbly introducing herself as:

> a woman, young, unlearned, unacquainted with any language but her own; possessing no other merit than a love of truth and virtue, an ardent desire of knowledge, and a heart susceptible to the affecting and elevated emotions afforded by a pure and rational devotion.[1]

Hays reinforced this deferential tone by signing her pamphlet as 'Eusebia', the Greek word for piety and a pseudonym that harked back to William Law's 1728 book-length challenge to Christians to live a life of active worship, *The Serious Call to a Devout and Holy Life*.[2] Hays thus aligned herself with the historical roots of Rational Dissent as well as with Law's 'good Eusebia', a learned widow who appeared in a chapter on the importance of improving women's education.[3] The pseudonym signalled Hays's learning while also shielding her identity from view. The ingenuous Eusebia earned praise from the reviewers for her insightful observations and religious devotion. However, the *Critical Review* remarked on her 'feminine weakness',[4] and the *Monthly Review* found 'nothing added to what is advanced by Dr. Disney except a reference to I Cor'.[5] As Eusebia, Hays found an opportunity to join public debate, but she was perceived by some to lack authority and originality.

The publication of *Cursory Remarks* also functioned for Hays as a symbolic rite of initiation into – and an announcement of membership within – the Dissenting community. Dissenting religious and literary networks offered women writers fellowship, mentorship and a built-in readership for their work,[6] and Hays's first text emerged from a decade-long tutelage under the guidance of Baptist minister Robert Robinson. By participating in the pamphlet debate sparked by Wakefield's opinions on public worship, Hays joined a print-sphere conversation amongst Dissenters that included the poet Anna Barbauld and the clergyman and theologian Joseph Priestley, with whom she became aligned. Like Barbauld, Eusebia emerged as a Dissenting figure opposed to Wakefield's version of Enlightenment rationality.[7] Eusebia's remarks induced the Unitarian Cambridge Fellow William Frend to write to Hays praising her work and initiating friendship. In a letter dated April 1792, Frend describes Hays's 'candour of sound reasoning' and delights that '[w]e seem to agree together nearly in our creed', though he also shows interest in discussing the points on which they disagreed.[8] By responding privately to a public text, Frend recognises Hays as part of the non-conformist intellectual community and establishes a personal relationship with her. Like the pamphlet war that debated the French Revolution, a smaller-scale conversation played out between Wakefield and his challengers. Frend's letter showcases the ramifications of Hays's *Cursory Remarks*, which both inaugurated (publicly) and solidified (privately) her membership in this group.

However, in spite of the accolades from the reviewers and the warm welcome from fellow Dissenters, Hays's deferential tone raised

Wakefield's suspicions. He found her profuse apologies for 'weakness' and 'incapacity for discussion' disingenuous,[9] and he judged 'Eusebia' as the common 'Artifice ... of assuming a female Name to escape the Lash of Criticism'.[10] Like the reviewers of Wollstonecraft's *Rights of Men*, Wakefield added mocking comments to his second edition, undermining the supposed female impersonator through sarcastic innuendo and ignoring her argument. Wakefield's reaction suggests his inexperience in addressing female critics in religious disputes.[11] The misunderstanding, for which he later apologised, also shows Hays's miscalculation and provided an early lesson to her about authorial credibility. This lesson was later echoed by Mary Wollstonecraft, who urged her friend to avoid apologising for defects and pleading for special indulgence[12] and warned Hays that positioning herself as an apprentice could backfire.[13] The reception of *Cursory Remarks* points to the benefits as well as the limitations of a reverential authorial persona like that of Eusebia.

## Personal and political affiliations

By signing her second work, *Letters and Essays, Moral and Miscellaneous* (1793), Hays strengthened her identity as a member of the Dissenting community. Like *Cursory Remarks*, this text also came out of her tutelage under New College mentors and her participation in the scribal culture in which writing circulated amongst friends for revision and discussion. The manuscript was read by friends such as George Dyer, William Frend and Mary Wollstonecraft, and the published text garnered praise from further afield. Hays's correspondence with her cousin Benjamin Seymour demonstrates that this favourable opinion extended to his Unitarian circle in Boston.[14] Unitarian minister and theologian Theophilus Lindsey also wrote to Hays in praise of her second work:

> Eusebia has led me to think highly of the author: but many things in the Letters and Essays have raised my ideas much higher ... I like both your metaphysics and divinity: but most of all, what appears in every page, the enlightened mind, turned to virtue and to God, and ardent to inspire others.[15]

Lindsey admires Hays's educational project, which aimed to make complex religious and political ideas comprehensible for women.[16] *Letters and Essays* offered a pioneering curriculum for women based on the New College programme.[17] Like contemporary Dissenting writers such as Elizabeth Coltman, Henrietta Neale and Anna Barbauld, Hays found a comfortable foothold within the emerging genre of educational literature designed for young female readers.[18]

Though these educational aims hardly marked Hays as a revolutionary, she indicated her radical affiliation through the signature and the paratexts. The decision to drop the Eusebia pseudonym distanced her authorial persona from the more explicitly pious voice of *Cursory Remarks*. Though many of her friends recognised Hays as Eusebia, the reviewers did not connect this second publication to her first. Moreover, the dedication of *Letters and Essays* to the Reverend John Disney, and her prefatorial endorsement of Wollstonecraft (referred to as the 'vindicator of female rights'), politicised her ostensibly didactic text. Hays further emphasised her allegiances by alluding and/or referring to Joseph Priestley, George Dyer and Robert Robinson. The recurring usage of charged words such as bondage, tyranny, chains and slavery also joined her to a politically radical subculture, and Eleanor Ty has connected Hays to Wollstonecraft and Charlotte Smith through their common use of revolutionary language.[19] Hays seems to adopt this register not only to highlight the political resonance of her ideas about female education but also to align herself with these contemporary writers. These strategies suggested to readers her theological and political radicalism[20] and help to explain how even a pedagogical text for women could become politicised in the 1790s.[21]

Consequently, the reception of *Letters and Essays* resembled that of other, more provocative works, with reviews dividing along predictable party lines. The conservative *English Review* mocks Hays as 'one of the boldest beneath the standard of Wollstonecraft', assumes that 'her political ideas are diametrically opposite to ours'[22] and dismisses her as 'a half-educated female'.[23] Several reviewers took umbrage at the section on Mrs Glasse's *Art of Cookery*, an example Hays had cited to illustrate how limited reading stifles women's mental, physical and social development. The *Critical* reviewer takes the

passage out of context, transforming it into an in-joke between men
at Hays's expense:

> [W]e freely acknowledge that the delicacies with which our good
> ladies have occasionally regaled us, have given us a great respect for
> the said Mrs. Glasse, and as, unfortunately, we are not possessed of
> the skill to make ourselves the various good things she treats of, we
> do hereby enter our protest against her treatise being left out of the
> library of any female, be she Unitarian, Trinitarian, Arian, or Supra
> lapsarian.[24]

This raillery forestalls engagement with Hays's argument. It reflects
a 1790s conservative backlash that perceived any impulse towards
feminine independence as an attack on the sacrosanct family unit and
its traditional roles and values.[25] Hays's affiliation, paratexts, allusions
and rhetoric worked to situate her second publication as a part of
contemporary radical political discourse. Only the radical *Analytical
Review*, wherein Dyer had discussed the review with Joseph Johnson
in advance, embraced the text on its own terms: as a practical guide
for women seeking a rational education.[26] Elsewhere, the reviewers
of *Letters and Essays* evinced a suspicious attitude to Hays's politics and
feminism and a scepticism about her intellect that was not present in
her reception as Eusebia.

Hays's strong alignment with Dissenting liberal thinkers was also
used to label her work as derivative, much as Burney's friendship with
Dr Johnson became a liability for her with the publication of *Cecilia*.
The *Critical* reviewer pegs Hays as 'a disciple of the Priestlian school
[sic]' and a 'professed admirer of the ingenious defender of the rights of
women'.[27] The *English Review* dismisses her as one of 'the pupils of Mrs.
Wollstonecraft', and the *Monthly* classes her as 'a devoted disciple' of
'the Priestleyan school [sic]' and 'a subaltern of Miss Wolstonecraft
[sic]'.[28] Given the political climate, it suited interested reviewers to
be able to side-line Hays as a plagiarising proselyte. Hays had secured
a position within Dissenting discourse, but the perception of her as
a follower (of Wollstonecraft, Godwin, Priestley, etc.) had already
become an issue in her reputation.

Still, Hays continued to forge relationships within the 'Priestleyan
school', and her interest in intellectual friendship was shaped by

norms within the Dissenting community. After her friend and fellow Dissenter William Frend recommended Godwin's *An Enquiry Concerning Political Justice* (1793), for example, Hays wrote to the philosopher in 1794 to request a copy.[29] Hays introduced herself as a 'disciple of truth' and asked '[his] assistance' in the project of a rational 'conversation' that would combat her 'worse than neglected, perverted, female education'.[30] In this respect, Hays participated in a longstanding tradition of Dissenting women who corresponded with prominent ministers, an intellectual mode of exchange visible in the published letters of Elizabeth Singer Rowe and Anne Dutton (and later Maria de Fleury) as well as the unpublished correspondence of Baptist Mary Steele and Caleb Evans, and of the Unitarian Mary Scott and Theophilus Lindsey.[31] Hays demonstrated the same enterprising spirit in her relationship with Wollstonecraft, whom she met not through Godwin, as some critics have suggested, but again through approaching her directly.[32] Hays wrote to Wollstonecraft in the summer of 1792 (before meeting Godwin) in praise of *A Vindication of the Rights of Woman*, and the two subsequently met. Hays had received her copy of *Rights of Woman* from George Dyer, another Dissenter who had taken her under his wing.[33] Though Hays took cues on reading from Dyer, Frend and other mentors, the contact with Wollstonecraft and Godwin resulted from her own initiative.

Through these relationships, Hays furthered her authorial career by contributing to the *Critical Review* in its short-lived liberal phase under the editorship of George Robinson and, by 1796, the *Monthly Magazine* and *Analytical Review* as well.[34] Like Wollstonecraft's early work for the *Analytical Review*, Hays's periodical contributions allowed her to develop her ideas, especially about women's position, and to hone her writing style. Her prominent role in the *Monthly Magazine* banter suggests that Hays increased her intellectual and professional standing during this time. Many of her epistle-essays responded to those of other contributors, such as 'J.T.', 'A.B.', and 'C.D.'. She may even have been enlisted specifically by the editor, Richard Phillips, to submit this work in order for the magazine to exhibit varied viewpoints and to promote discussion.[35] Hays's participation in this textual back and forth may indicate not only the 'collegiality of the men who wrote for the *Monthly* with Hays', as Walker suggests, but also her standing in the eyes of Phillips, the editor who would later publish her *Female Biography*.[36] This period in Hays's career saw the consolidation of her literary reputation within the overlapping London networks at St Paul's Church-Yard and New College Hackney. However, many of her *Monthly Magazine* pieces were signed as 'M.H.' or 'A Woman', decodable only to those who already knew her. As was the case in Mary Wollstonecraft's early career, the impact of these developments on Hays's wider public image was negligible, and Hays remained a minor figure in 1793.

## Changing reputations

Mary Hays's *Memoirs of Emma Courtney* (1796), a novel based on her own recent romantic disappointment with William Frend, transformed her into a figure of notoriety. The novel's eponymous heroine not only champions revolutionary principles but also offers herself to her lover outside of marriage – a step too far even for many Jacobin writers. The novel's provocative content was intensified by its form. Epistolary novels were seen as dangerously effective in fostering sympathetic identification between heroines and impressionable (female) readers. Moreover, fiction was common fare amongst radical writers like Godwin, Wollstonecraft, Thomas Holcroft and Matthew Lewis but *not* among Dissenters (especially not Dissenting women).[37] Although *Emma Courtney* shared many of the moral and political concerns of Hays's earlier writing, her foray into fiction set her apart from other Dissenting women writers, and her transgressive heroine scandalised readers across the political spectrum. Many readers assumed that the story had its basis in the author's life and took it as a confession of Hays's own transgressions.

Like Godwin's biography of Wollstonecraft, Hays wrote *Emma Courtney* for reasons at once personal, philosophical and political. Hays strove, first of all, to cope with her real-life rejection by William Frend, whom she had loved and (unsuccessfully) pursued. Since his laudatory letter to 'Eusebia' in 1792, they had corresponded and met regularly, and their friendship had deepened. Marilyn Brooks speculates that '[t] his intertwining of ambitions; political, philosophical, sexual and so on, helps explain the extent of her response to Frend's final rejection of her'.[38] Hays's letters to Godwin during this period suggest that this rejection happened immediately after Hays disclosed her feelings for him.[39] Hays was heartbroken, and in February of 1796 she told Godwin of her wish 'to employ [her]self in a work of fiction, to engage [her] mind, to sluice off its impressions'.[40] This idea of turning to composition as a form of therapy fit with Dissenting conceptions of life writing as a means to self-understanding and moral truth.[41]

The novel also served a more outward facing function. Hays confesses:

> My MS was not written <u>merely</u> for the public eye__another latent, & perhaps stronger, motive lurked beneath ... I have a melancholy satisfaction in presenting to the stubborn heart, which I sought in vain to melt, a just, but far from an exaggerated picture, of its own cruel & inflexible severity__yet tho' "cruel" he was not "worthless"__I urged him too far.[42]

Hays wanted to force Frend to recognise the effect of his actions, and by expressing her sense of her own culpability, to make an apologetic gesture as well. For this reason, she refuses to tamper with at least one aspect of her '<u>too real</u>' story, insisting that she '[could] not violate its truth, by making Augustus either a coquet or a lover', modifications Godwin probably proposed.[43] In her correspondence with Godwin, Hays often seems more concerned with these personal motives – how the text would help her and how it would be read by Frend – than with its impact further afield.

Hays also utilised her experience of romantic disappointment in *Emma Courtney* to explore a revision of Godwinian philosophy.[44] Hays reproduces much of her correspondence with Godwin verbatim in the novel. In their wrangling over the powers and limits of rationality, Hays repeatedly cited her own encounter with Frend as grounds for critiquing Godwinian conceptions of sincerity, rationalism and passion. For example, when Godwin chides her for having 'sacrificed at the shrine of illusion' rather than 'at the altar of reason', she retorts that her 'conduct was not altogether so insane' given the inconsistent, secretive and, therefore, confusing behaviour of her would-be Romeo.[45] Bristling with indignation, Hays picks holes in one of Godwin's most far-reaching premises, his 'faith in the individual's

ability to develop his reason and natural benevolence so that he could
live peaceably and usefully with other men, without the restraints of
laws or governments':[46]

> I deeply reason'd & philosophised upon the subject … <u>I was the dupe
> of my own reason!</u> Even now, the affair, <u>altogether</u>, appears to me a
> sort of phenominon [sic] which I am unable to solve__I doubt, if there
> be another man in existence who cou'd have acted, exactly, the part
> this man has done __ how then was I to take such a part into my
> calculations?[47]

Her own life supplies an exception to Godwin's logic.

For Hays, converting painful experience into fiction had public
utility. In his theoretical account of nervous complaints as a means of
conveying social criticism, Peter Melville Logan situates *Emma Courtney*
as a response to Godwin's *Caleb Williams*, showing 'how late Georgian
social conditions create a psychology that is unique to women and that
results in a debilitating form of romantic love'.[48] Hays's own account
of her novel confirms this reading:

> My aim was merely to shew, & I searched into my own heart for the
> model, the possible effects of the present system of things, & the
> contradictory principles which have bewilder'd mankind, upon private
> character, & private happiness.[49]

As Tilottama Rajan suggests, the novel remains 'strategically rather
than essentially about female sexuality' for 'Emma's passion causes her
to rethink the social structures that condemn passion as outrageous'
and therefore to provide 'the site of her emergence as a political
subject'.[50] Hays's multifaceted use of life writing seems influenced
by the literary and religious culture of Rational Dissent, where its
applications for personal, philosophical and political purposes were
widely embraced.[51]

Hays's decision to incorporate real letters (to Frend and Godwin)
in *Emma Courtney* made this mixture of the personal and political
dangerously resonant. Letters were thought to originate in one's
core self, and correspondence thus involved great confidence and
intimacy.[52] Because people were seen to be embodied in their letters,

moreover, the link between this emotional intimacy and that of a sexual kind was very close.[53] The urgent desire and painful humiliation so palpable in Hays's novel could be seen to facilitate a strong connection between heroine and audience, especially the uneducated female reader who was already a site of anxiety.[54] Lucy Newlyn suggests that through such 'excessive readerly sympathy', it was feared that readers would 'become tainted by escapist fantasies in which conventional codes of morality were suspended'.[55] Although Hays's preface frames Emma as 'a *warning*, rather than as an example', the text luxuriates in her pained passions and in at least one sense vindicates its heroine: she is ultimately proved right in her hunch that Harley returned her love all along.[56] The reader is therefore left in some uncertainty as to how to judge Emma.[57] This ambiguous characterisation contributed to the controversy surrounding the text. Hays's concerns with self-expression, introspection and political critique led to a scandalous mixture of radicalism, sexuality and seeming authenticity that had far-reaching consequences for her reception.

### Mixed reactions

Published in November of 1796, *Emma Courtney* was widely read and reviewed and elicited strong reactions. According to Walker, 'readers of every political and religious persuasion were horrified by the "fiction" that was widely – and correctly – believed to be autobiographical'.[58] However, the more sympathetic Reviews tempered their reservations with praise for the 'intellectual powers' of the novelist and looked for a moral message.[59] Taking Hays's preface at face value, the *Monthly Magazine* endorsed the novel as a warning about the pernicious effects of unchecked sensibility.[60] The *Analytical* reviewer finds 'much good sense and much liberal principle', even if it 'cannot give an *unqualified* approbation of the character'.[61] After a five-page extract that includes the most shocking line of the novel (*'My friend – I would give myself to you'*), the *Monthly* reviewer defers to the reader 'to form his or her own judgement, on perusal'.[62] Others, such as the *Critical Review*, denounce Emma's conduct positively and seem uneasy about Hays's relationship to the narrative: 'we do not hold up Emma Courtney as a character for general imitation, any more than, we presume, the authoress herself would'.[63] The *British Critic* went furthest in its attack. It condemns the novel for 'sacrific[ing] morality at the shrine of passion' and disapproves of the 'books and men' by which Hays has been influenced.[64]

Private correspondence from within Hays's social circles confirms that the book provoked discussion and divided opinions. According to Hays's close friend Henry Crabb Robinson, the novel gained 'some reputation as a novel of passion, but was thought to be heretical on the great question of marriage'.[65] Predictably, friends such as George Dyer, Mary Robinson and Mary Wollstonecraft appreciated the novel.[66] Despite listing a string of faults and proposed revisions, Godwin also praised it. In a letter to Wollstonecraft, Amelia Alderson (later Opie) enthused: 'I am delighted with Hays's novel [!] I would give a great deal to have written it, tho [sic] as society now is, it is something to be capable of admiring it.'[67] Alderson's exclamation communicates her sense of Hay's boldness and her sympathy with Hays's radicalism. However, in a letter to Godwin written during the same period, she situates Hays as one of his acolytes: 'Upon my word General Godwin, you have a very skilful aide de camp in Captain Hays'.[68]

Others within Dissenting circles also noted *Emma Courtney*'s debt to Godwin and condemned the novel outright. The Dissenting minister Rochemont Barbauld disapproved of it so strongly that Wollstonecraft felt compelled to defend both text and author. Wollstonecraft reports that Barbauld 'stigmatized [Hays] as a Philosophess___a Godwinian' and that he judged the book antithetical to religion.[69] The Unitarian minister Theophilus Lindsey, who had praised Hays's writing in 1793, likewise viewed *Emma Courtney* as anti-religious and saw its author as having fallen under the unfortunate influence of Godwin:

> I am sorry to mention that these zealous antichristians have had but too much success in proselyting [sic] some of the other and better sex ... . There is also lately come forth a novel, Emma Courtenay [sic], by Mary Hays. You may perhaps have met with this ingenious young woman, a Dissenter ... I am told, for I have not read it, that this book ... retails too much of the principles of Helvetius and other french [sic] writers, as well as M[r] Godwin, all of whom she frequently quotes.[70]

The Jacobin novelist Thomas Holcroft, also a personal acquaintance of Hays's, objected, based on hearsay, that 'Emma Courtney did inculcate certain opinions relative to love … which his judgement disapprove[d]'.[71] Though anecdotal, these reactions foreground trends in Hays's reputation: her negative, derivative association with leading male thinkers; her difficulty in straddling Dissenting and radical values and genres; and her increasing prominence in the rumour mill.

Disapproval amongst Dissenters may also have been based on other factors, however. As Jon Mee observes, Rational Dissent struggled against the taint of 'enthusiasm', that fiery brand of affective religious sentiment that Samuel Johnson explicitly linked to 'private revelation', 'heat or imagination', 'violence of passion' and '[e]levation of fancy; exaltation of ideas'.[72] Enthusiasm was construed as a dangerous mania of the senses through which the passions could circumvent rationality, and it was associated with a confusion of religious agape for its sexual counterpart, eros. Although even a respected scientist like Priestley could be accused of enthusiasm, women were considered particularly vulnerable to the phenomenon, which was thought to make them mistake 'physical desires for illapses of the spirit'.[73]

Though *Emma Courtney* does not deal with religious devotion, the behaviour of its protagonist bears the hallmarks of an enthusiasm regarded as disruptive and contagious. Characterised by her passion, obsession, candour and convulsion of the senses, Emma Courtney often curses her own 'distempered imagination' but validates feelings 'prone to enthusiasm' and considers 'passions, but another name for powers'.[74] Her self-analysis aligns with the Anglican understanding of enthusiasm as 'a product of diseased minds', a 'pathology' or 'Distemper'.[75] Moreover, passion like Emma's provided a slippery slope to licentiousness, which Hays underlined with her heroine's brazen unorthodoxy. In the character of its heroine, Hays's *Emma Courtney* could be seen to substantiate suspicions that Rational Dissent was infected with enthusiasm. Reactions to the text like those of Reverend Barbauld may be best understood in light of popular associations apparent to contemporary readers.

Hays's epistolary novel also accorded poorly with traditions in Dissenting publication. Women in Hays's nonconformist network published in a variety of genres including moral tales, life writing, history, essays, correspondence and political tracts, but no other Baptist women wrote novels in this period.[76] Hays's later work is often regarded as a 'retreat' from the radical position of her 1790s fiction, but in fact her two novels may be the aberration in a lifelong career in nonfiction that otherwise fit well within the parameters of Dissenting culture. The autobiographical nature of *Emma Courtney* was also problematic. Walker suggests that the novel breaches 'the tacit understanding among Unitarians and Rational Dissenters to avoid public discussion of unseemly private matters' and could have been seen to confirm 'longstanding predictions that theological heterodoxy would lead to immorality'.[77]

The perception of *Emma Courtney* as a confession of Hays's own sexual transgressions undoubtedly damaged her public reputation. The most widely documented instance of this reaction comes from the temperamental poet and novelist Charles Lloyd, who later responded to *Emma Courtney* with his own *Edmund Oliver* (1798). Letters from Robert Southey, Samuel Taylor Coleridge and Charles Lamb show that Charles Lloyd not only judged Hays harshly but also spread rumours about her. Lamb reports what Lloyd told Hays:

> I had heard several times repeated, that you had loved both Godwin and Frend, moreover I had heard several times repeated, that all your first novel was but a transcript of letters sent by yourself and the latter Gentleman. ... I most <u>wickedly</u> exprest myself as if I thought you would in conduct demonstrate all that you had proposed in speculation! ... I have interwoven my abhorrence of your principles with a glanced contempt for your personal character.[78]

Southey corroborates that 'Lloyd has behaved very ill to [Hays]' and Coleridge, despite a personal antipathy towards her, agrees that 'Charles Lloyd's conduct has been atrocious ... Lies, Treachery, & Rascality'.[79]

Hays had an extensive network of family and friends, however, and she was not without defenders. According to Crabb Robinson, Dr Reid 'resented Lloyd's satirical attack on Miss Hays in his *Edmund Oliver* by a very bitter review in the *Analytical Review*'.[80] Crabb Robinson himself wrote to his friend Catherine Clarkson (who knew Lloyd) in early

1800 'with a few words in vindication of my ffriend [sic] Miss Hays against the wilful calumnies [of Llloyd]'.[81] Crabb Robinson not only affirms Hays as 'pure & chaste even to excess' but recounts how she boldly rebuffed Lloyd:

> Miss H renounced his acquaintance and answered his letter in so severe & unmerciful a style that his wife declares he flew into a rage … . In revenge it seems he has repeated the outrage And Miss Hays in self-defence has circulated his letters.[82]

As Crabb Robinson notes in his diary in 1799, Hays 'became the friend of Wollstonecraft, and professed her opinions with more zeal than discretion. This brought her into disrepute among the rigid, and her character suffered, but most undeservedly.'[83] Though anecdotal, Crabb Robinson's comments about Hays show that her friends continued to support and accept her. Moreover, Hays's 'self-defence' suggests a woman who proudly held her head up and was not cowed by the rumours.

## Conflation and condemnation

Hays's continued association with Wollstonecraft contributed to the perception that she was a sexually transgressive radical. Hays reinforced this association when, in October 1797, she added her name to the obituary of her friend that had appeared unsigned in the September *Monthly Magazine*. According to B. P. Pollin, Hays's effusive style and reverent tone denote 'the distress of a loyal friend and disciple'.[84] Lionising her friend's achievements, Hays aligned herself with Wollstonecraft's views. The first edition of Godwin's *Memoirs*, issued in January of 1798, again reaffirmed the connection. Although the *Memoirs* did not dwell on Hays, who was often relegated to the footnotes, Godwin did cite her as the friend who had re-introduced him to Wollstonecraft. As we have seen, Hays's views on women and politics had been linked to Wollstonecraft since 1793 at least; the *Memoirs* encouraged readers to draw private-life parallels as well. Hays thus became linked with the sexual improprieties Godwin had revealed about Wollstonecraft. R. M. Janes argues that 'Wollstonecraft's reputation collapsed as a consequence of two separate events: the course of the revolution in France ... and Godwin's publication'.[85] This publication also resituated *Emma Courtney* as Hays's autobiographical counterpart to Godwin's *Memoirs* of his now deceased wife.

The perceived differences between Hays and Wollstonecraft were even less flattering than the similarities. Walker reminds us that physically 'it was Hays's misfortune to present a striking contrast to Wollstonecraft, who appeared to many as the alluring embodiment of a forthright public intellectual woman'.[86] In a letter to Wollstonecraft, Amelia Alderson recalled that Stephen Weaver Browne had described Hays as 'old, ugly & ill-clad' and Coleridge likewise referred to her as 'a Thing, ugly & petticoated'.[87] Her unattractiveness and unkempt self-presentation were complemented by idiosyncratic habits (what Crabb Robinson terms 'precise manners') that could make her appear awkward.[88] According to Crabb Robinson, she also 'made herself disagreeable in company by preaching' and 'by her complaining tone of conversation'.[89] Her reputation as a disciple set her apart from the trailblazing originality associated with Wollstonecraft. Robert Southey summarised this view when he alluded disparagingly to Godwin as a philosopher who 'talks nonsense about the collision of the mind, and Mary Hayes [sic] echoes him'.[90] The most unfortunate difference between Hays and Wollstonecraft, however, may have been that Hays was the one still living. In the reactionary climate of the late 1790s, with its accelerating anxieties about spies, Jacobinism and 'French' morals, Hays was positioned as a perfect scapegoat.

## Public hostility

A series of printed attacks on Hays, starting with Charles Lloyd's anti-Jacobin novel *Edmund Oliver* (1798), shows how her public reputation suffered. Lloyd assailed Hays's philosophical position on marriage and caricatured her as the fallen Lady Gertrude Sinclair, a heroine who spouts lines from *Emma Courtney* verbatim. Even from her first letters, where Gertrude explains to her revolutionary paramour, Edward D'Oyley, that she no longer loves her childhood sweetheart, Edmund Oliver, her erroneous conduct emerges clearly. In unsubtle echoes of *Emma Courtney*, she relinquishes her attachment to Oliver by forswearing all vows as 'ministers of perdition to the weak and inexperienced' and by identifying herself as an intellectual who acts 'from the conclusions, and calculations of the moment'.[91] However, her jargon-laden justification, punctuated with short exclamations – 'I have seen Oliver! … I am satisfied! … Edward I am thine!' – gives away her guilt at betraying her 'pure of soul' Edmund. Such justifications derive from the same radical views that later impel her to cohabitate with D'Oyley, who will forsake her, pregnant and unwed, for another woman. Gertrude's false principles allow D'Oyley to take advantage of her and play out tragically in the denouement of the novel, where she commits suicide. They comprise Lloyd's didactic defence of marriage and account for his objections to Hays's *Emma Courtney*.

Lloyd's portrayal of Hays links her with the scandalous conduct of Wollstonecraft. Indeed, Lady Gertrude's narrative arc often smacks of Wollstonecraft more than Hays. Lloyd began work on the novel in October 1797, three months prior to the issue of Godwin's *Memoirs*, so it is unlikely that he modelled Gertrude directly after Wollstonecraft.[92] Rather, Lloyd resituates the prototypical lifeline of the fallen woman within the context of the liberal tenets espoused by Hays in *Emma Courtney* (also later obvious in the life of Wollstonecraft, as revealed in 1798).[93] Lloyd's 'Advertisement' to *Edmund Oliver* clarifies Gertrude's role:

> The domestic connections, which are only coeval with the existence of marriage, are the necessary means of disciplining Beings […] to a rational and enlarged benevolence. … In the character of Gertrude I have endeavoured to portray a woman of warm affections, strong passions, and energetic intellect, yielding herself to these loose and declamatory principles, yet at the same time uncorrupted in her intentions, unfortunate from error, and not from deliberate vice.[94]

Gertrude appears the apotheosis of feminine sensibility, with a 'spirited and majestic figure' and eyes brimming with 'earnestness and enthusiasm'.[95] Distracted by her 'impetuous' passions, she becomes the dupe of D'Oyley's democratic philosophies, by which she destroys her own reputation and breaks Edmund Oliver's heart. In advancing the case for traditional marriage values, however, Lloyd employs the (melo)dramatic dialect of sensibility that also prevails in

*Emma Courtney*. He condemns Hays's philosophy in her own idiom, yet
he lacks her aptitude for the epistolary genre, and his novel received
mixed reviews even in the conservative press. Nevertheless, the novel
constitutes an important forerunner of the more successful subsequent
attacks on Hays.

Though later criticism of Hays likewise objected to her radical
views, it substituted the language of sensibility for that of satire.
This material took its cues from the strategy used in the counter-
revolutionary *Anti-Jacobin Review*, where monstrous revolutionary
principles were pinned on biographical personae in comical
drawings.[96] Richard Polwhele's verse-satire, *The Unsex'd Females: A
Poem* (1798) performs a similar personification strategy to anti-Jacobin
ends, taking aim at radical women writers. Yoking licentiousness
and republicanism, Polwhele was indebted to Godwin's *Memoirs* for
supplying a convenient target in the form of Wollstonecraft.[97] In heroic
couplets, Polwhele points the finger at Wollstonecraft as an unnatural
woman whose immorality and (Gallic) political incontinence has,
in turn, brainwashed a whole 'female band despising NATURE's
law', including Anna Laetitia Barbauld, Mary Robinson, Angelica
Kauffman and Mary Hays.[98] They are juxtaposed with a retinue
of worthy women writers exhibiting virtue and genius, such as
Hannah More, Elizabeth Carter, Frances Burney and Ann Radcliffe.
Assigning names and faces to the rival camps of 'Gallic freaks' and
'female genius', Polwhele makes radicalism the province of debased
women. Hays appears as the disciple of Wollstonecraft: 'Now stole
the modish grin, the sapient sneer, / And flippant HAYS assum'd a
cynic leer.'[99] Polwhele's rhyming nouns 'sneer' and 'leer' poke fun
at a masculine Hays whose arrogant expression of self-satisfaction
ironically implies a dearth of all things 'sapient'. This manliness
heightens the comic effect while also emphasising her unnaturalness
as a woman of perverted morality and politics. Polwhele's economical
couplet reduces Hays to a laughable caricature. Like so many of her
earlier detractors, Polwhele figures Hays as a Wollstonecraft sidekick
rather than the prime target.

With Wollstonecraft gone, however, Hays soon became a symbolic
target in her own right. The May 1799 *Anti-Jacobin* reviews both of
Hays's novels in an article tellingly titled 'The Reviewers Reviewed'.

The article indicts Hays and her fiction in order to chastise the liberal media for their moral laxity. It opens with an excerpt not from Hays or *Emma Courtney* but from the *Monthly Review*'s complimentary response to her novel in its May 1797 issue. The *Anti-Jacobin* castigates the *Monthly* for inculcating 'a corrupt and vicious system of education' that trains women to be 'revolutionary agents' or 'heroines' rather than 'dutiful daughters, affectionate wives, tender mothers, and good Christians'.[100] This critic blames 'the Monthly Reviewers, and their liberal fellow-labourers' for praising a book in which 'the mistress is, in all respects, as honourable as the wife'.[101] Hays's narratives are made to stand for all that threatens female chastity and domestic duty. Hays is re-imagined metaphorically in the article's final lines: 'On the *style* of her writings it is needless to remark; who stays to admire the workmanship of a dagger wrenched from the hand of an assassin?'[102] Hays mutates here into an 'assassin' whose deft authorial 'workmanship' is refigured as an instrument of annihilation. The analogy positions the *Anti-Jacobin* reviewer himself as the heroic protector of public safety who valiantly 'wrenche[s]' the dagger from her grasp. Though ostensibly about *Emma Courtney* and *The Victim of Prejudice*, these scathing five pages actually criticise Hays as an emblem of 'her party', which extends to 'Godwin, Holcroft, Mary Wollstonecraft, Helvetius, Rousseau, &c'.[103] Hays and her writing symbolise the jeopardy in which radical philosophy places not only individual women but also the upstanding institutions of print culture and the moral fabric of society.

## Satire and self-defence

The most effective critique of Hays came from the satirical genius of Elizabeth Hamilton, whose *Memoirs of Modern Philosophers* (1800), a send-up of radical philosophy, became a bestseller. Though *Modern Philosophers* contains a string of caricatures, including Wollstonecraft (the Goddess of Reason), Holcroft (Mr Glib) and Godwin (Mr Myope), its unlikely protagonist, Bridgetina Botherim (Hays), occasions the most comedy and comes in for the most criticism. In Bridgetina, Hamilton shows the hazards – and the humour – that result from the misapplication and/or manipulation of radical beliefs.

Hamilton refashions Hays as the unbecoming Bridgetina Botherim, giving her physical qualities that undercut Emma Courtney's menacing sexual unorthodoxy and radical beliefs. Bridgetina has an 'unfortunate squint', a 'craggy neck', a 'homely plainness of countenance', 'shrivelled parchment-like skin' and legs of noticeable 'shortness'.[104] Her physical endowments aim for comic, rather than pathetic, effect. Hamilton encourages this effect by placing Bridgetina in farcical scenes that leave her covered in mud, surrounded by pigs or entrapped by prostitutes. Depicting Bridgetina as a hag or old maid, Hamilton uses masculine textual conventions for controlling a disruptive female figure.[105] The idea of free love becomes far less dangerous on the lips of the grotesque Miss Botherim than coming from the sensuous Emma Courtney. Hamilton nullifies Emma's affective appeal with the repulsive and ridiculous physique of Bridgetina Botherim.

Meanwhile, Hamilton derides Hays as a misreader of both philosophical and social discourse. Bridgetina misconstrues Henry Sydney's love confession, believing he returns her own feelings when in fact he is attached to the fair and just Harriet Orwell. Labouring under this misapprehension, Bridgetina follows Henry to London to pester him with lengthy love letters, one of which proclaims:

> I have reasoned, I have investigated, I have philosophised upon the subject ... . My interest, my pleasure, is all centered in your affections; therefore I will pursue you, nor shall I give over the pursuit, say what you will. ... Why should I despair of arguing you into love?[106]

In a layered pantomime of *Emma Courtney*, Bridgetina copies Emma's letters to Harley (just as Hays incorporated her own letters into the novel), using them to hound Henry with declarations of her love.[107] Like Gertrude in *Edmund Oliver*, Bridgetina's misguided actions in the name of love derive from her reading of *Emma Courtney*, yet Hamilton makes them comic rather than tragic. *Modern Philosophers* not only warns against narcissistically reading *Emma Courtney* as Bridgetina does but also raises the suspicion that Hays herself may have misinterpreted her own real-life interactions. In Bridgetina, Hamilton rewrites Hays as a desperate and self-deluded clown whose *Emma Courtney* can be deposed as an absurd – rather than subversive – autobiographical fiction.

However, the didactic thrust of the novel is encapsulated not in Bridgetina but in the disastrous misreadings of another character, the beautiful and impressionable Julia Delmond. Hamilton uses the villainous Vallaton to show how a self-seeker can manipulate New Philosophical ideas to seduce a susceptible girl.[108] The eventual demise of Julia contrasts with a happier ending for Bridgetina. In a Fielding-inspired final chapter, the narrator facetiously confesses his inability to marry off the principal protagonist, pleading that 'this is far from being our fault' as 'she is neither *rich* nor *handsome*'.[109] Bridgetina is later advised by Mr Sydney that Julia's ruin

> has been wrought … by the same delusive principles that have seduced you from the path of filial duty. Had nature bestowed on you a form as beautiful, or a face as fair, you too would have been the prey of lust, and the victim of infamy.[110]

Bridgetina's hideous looks preclude her sexuality from posing a threat and separate her mock-heroic failures from the tragic fate of Julia. Hamilton's epistolary prelude to *Modern Philosophers* frames the novel as an interrogation of 'opinions, not persons', yet its satirical punch lies in the transformation of Hays into the ridiculous Bridgetina.[111] By replacing the philosophically and sexually revolutionary mystique of Emma Courtney with the foolish whims of Bridgetina Botherim, Hamilton repositioned Hays as a figure of mockery.

Nonetheless, Hays continued to publish, and to make a profit from, politically progressive writing. In her second novel, *The Victim of Prejudice* (1799), Hays uses the abduction and rape of the virtuous and unprotected heroine Mary Raymond to comment on institutional biases and social prejudices that determine female worth according to reputation rather than individual merit.[112] The novel demonstrates how a tarnished name becomes an insidious obstacle to a woman's independence. Although Mary Raymond looks back 'with complacency on a spotless life', her violation at the hands of Sir Peter Osborne stains her irrevocably, rendering her unable even to find work by which to support herself.[113] Her loving guardian, Mr Raymond, had advised her, before he died, to cherish virtue as the supreme good:

[T]he good opinion of our fellow-beings is desirable: it is connected
with usefulness, and ought not to be contemned. … yet reputation is
but a secondary good; it wears the semblance of virtue, but, if prized
before the substance, may accelerate the evil it was meant to avert.[114]

Nevertheless, Mary's upright conduct cannot preserve her in the face
of the persecution and abuse of Osborne. It is ultimately Jean-Jacques
Rousseau's words – not Raymond's – that hold true:

Worth alone will not suffice, a woman must be thought worthy …
. A woman's honour does not depend on her conduct alone, but on
her reputation … . A man has no one but himself to consider, and so
long as he does right he may defy public opinion; but when a woman
does right her task is only half finished, and what people think of her
matters as much as what she really is.[115]

Hays protests against this double standard in the *Victim of Prejudice*,
where Mary Raymond bears responsibility not only for her own
actions but for those which are done to her (even if against her will).

This novel can thus be read as an attempt to theorise the problematic
dynamics of female reputation and perhaps to defend herself as
well. The sexual violation of Mary Raymond and her subsequent
ignominy may contain a veiled reference to the rumours and slander
that followed in the wake of *Emma Courtney*. Like Mary Raymond,
Hays suffered not because she was unchaste but because people
*thought* she was (based on reading her novel). Hays thus transplants
into fiction a predicament that she herself experienced, though in
altered circumstances, protesting a wider injustice as well as her
personal experience of it. Though the conservative climate of the late
1790s meant that her second novel fared poorly in the Reviews, it
nevertheless earned £40 and led to further work.[116] More importantly,
it shows how Hays, who had long been branded a follower, conflated
detrimentally with her own fictional protagonist or satirised in those
of others, was beginning to redirect such associations in her writing.

## The biographical (re)turn

Hays believed in the potential of life writing to be used for polemical,
educational and self-reflective purposes. In her *Monthly Magazine*

essays in the mid-1790s, she had invoked the lives of eminent ladies to prove the equal capability between the sexes and to protest against the poor state of women's education. Given the opportunity, Hays argued, women can shine just as brightly as men:

> Amidst the disadvantages under which the heroines of antiquity, Semiramis, Zenobia, and Boadicea –the Catherines of the North, and Elizabeth of England; the Lesbian Sappho, the Grecian Hypatia, Madame de Chatelet, the commentator upon Newton; Dacier, the translator of Homer; and Macauley [sic], the English historian … have afforded proofs of powers and capacities, perhaps, little less extraordinary than either those of Homer, Newton, or Shakespeare.[117]

Here Hays cites individual female lives not only as sources of inspiration but also as material for political analysis. This approach to life writing appeared in her *Letters and Essays* (1793) and in her fictionalised self-portrait in *Emma Courtney* (1796).[118] After 1800, she continued to develop it in new generic forms.

Hays's approach to life writing overlapped with Godwin's. As we saw in Chapter 2, Godwin believed that a 'minut[e]' acquaintance with 'illustrious men' could inform and inspire readers and thus promote social change.[119] The narrator must follow the subject behind the scenes in order to provide a candid account. Hays, similarly, had written in 1796 about the importance of such intimate personal history:

> Were every great man to become his own biographer, and to examine and state impartially, to the best of his recollection, the incidents of his life, the course of his studies, the causes by which he was led into them, the reflections and habits to which they gave birth, the rise, the change, the progress of his opinions, with the consequences produced by them on his affections and conduct, great light might be thrown on the most interesting of all studies, that of moral causes and the human mind.[120]

It is no surprise therefore that Hays's 'Memoirs of Mary Wollstonecraft' (1800) resembled Godwin's earlier version, as the two writers shared a conviction in the importance of life writing as a socially beneficial enterprise.

Hays and Godwin resisted the biographical conventions which had reigned from mid-century and which tended to celebrate well-

educated women as markers of cultural progress and sources of
national pride. George Ballard's *Memoirs of Several Ladies of Great Britain*
(1752) comprised the transitional text 'between the more generalized
celebrations of the 'BRITISH FAIR' of the first half of the century ...
and the emergence of a national canon of celebrated women'.[121] Ballard
commemorates eminent female citizens of Britain who have displayed
refinement of education. Though implicitly he assumes learning to be a
boon, Ballard elides the contemporary debates on women's education,
emphasising it instead as a feminine accomplishment.[122] In his ability
to appreciate these great women, Ballard underscores his own level
of cultivation. These learned ladies function as 'sign[s] of the civility
of the national institutions of taste and critical judgement' which are
to be admired.[123] In contrast to Ballard, Hays and Godwin understand
personal history as a process of discursive individuation that subjects
an exemplary human life to philosophical and psychological scrutiny.
They depict the lives of women to educate and inspire the reader.

Despite these similarities, Hays and Godwin had different emphases
in their practice of biography. Where Godwin wished readers to
rethink social and political relations, Hays was more specifically
concerned with issues of sexual equality. Walker explains that Hays
'envisions her [Wollstonecraft's] life from their shared perspectives
as women and emphasizes the role resistance to gender prejudice
played in Wollstonecraft's development'.[124] In 'Memoirs of Mary
Wollstonecraft', Hays narrates the long road to the domestic peace
that Wollstonecraft achieved with Godwin:

> It was now that her exhausted heart began to find repose ... her ideas of
> rational happiness had ever been concentered in the circle of domestic
> affections, in seeking to realize her plans, she had till this period been
> involved in undeserved calumny and distress; ... . Had the sensibility
> of this extraordinary woman early found its proper objects, softened
> by the sympathies, and occupied by the duties of a wife and mother,
> she had serenely pursued her course.[125]

According to Mary Spongberg, Hays emphasises Wollstonecraft's
'religiosity', shows her 'action and politics as being shaped by the
typical experience of being a woman' and, most importantly, allows her
own letters 'unfiltered' to dominate the narrative.[126] In this way Hays

not only contests the authority of Godwin's *Memoirs* but also connects 'Memoirs of Mary Wollstonecraft' with *Emma Courtney* through their mutual fixation on a romantic attachment. Hays sympathises with Wollstonecraft and denounces a system in which women 'overste[p] the bounds prescribed to them' and 'by a single error … become involved in a labyrinth of perplexity and distress'.[127] Godwin had chafed at the reigning 'hypocrisy' that allowed his wife's friends to accept her while pretending to believe her married (to Imlay) but to snub her once the official union with Godwin made her previous status as an unwed mother undeniable.[128] Godwin aimed to excite anger at a sanctimonious orthodoxy he wished to reform. In contrast, Hays uses a more sentimental lexicon, enlisting the sympathy of the reader for female victims of an unjust status quo.

'Memoirs of Mary Wollstonecraft' provides an empathic analysis of one woman's life as the symptom of comprehensive gender inequalities. It fits into what critics such as Greg Kucich call 'an emergent feminist historiography'.[129] Kucich places Hays alongside other women writers who pioneer alternatives to the practice of traditional masculine history. According to Kucich, these women 'humaniz[e] the past by replacing the abstractions of universal history with sustained evocations of the interior lives and domestic communities of those individuals, particularly women, who have been victimized by the grand sweep of official historical process'.[130] Hays's compassionate, woman-centred recasting of Wollstonecraft's life turns on its ability to evoke a personal response with political implications. Again, Hays may also be writing self-reflexively, encouraging readers to think sympathetically about how women's decisions are informed by their disadvantaged social circumstances. Hays's 'Memoirs of Mary Wollstonecraft', along with her earlier two-page *Monthly Magazine* obituary of 1797 (published anonymously but later signed), boldly reaffirmed their affiliation and worked to reshape, however minutely, the reputations of both women.[131]

Hays's memoir of Wollstonecraft thus reveals the polemical and personal concerns in her approach to life writing which span her career. Hays uses biography much as she had used her own life in *Emma Courtney*: as investigation, self-expression and teaching tool. Walker argues that Hays's interest in 'female consciousness' was 'epistemological as well as sociological and psychological', and that she began to 'experiment with, chronicle and assess her own awareness' in *Emma Courtney*.[132] Afterward, as Miriam L. Wallace observes, she 'moved away from transmuting her own life into fiction so directly' and turned to 'writing more obliquely the lives of women'.[133] In a 1797 essay for the *Monthly Magazine*, Hays theorised:

> Gradations, almost imperceptible, of light and shade, must mingle in every true portrait of the human mind. Few persons are either wholly or disinterestedly virtuous or vicious; he who judges of mankind in masses, and praises or censures without discrimination, will foster innumerable prejudices, and be betrayed into perpetual mistakes.[134]

Here Hays emphasises that biography has to include three-dimensional, lifelike portrayals of its subjects rather than one-note paragons of virtue or vice. Hays had brought this standard to bear in her fiction and her writing on Wollstonecraft, and she returned to it in *Female Biography*, with consequences for her reputation and literary legacy.

## Female Biography

The Preface to Hays's *Female Biography* (1803) echoes sentiments expressed in her *Monthly Magazine* contributions, *Letters and Essays* and *Emma Courtney*. Hays claims: 'My pen has been taken up in the cause, and for the benefit of my own sex. For their improvement, and to their entertainment, my labours have been devoted'.[135] In the six volumes that follow, Hays details the lives of over 300 women from various countries, periods and social backgrounds, championing their achievements and holding up her subjects as complex, flawed humans with whom readers can sympathise and through whom they can learn about history. This epic biographical dictionary represents Hays's attempt to redress the absence of women from the Enlightenment *Encyclopédie* and stands at once as a landmark in Romantic-period historiography and an innovation in life writing.[136] Moving away from the earlier assessments of *Female Biography* as 'hack work'[137] or a 'retrea[t] from her most radical feminist position',[138] scholars have now begun to situate it as a bridge between Enlightenment reason and Romantic ideas about self-expression,[139] a feminist intervention[140] and a vindication of Hays's own life.[141] Hays's unorthodox approach to narrating women's lives and her inclusive principles of selection have been noted. Yet few modern critics analyse more than one entry, as Spongberg has observed, and little attention has been paid to how the form of *Female Biography* links with Hays's feminism, her innovative approach to history writing or her own self-fashioning.[142]

The structure of *Female Biography* may appear flawed to modern eyes. The alphabetically arranged entries are uneven in length and inconsistent in format and content. The text can feel at once repetitive and chaotic, as if Hays tells the 'female story ... over and over',[143] but in no apparent order. However, the encyclopaedic form of *Female Biography* has several features which affect the experience of reading the text profoundly, including alphabetical juxtapositions that reveal previously unseen relationships, intersecting cross-references that ask readers to make connections between entries and recurring themes and conflicts that render female experience as circular rather than linear. These formal features link directly to Hays's feminist project, not only cultivating a reinterpretation of women's roles and representation in history but also encouraging active reading practices in her female audience. Moreover, attention to the form of *Female Biography* shows it as a descendant of Hays's earlier experiments in life writing, such as *Letters and Essays*,[144] *Emma Courtney* and 'Memoirs of Mary Wollstonecraft', and a product of her hard-earned insight into how lives are read, appraised, compared, conflated and appropriated.

Hays's choice of alphabetical arrangement, highlighted in the subtitle, suggests that she expected *Female Biography* to be read as a reference work.[145] In other words, readers would not necessarily peruse the text from start to finish but might dip in and out as desired. By 1800, alphabetical order had begun to replace chronological and thematic principles of organisation in dictionaries and encyclopaedias on account of its perceived convenience for readers. John Aikin and William Enfield highlighted the benefit of their own alphabetised *Biographical Dictionary* by reminding readers that 'no time is lost in searching after knowlege [sic] ... at the moment when it is required'.[146] A biographical dictionary would be consulted in a 'moment' of need, not read end to end like a conventional biography or narrative work. Like their more complex encyclopaedic counterparts, biographical dictionaries aimed for efficiency and accessibility and prioritised the learning needs of a general reader who might want an aid to memory or an introductory overview.[147] In his didactic *Emily: A Moral Tale* (1809), Reverend Henry Kett advises that girls study history and biography as part of their moral education, and he recommends Hays's *Female Biography* as a useful primer. Kett isolates nine entries which will be particularly edifying and enjoyable for his young readers. This list indicates his assumption that readers would choose the entries within *Female Biography* that interested them, rather than reading it in a linear fashion.

This non-linear reading comprises part of a wider Enlightenment intellectual project that envisioned an active, self-directed reader who would forge a unique path through the text and construct his own interpretation of the material accordingly. In employing an alphabetical arrangement in *Female Biography*, Hays joined dictionary writers such as Andrew Kippis and William Boyd, as well as encyclopaedists like Ephraim Chambers, Denis Diderot and Jean d'Almbert, in endorsing this unregimented reading.[148] Hays implicitly rejected other principles of organisation, such as the didactic arrangement by character type favoured by Mary Pilkington's *Biography for Girls* (1799); the 'classical' arrangement which grouped entries into sections indicating how they were to be interpreted (i.e. imitation or warning);[149] the chronological design of standard historical texts; or the 'rational' arrangement which prescribed the order in which readers should study the material so as to help them master a series of concepts.[150] With entries assembled in alphabetical order, *Female Biography* moved away from the use of biography as a form of didactic control, instead refashioning it as a means of autonomous intellectual development.

Yet Hays subtly directs and stimulates this intellectual development through her usage of what I will term *cross-references*. Though these links between entries are not as overt or as sophisticated as the *renvois* in the *Encyclopédie*, they serve, similarly, to draw readers on from one subject to another and to encourage comparisons between them.[151] Hays's entry on Agnes Sorrel, for example, details how Charles VII's mistress used her feminine wiles to 'rouse him to the recovery of his dominions, which the English were wresting from his hands'.[152] Hays praises Sorrel for her 'stratagem': she teasingly threatens to leave her royal lover for a 'great' monarch (such as his rival, Henry VI of England). Deliberately making him jealous as a way of spurring him to action, Sorrel wields a private 'influence' which had far-reaching public consequences. Hays not only demonstrates the significance of Sorrel, whose manoeuvres might be overlooked in conventional histories, but also links her to another important female contemporary: 'Charles owed his success and his restoration to women. While Agnes urged him to resistance, the heroic Joan d'Arc fought his battles'.[153] In this cross-reference, Hays makes a comment that cannot be fully understood without turning to another entry within *Female Biography*. This comment invites the reader to turn (back) to the account of Joan of Arc, where she will find a contrasting model of female agency.

At first glance, the French peasant Joan of Arc could not appear more different than the alluring and aristocratic Sorrel. According to Hays, the 'robust and hardy' Joan becomes deeply 'interested in political affairs'.[154] She determines to intervene in national events by winning the trust of Charles VII and leading his troops in combat. A military 'heroine' and a strategic advisor, Joan of Arc assumes martial and diplomatic roles that contrast with Sorrel's behind-the-scenes measures.[155] The two women offer opposite examples of historical agency, the former of private feminine 'influence', the latter of masculine public leadership. Yet both are presented as laudable despite their transgressions. As Charles's mistress, Sorrel's 'ambition', 'vanity' and debt to her 'senses' mark her as sexually fallible, but she is praised for using her illicit sway to thwart Charles's own 'voluptuous effeminacy'.[156] Though chaste, Joan violates gender roles in a different way: 'assuming the habits and the command over men' and 'boldly avow[ing] and justif[ying] the purpose'.[157] Hays celebrates Joan's 'heroism' in the context of the Hundred Years' War. She faults Charles, who hypocritically failed 'to rescue from destruction the deliverer of himself'.[158] In both entries, the violation of feminine ideals functions to highlight the much greater failings of Charles VII, who appears weak and selfish in comparison. Hays's attention to the flaws of her subjects serves to humanise, authenticate and individuate them but not to detract from the import of their actions. Hays revises the historical record, showing women as three-dimensional individuals and agents of historical and political change.

Just as in the *Encyclopédie*, where the meaning of any given subject emerges through a consideration of separate, related entries,[159] the full critique, both of Charles and of traditional gender roles, only surfaces when these entries are considered in tandem. Hays's *Female Biography*, like the Enlightenment encyclopaedias that preceded it, invites readers 'to coordinate related entries and put together their hidden … shape'.[160] In doing so, Hays risks that the reader will miss or ignore her prompts, but if the reader does follow them, Hays has not only transmitted information but has also facilitated an intellectual process of investigation and analysis. By concluding each entry with a list of sources, Hays directs the inquisitive reader to further material for study and comparison. As Miriam Wallace suggests, 'Hays seeks not only to change the ways of writing public lives and history, but to teach us to read the past differently'.[161] It is significant that she does so not only through the content but also through the form of her collection.

The cross-references also direct readers to different perspectives on the same events. That the entries for Agrippina (Volume I) and Livia Drusilla (Volume IV) contain references to one another remains unsurprising. The two women were contemporaries, and their lives were personally and politically intertwined. According to Hays, Livia Drusilla and her son, the Emperor Tiberius, joined in orchestrating the murder of Agrippina's husband Germanicus.[162] In the twenty-four-page account of Livia Drusilla, this assassination illustrates the 'triumph of Tiberius and his mother' over 'justice' and 'humanity' and a crucial juncture in Livia's self-willed climb to power.[163] The 'noble' Agrippina appears a victim who 'in vain solicited of the senate vengeance on her husband's murderers'.[164] However, the entry on Agrippina, though much shorter, adds further details. In this account, Agrippina appears 'proud, aspiring, inflexible' and Hays reveals that the 'tears and tenderness of [the] widow gave place to a thirst for vengeance: she attacked Piso, whom she suspected to be the murderer, and compelled him to take shelter from her fury in death'.[165] Here, Agrippina seems far more assertive and formidable. Livia, by contrast, appears simply as a jealous rival.[166] On balance, Agrippina is portrayed more positively than Livia, but both women have strengths and weaknesses, and both explicitly manifest what Hays terms 'masculine' qualities.[167] Reading one entry provides only part of the story. However, if the curious reader follows the trail of Hays's cross-references, she supplements her knowledge of the first woman through her reading of the second.

In this way, the cross-references not only support active reading practices and teach a complex historical understanding[168] but also mimic the entertainment quality of fiction. Instead of binary examples of good or bad conduct, Hays offers a polyvocal, 'affective view of the past'[169] which complicates simplistic 'cause and effect' models of history.[170] *Female Biography* participates, like much of Richard Phillips's non-fiction stable, in the shift towards a new historical consciousness that emerged in the Romantic period.[171] Paradoxically, this historiographical shift is often most evident in parahistorical genres like educational history, life writing, journalism, criticism and fiction.[172] *Female Biography* bears one of the hallmarks of Romantic historiography: it 'addresse[s] … the need to hold attention and to keep a reader reading' by making 'history learn from literature'.[173] Hays's cross-references stimulate and reward curiosity, encourage sympathetic identification with historical characters and invite readers to think critically about events. In these ways *Female Biography* resembles epistolary novels such as Burney's *Evelina* (1778) and prefigures historical fiction like Walter Scott's *Waverley* novels (1814–31) and experimental gothic narratives like James Hogg's *Confessions of a Justified Sinner* (1824).

In addition to cross-references, *Female Biography* also promotes connections between entries through physical juxtapositions. As noted by Felicity James, 'mistresses, novelists, queens, Revolutionaries, Roman matrons, courtesans, intellectuals and Dissenters all take their place in Hays's biography, rubbing up against one another in a fertile cross-period jumble thanks to her alphabetized, non-chronological layout'.[174] This layout allows for an entertaining and edifying promiscuity of association, a quality that Ephraim Chambers's Preface to his *Cyclopaedia* (1728) praises: 'Where numbers of things are thrown precariously together, we sometimes discover relations among them, which we should never have thought of looking for'.[175] In Volume VI of *Female Biography*, for example, Laura Sade, the unrequited love of the poet Francesco Petrarch, is followed directly by Sappho, the ancient Greek poet known for her sexually charged verse. According to Hays, Laura is married when she meets Petrarch but she 'conceal[s]' her true sentiments in order to preserve her chastity.[176] Not unlike Petrarch himself, Hays focuses on the male poet's feelings and the impact of Laura on him; Laura's voice is audible only at the end of the entry, before she dies. The beautiful, virtuous, suffering and (mostly) silent Laura seems to symbolise a feminine ideal. Sappho, by contrast, resembles Petrarch more than Laura. She is introduced as a poet of 'genius and talents', who created new metrical forms to lyricise her passions.[177] Hays salutes her endeavour 'to inspire the Lesbian women with a taste for literature' and also defends her reputation, suggesting that it is not 'always a true criterion to judge of a writer by his works'.[178] In what is tempting to see as a self-reflexive comment, Hays makes clear that 'voluptuous' poems do not necessarily mean a 'voluptuous' poet. If Laura represents the archetypal love object, Sappho becomes the transcendent writing subject. Each should be judged – or admired – on her own terms. The juxtaposition of Laura Sade and Sappho implies that there are different ways that women can gain poetic immortality.

The radical levelling effect of this kind of juxtaposition was not lost on readers of Hays's *Female Biography*. In 1803, Lucy Aikin compared it to 'a great London rout, everybody is there, good, bad and indifferent, visitable and not visitable, so that a squeamish lady scarcely knows whom she may venture to speak to'.[179] Aikin's comment reminds us of the controversial inclusiveness of Hays's work. It also points to the randomness of the juxtapositions. A young lady may set out to 'speak to' Laura Sade, and accidentally end up face-to-face with the 'not visitable' Sappho. The extended metaphor of the social gathering signals the anxieties about women's reading, which was seen as having the same dangerous influence of mixing in 'bad' company.[180]

The juxtapositions in *Female Biography* not only contrast opposite 'types', as seen in the Sappho/Sade discussion above, but also bring to light more subtle variations as well as unexpected parallels. The entry for the sixteenth-century poet Laura Ammannati, who 'united with her husband in his studies and pursuits', precedes that of Isabella Andreina, an Italian actress whose 'talents' and 'dramatic powers' thrived while acting in her husband's company.[181] In both cases, the cooperative marital partnership is linked to domestic happiness and artistic achievement. Family collaborations of a military nature emerge in the adjoining entries of Maria D'Estrada and Ethelfleda in Volume IV. The latter, an English warrior queen who fought alongside her father, Alfred the Great, seems to echo the former, a Spanish warrior who joined her husband in battle in Mexico. The juxtapositions of these collaborations in learning, acting and fighting affirm the potential of equitable gender relationships within families.

Consecutive entries also reveal alternative outcomes in similar scenarios. In Volume I, Anne Askew and Aspasia show how learning can be turned toward noble or ignoble purposes, and in Volume III, the juxtaposition of Helen Lucretia Cornaro and 'Anonymous' showcases the different personalities of two female 'doctors'. Cornaro, whose celibacy and severity in devotion to her studies are viewed as extreme, contrasts with the more pleasing 'Anonymous' daughter of an Italian gentleman who became a professor of law but was able to maintain 'the elegance of her sex'.[182] In Volume VI, the third-century Roman Empress Valeria and the seventeenth-century French mistress of Louis XIV, Mademoiselle De La Valliere, are both subjected to the cruel and fickle whims of autocratic rulers. Valeria, who refused to remarry the 'tyrant' Maximin after the death of her husband, was persecuted and then beheaded for her resistance.[183] Similarly, after many years as the King's favourite, La Valliere eventually becomes a 'victim of his caprice' and is banished to a convent.[184] The positioning of these pairs allows readers to consider them in relation to one other and to muse on the positive effects of equitable family partnerships, the possible outcomes of female education or the appalling abuses of royal power.

Of course not every reader will notice these juxtapositions or draw the same conclusions, nor will they necessarily follow the paths prompted by the cross-references. As in case of the *Encyclopédie*, the reader's sequence through, and interpretation of, the text remain out of the author's hands. However, certain types and tropes recur with such frequency in *Female Biography* that it is unlikely that readers will miss them.[185] Again and again, we meet heroic women who demonstrate leadership in the absence or defence of their husbands. This scenario surfaces in the entries for Aldrude, Lady Arundel Blanche, Countess of Derby, Margaret De Foix, Phillipa, Eponina, Catherine Sforza and Zenobia, to name a few. More troubling, perhaps, is the repeated situation in which women become victims or pawns in the hands of masculine power struggles, visible in the adjacent entries of Valeria and La Valliere discussed above, as well as those of Isabella of Aragon, Berenice, Elizabeth of France, Octavia (wife of Anthony), Lady Jane Grey, Sophronia, Lady Arabella Seymour, Tymichia and Countess de la Suze. In the first group, the lack of a male figure opens a power gap that these women rise to fill; in the second, unchecked male dominance allows for brutal treatment of women. Despite great differences in period, place and personality, these women experience remarkably similar trajectories. As Wallace notes, the alphabetical arrangement collapses distinctions of 'time, nation, or social standing' and foregrounds 'interconnections' with an important effect: 'Rather than a narrative of feminine progress or growth, the impression is of an expansive and expanding category of "women".'[186] In other words, women's situation – both the ways in which they acquire power and the ways in which they are rendered powerless – has not 'progressed' over time. Hays thus joins Catharine Macaulay as well as Charlotte Smith, Lady Morgan and many other Romantic women writers in an early feminist critique of the linear progress narrative of mainstream masculine historiography,[187] using generic innovation to do so.[188] Hays's critique operates not only thematically but structurally as well, as she fosters the 'advancement' of her female readers through a dynamic reading and thinking process directed by *Female Biography*'s cross-references, juxtapositions and repetitions.

## Speaking by proxy

Another repetition within *Female Biography* is Hays's privileging of women's self-writing, which Walker defines as a vital element of the text.[189] Scholars have long recognised that Hays moves beyond the women worthies model[190] by including rounded characters capable of good and evil[191] and by daring to include such morally dangerous 'exemplars' in her collection. Equally significant, perhaps, are the women, such as Henrietta of Bourbon, Countess de Bregy and Ann Clifford, for example, whose candid and idiosyncratic self-portraits Hays quotes within her entries. The embedded first-person accounts render these entries some of the most nuanced and relatable characters in the collection. In an excerpt from her six-volume memoir, Henrietta plainly owns that her 'defects are not few', before listing them: 'I dress negligently ... I talk a great deal ... I confess I love praise ... I resent warmly, and do not easily pardon ... I love to provoke and irritate ... I am not devout'.[192] Countess De Bregy likewise proclaims her shortcomings: 'I love praise ... I am not only proud but indolent; and these defects have been productive of others. I take no pains to court favour [...] I am resolute, persevering to obstinacy, and secret to excess ... I wish evil to those who conform not to my desire'.[193] Though Ann Clifford does not catalogue her weaknesses as such, her journal records the 'contradictions and crosses' of her two marriages, in which defiance of her husbands' demands led to 'dissension'.[194] In her first marriage, she refused to sell her lands to compensate for her husband's 'profuseness in consuming his estate' and 'other extravagances'; in her second, she declined to force her youngest daughter to marry her stepson.[195] In unemotional prose, these women discuss their unfeminine qualities and actions with surprising levels of self-awareness.

In similarly dispassionate terms, all three also identify their own gifts, both mental and physical. Henrietta stresses that she has 'a noble and an upright mind' and 'strength' which 'nothing fatigues, dejects or discourages'.[196] De Bregy emphasises her 'penetrating, delicate, solid, and reasonable' mind and 'native good sense', and Clifford her possession of a 'strong and copious memory, a sound judgment, a discerning spirit, and an imagination so strong'.[197] In depicting their external appearances they seem even more self-satisfied, with Clifford describing her dark and 'lively' eyes and her 'exquisite shape', and Henrietta her 'handsome' neck and 'good hands and arms'.[198] De Bregy goes even further: 'I am one of the finest women of my size.

My eyes are fine … My air is lovely and delicate. My glass persuades me that I see nothing superior, if equal to the image which it presents to me'.[199] Yet even De Bregy does not seem to be boasting so much as attempting to paint herself as accurately and meticulously as possible. Though not published in their lifetimes, these women's self-descriptions are remarkable for their detail and lucidity. By inscribing the writing of these women in *Female Biography*, Hays endorses them both as unapologetic autobiographers and as flawed but self-reflective human beings. Spongberg has suggested that the 'women most admired by Hays were those who represented both '"rational womanhood" and "domestic heroism"', and that 'the women who received most praise … were models of Roman republican virtue'.[200] However, it could be argued that Hays's greatest tributes can be found where her voice recedes and she allows her subjects to speak for themselves.

Furthermore, entries such as these, which include first-person excerpts, often seem more real and 'present' than others in the collection. According to Mark Salber Phillips, 'every historical account must position its audience in some relationship of closeness or distance to the events and experience it recounts'.[201] The author modulates this 'distance' through ideological, formal and aesthetic choices that in turn shape the reader's political and emotional engagement with the material. Phillips stresses, however, that levels of engagement vary even within a single work, and authors may render certain moments – or subjects – more 'close and pressing' in order to 'intensify … the affective, ideological, or commemorative impact'.[202] Hays's inclusion of her subjects' life writing within *Female Biography* represents one of the strategies by which she makes these subjects particularly 'close and pressing', that is, realistic and relatable. Hays was not alone in incorporating such accounts into her text. Romantic historiography and literary biography – like fiction – sought increasingly to offer access to feelings and individual experience through first-person documents.[203] Romantic historical and parahistorical writers, including not only Hays but also Ann Yearsley, Elizabeth Benger, Charlotte Smith, Catharine Macaulay and Joanna Baillie, were beginning to represent experience as well as action.[204] Kucich highlights, for instance, how the representation of female suffering works to 'mobilize "sympathizing tenderness" for the historical plight of women ... to critique sex/gender systems past and present'.[205] Hays's *Female Biography* joins the historiographical experiments of her contemporaries in changing historical consciousness, providing a revisionary history based in sympathy for the suffering of individuals from history.[206]

Yet the entries for Clifford, De Bregy and Henrietta of Bourbon do not primarily dwell on pain, nor do they elicit pity. Henrietta stresses the magnitude of her 'vexations and chagrin' but affirms that 'God has been merciful and good in endowing me with sufficient strength'.[207] Clifford expresses a near identical sentiment: 'by a happy genius I overcame all these troubles'.[208] These women show courage and resilience in triumphing over adversity; they are not passive victims but empowered historical agents. They do not think themselves perfect (and nor does Hays), but their quirky, candid prose remains neither confessional nor sentimental so much as analytical. As rational subjects, they appeal to readers' empathy rather than sympathy. If Hays has exemplars in mind in her *Female Biography*, it is tempting to see them in these entries, not so much in the contours of these women's lives but in their ability to understand themselves and communicate this experience in their writing. Through her use of women's self-narratives within selected entries, Hays endorses active reading and suggests the importance of writing as a means of understanding history and one's own place in it.

Hays may also use certain subjects to 'intervene' more specifically in her own public narrative, with some entries functioning almost as avatars. Felicity James situates the account of Susanna Perwich, for example, as a 'rewriting' of the original source and 'an act of "autonarration": a version of Hays's own life narrative, and a vindication of her personal life choices'.[209] Here, James applies Tilottama Rajan's concept of 'autonarration', a self-conscious form of life writing in which the author records personal experience within a text, therefore highlighting the relationship between experience and narrative and recognising lives as textually constructed.[210] According to James, by revealing the devout female exemplar of John Batchiler's 1661 obituary as 'cramped, repressed and fatally thwarted', Hays performs a 'sympathetic recovery' of her Dissenting predecessor and a defence of her own decision to 'move into the public sphere'.[211] Hays's 'Mary Wollstonecraft' (1800) may have served as a similar self-vindication three years earlier.[212] As Wallace puts it, 'biography here is in the service of autobiography in the sense of making a "self" rather than merely recording a pre-existing selfhood'.[213]

The entry on Catharine Macaulay (1731–91), one of the most contemporary figures in the collection and one of only a few for which Hays undertook original research,[214] also seems to work as both revisionary commemoration and personal vindication. Hays refuses to focus on Macaulay's much ridiculed second marriage to the twenty-one-year-old William Graham (which is glossed in a single sentence), nor does she name the accusation made in D'Israeli's *Dissertation on Anecdotes* (1793) that Macaulay defaced manuscripts in the course of her research at the British Museum.[215] Instead, Hays alludes to these 'petty and personal scurrilities' as attempts to subdue the 'female historian' who 'seemed to have stepped out of the province of her sex'.[216] Hays deconstructs the attacks on Macaulay: 'Her talents and powers could not be denied; her beauty was therefore called into question'; her 'adversaries' pronounced her 'deformed' and 'unfortunately ugly'.[217] Hays explicitly links this personal slander with the perception that Macaulay's historical writing 'encroach[ed] upon the province of man'.[218] In the remainder of her twenty-page account, Hays emphasises the importance of Macaulay's 'writings', the 'powers of her mind' and her admirable 'character', as attested by her intimate friend, Mrs Arnold, whose testimony is quoted at length.[219] This championing of Macaulay resonates self-reflexively, as Hays's appearance was also mocked to discredit her. Hays suggests that such containment strategies mobilise gender prejudices against women who dare to contend with men as intellectual equals. Like her writing on Wollstonecraft and portrayal of Mary Raymond in *Victim of Prejudice*, the biography of Macaulay thus doubles as self-defence.

Ironically, the Reviews manifested exactly the kind of gendered response that Hays explodes in her Macaulay entry and that she herself had experienced previously. The *London Review* criticises Macaulay for 'inconsistency of character, both as an historian and a woman', and Hays for 'sacrific[ing] her own judgment to the partial communications of a warm female friend of the late Mrs. C. M. Graham'.[220] Through phrases like 'as a woman', 'her own judgment' and 'female friend', this reviewer emphasises the gender of the subject, source and scribe in order to interrogate the reliability of the account. The *Critical* reviewer likewise questions Hays's 'biographical fidelity', complaining about the omission of Macaulay's age and of the dates of her marriages and calling the entry a 'panegyric' that is 'worked up *con amore*'.[221] Though the reviewers may not have read the Macaulay entry as a direct avatar for Hays, they resisted its progressive thrust.

Still, criticism of *Female Biography* was mixed with praise, with reviewers disapproving of Hays's principles of selection and unorthodox characterisation but highlighting the merits of the collection as a whole. Despite its concerns about the Macaulay entry, for example, the *Critical Review* reprinted a six-page excerpt from it (which took up the bulk of the essay's ten pages) and hailed *Female Biography* as 'copious in entertainment', though unsuccessful in its 'higher purposes'.[222] The *Monthly* reviewer wished the 'vicious and defective traits of several females … more shaded' and thought 'some of the lives … might have been as well omitted'.[223] The *London Review* expressed similar reservations about 'mixing dross with sterling ore' but stressed 'the high esteem in which we hold the work, independent of the defects'.[224] That the *London Review* devoted three separate essays to *Female Biography* suggests the respect it accorded to Hays's text. The *Monthly Register* also endorsed the collection, but not before raising objections to its radical undertones: 'something *lurks at the bottom of this*; we are reasonably in dread of this *champion of woman kind*; we are afraid, lest we find in Mrs. Hays another Mrs. Woolstonecroft [sic]'.[225] Spongberg has suggested that *Female Biography* was poorly reviewed, but on balance, it seems fairer to say that the reviews were mixed.[226]

## Respect and 'retirement'

Moreover, *Female Biography* was, by many other standards, a resounding success. It was reprinted in the United States in 1807 and widely reviewed in the United States, the United Kingdom and France.[227] Anecdotal evidence suggests that it was read and recommended as an educational text for girls at home and in schools. It also netted a sizeable financial profit[228] and led to further historical writing for Hays published by Phillips.[229] It may even have helped to repair the damage to Hays's reputation that followed the sensational *Emma Courtney* and its best-selling send-up *Memoirs of Modern Philosophers*. In an 1805 letter, Crabb Robinson reflects on his friend's situation and status two years after the publication of *Female Biography*:

> Miss Hays lives in retirement, an highly respected character. She pursues literature as a profession; she does not estimate her productions above their value; she is content to be a useful writer and does not lose feminine excellence and virtues while she seeks literary fame.[230]

This description suggests an esteemed writer who has learned to balance the pursuit of 'literary fame' with the management of her public 'character'. It is true that Hays did not maintain the visibility she had in the 1790s: Crabb Robinson describes her in 1819, for example, as 'one of the minor *literati* of that generation, now forgotten'.[231] Yet she continued writing for nearly two decades after *Female Biography*, publishing *Memoirs of Queens, Illustrious and Celebrated* (1821) at the age of sixty-two. Though this collection was once dismissed as 'a sanitised abridgement of *Female Biography*',[232] research now suggests that Hays added at least twenty-eight new subjects, including Queen Caroline, wife of George IV (the obvious selling point of the volume) as well as Catherine Parr; Margaret, Queen of Scotland; and several non-Western figures.[233] Walker argues that *Memoirs of Queens* demonstrates the ongoing 'optimism of [Hays's] Unitarian convictions', her continued investment in women's 'political participation' and her innovative use of sources.[234] However, further work is needed to situate this text within contemporary debates about royal lives, politics and the position of women.

Timothy Whelan's genealogical and archival research clarifies, moreover, that Hays may have lived in 'retirement' but never in isolation or poverty.[235] Until her death in 1843, she remained an active participant in the religious, literary and family circles in which she had long mixed. During the second half of her life, as before, she often lived with or near relations and enjoyed warm relationships with them. During at least two separate periods, she helped to educate her nieces. While at Park Street, Islington, in 1806–10, she lived near her sisters Sarah and Elizabeth and taught the daughters of her older sister Joanna (who had died in 1805) and John Dunkin; while living with the family of her younger brother, John Hays, at 11 Grosvenor Place, Camberwell, in 1832–39, she taught his daughter, her precocious namesake Matilda Mary Hays.[236] The longstanding emphasis on Hays's writing of the 1790s and the lack of scholarly attention (and incomplete access) to her life and work after 1800 have fostered a mistaken impression that Hays descended into straitened conditions, became a loner and vanished into obscurity. Marilyn L. Brooks's *Oxford Dictionary of National Biography* entry, for instance, perpetuates this interpretation of Hays: 'Towards the end of her life she confessed to Henry Crabb Robinson that "I have done with systems. I am a complete and indifferent skeptic"'.[237] It is misleading to suggest that a letter written in 1802 represents Hays's feelings 'toward the end of her life' given that she lived for another four decades. It would be more accurate to see her frustrations here as coming at the 'end' of a very difficult and tumultuous period – or at the beginning of a new one. Whelan has challenged the narrative about Hays's 'buried life' and suggests that full access to Hays's correspondence with Crabb Robinson (of which only seven out of 170 letters have been published) will be invaluable in re-examining perceptions of Hays's mature years.

Furthermore, there is evidence that Hays's *Female Biography* had a lasting – if not yet fully documented – influence on nineteenth-century women writers.[238] Despite Lucy Aikin's ostensible disdain for Hays's methods, Mary Spongberg suggests that her *Epistles on Women* (1810) overlaps substantially with *Female Biography*. Lady Elizabeth Austen Knight, Jane Austen's sister-in-law, received a copy of *Female Biography* in 1807, and it is likely that Austen consulted it in her visits to her brother Edward at Godmersham, where she composed and edited her novels.[239] Mary Shelley also knew and respected Hays's work,[240] as did Victorian writers such as Elizabeth Gaskell.[241] For Walker, Mary Hays's writing anticipates that of Gaskell, Harriet Martineau and George Eliot, supplying a 'missing link' between Enlightenment feminism and the women's movement that emerged in the nineteenth century.[242]

Hays's legacy can also be seen in the life, writing and activism of her niece, Matilda Mary Hays (1820–97), whom she mentored both textually and personally.[243] Between the ages of twelve and nineteen, Matilda Mary was taught by her aunt. During these seven years, Hays lived in Camberwell with her brother John and his three children, and even after she moved into her own lodgings in 1840, she visited John's family and wrote to Matilda Mary frequently. Hays enjoyed strong relationships with the children of all her siblings, but Matilda Mary was her favourite.[244] Her teaching seems to have inspired Matilda Mary, who by the age of eighteen (while Hays was still living with and educating her) had decided to take up her pen in service of the advancement of women.[245] Like her aunt, Matilda Mary worked in various genres, contributing to periodicals, writing fiction and translating into English the oeuvre of George Sand, the pseudonym of the scandalous contemporary French novelist and memoirist Amantine-Lucile-Aurore Dupin. Just three years after Mary Hays died, Matilda Mary published her first novel, *Helen Stanley* (1846), and the next year she edited and translated the six-volume *Works of George Sand* (1847). She later published a partly autobiographical novel titled *Adrienne Hope:The Story of a Life* (1866).

Matilda Mary's aims for *The Works of George Sand* resemble Hays's for *Female Biography*. An 1845 'Advertisement' for the former explains the translator's desire 'to afford an opportunity for readers of all classes to judge for themselves, whether the productions of the greatest female genius of the day are deserving of the condemnations … or whether the time has not come when an unmerited stigma … should be removed'.[246] Like her aunt, Matilda Mary seeks to widen access to Sand's progressive writing and to rescue the reputation of her French contemporary from rumour and 'stigma'. Though Hays does not frame *Female Biography* in such explicit terms, the overlap in their goals is evident. Moreover, in her 'Introduction' to Volume I, written in December 1846, Matilda Mary praises Sand for her lifelike pictures of 'human nature', which include 'good in evil, and evil in seeming good'.[247] Both niece and aunt favour realistic, three-dimensional accounts of women because they allow the reader to draw her own conclusions.

Matilda Mary also, like her aunt, values life writing for its intellectual, affective and political potential. Volume VI of *The Works of George Sand* contains Sand's memoir, *Letters of a Traveller* (translated by Edmund Larken and edited by Hays), along with three important paratexts: a brief 'Advertisement' by Matilda Mary, an 'Introduction' by the Italian revolutionary writer and politician Giuseppe Mazzini and a translation of the original 'Preface' by Sand.[248] Matilda Mary's 'Advertisement' reiterates her desire to restore Sand to her rightful public status as one of 'the noblest social reformers of the age'.[249] Mazzini echoes this endorsement, linking Sand's memoir to the fight for '*progress*'.[250] Mazzini refers explicitly here to the political resonance of Sand's writing. Yet his introduction suggests a personal response to the 'secret biography of a powerful intelligence' which is 'the most attaching to the heart, and … the most important for the intellect'.[251] Comparing Sand's memoir to Rousseau's *Reveries of a Solitary Walker* (c. 1776–78), Mazzini situates emotional engagement with life writing as integral to its effectiveness in promoting 'progress'.

But it is Matilda Mary's translation of Sand's own 'Preface' that recalls *Female Biography* most clearly. Sand reflects explicitly on the dialogic function of life writing:

> My soul, I am sure, has served as a mirror to many who have cast their eyes upon it. … seeing so much weakness, so much terror, irresolution, mobility, humiliated pride and powerless strength, they cry out that I am an invalid, a fool, an exceptional case, a prodigy of pride and scepticism. No, no, I am like yourselves, ye men of bad faith; I only differ from you in not denying the evil.[252]

Like Henrietta of Bourbon, Countess de Bregy and Ann Clifford, whose self-writing Hays quotes in *Female Biography*, Sand admits her flaws: 'I am not at all surprised at finding myself ignorant, sceptical, sophistical, inconsistent, unjust'.[253] Sand's *Letters* becomes reflective and confessional as well as educational, supplying not only entertainment but also a 'mirror' for the reader's own struggles. Sand emphasises the emotional impact of self-writing which consoles, encourages and instructs readers, thereby allowing them to understand themselves and to act with compassion to others. The

Romantic ideals and radical thrust of Sand's *Letters* are emphasised in the paratexts. Though Matilda Mary does not reference Hays by name, she implicitly invokes her. Both Hays and her niece see the social, political and personal value of life writing in allowing women of different times and places to connect.

Matilda Mary Hays experienced negative press on account of her radicalism and her unorthodox lifestyle, and like her aunt, she experimented with life writing to express and to defend herself. In addition to writing and translating, Matilda Mary worked with Bessie Rayner Parkes and Barbara Leigh Smith to found the feminist *English Woman's Journal* in 1858, the Langham Place offices for which became a centre for the Society for Promoting the Employment of Women and the Victoria Press.[254] Matilda Mary also lived, for a time, with the American actress Charlotte Cushman in a 'female marriage' and later had another lesbian relationship with the poet Adelaide Procter.[255] As one might anticipate, Matilda Mary was attacked satirically in the press. The poem 'Love in a Haze', which appeared in *Punch* and was reprinted in *Littell's Living Age*, mocked Matilda Mary's complaint that 'Woman has no share of the World's work'.[256] Using word play on the homophones 'Haze' and 'Hays', as well as feminine and imperfect rhymes, the first stanza asks: 'What platform will plaze / Miss Matilda M. Hays, / Who considers that women are gabies / If content with a mate / And a home *tete-a-tete*, / Or a room full of babies?'[257] The poem ridicules Matilda Mary as a 'Spinster' with outmoded and un-English ideas. 'Love in a Haze' resembles Hamilton's *Modern Philosophers* in its usage of comic techniques to contain and undermine its target.

Like her aunt, however, Matilda Mary refused to be intimidated, publishing her second novel, *Adrienne Hope* (1866), a few years later. Though the novel contains some autobiographical elements – particularly at the start when the newly married couple travels to Rome and enters into a circle of artists there – it is perhaps more significant in its extended thematic engagement with Mary Hays's *Memoirs of Emma Courtney*. In *Adrienne Hope*, there is an echo of Emma's scandalous offer of herself to Augustus Harley outside of marriage. Matilda Mary's protagonist allows herself to become 'wife' to her beloved – and mother to his child – in a clandestine relationship which may or may not have a legitimate marriage to back it up (an ambiguity which is left open until the end of the novel). *Adrienne Hope* demonstrates what happens when a woman risks a sexual relationship outside the normal parameters of Victorian conventions, putting her faith in a man's promise and staking her happiness and reputation on his honour. The outcome is dire: the child dies, as do both Adrienne and her husband, who ends up committing bigamy. Though sentimental rather than radical in its tone, *Adrienne Hope* continues the critique of women's education, marriage and patriarchal power that had been put forward so passionately in her aunt's novel nearly three-quarters of a century earlier. Though more research is needed to understand the writing and reception of Matilda Mary, her work provides an example of Mary Hays's influence on Victorian women's writing.

## Conclusion

The reform agitation that peaked in the early 1790s was, by the end of that decade, repressed and dispersed, with Britain emerging from William Pitt's Tory administration as a far more conservative country. The defeat of this reform movement, according to Kenneth R. Johnston, 'also registered in the ruined lives and careers of the 1790s reformers' who were punished for their 'political heterodoxy' and 'became Britain's first "lost generation"' of writers.[258] Johnston documents myriad effects of the official or unofficial conflict with the repressive authority of Pitt's government, including death by execution or from the effects of imprisonment; transportation; self-exile; arrest; financial penalty; harassment; psychological damage; silencing of literary production; public ridicule; unexplained silence or disappearance; pseudonymous, anonymous or long-delayed publication; change in choice of literary topics or formal expression; and drastic shifts in or recanting of former opinions. Like Robert Bage, James Montgomery, Elizabeth Fenwick, Anna Barbauld, Joseph Priestley and many others, Hays's authorial career may seem to fit into the narrative of the 'almost famous', those radicals of this 'lost generation' whose reputation and authorial careers never recovered from the injuries suffered at the turn of the nineteenth century.

However, as this chapter has demonstrated, Hays's career can be interpreted differently. It is undeniable that her reputation was dented by the scandal that erupted in the wake of *Emma Courtney* (1796) and that she suffered many effects on Johnston's list, such as harassment, psychological damage and public ridicule. Nonetheless, Hays weathered the storm. Though she left fiction to return to the non-fiction genres with which she had started, she did not abandon her lifelong interest in the education, representation and promotion of women. She went on to publish arguably her most significant text, *Female Biography*, a milestone in life writing, historiography and feminism, in 1803. This epic biographical dictionary shows continuity with her early experiments in life writing, yet its pioneering form allowed Hays to push for political and pedagogical reform as well as to defend herself. It goes without saying that Hays encountered setbacks in the 1790s and that the scope and shape of her later work (like that of all radicals of her day) would have looked different had the reform movements succeeded. Despite the high-profile attacks on Hays in the 1790s, however, her career ironically may not have suffered to the same extent as those of the other radicals mentioned by Johnston. If Hays is considered not only in the context of 1790s radicalism but also within the religious and literary subculture of Rational Dissent, and if equal weight is given to her work and life after 1800, her trajectory seems less broken and more successful. Hays did not achieve the fame of the other women considered in this study, and hers was not a household name in the nineteenth century. However, the impact of her work on that of contemporaries such as Lucy Aikin and Jane Austen, as well as Victorian writers like Gaskell and, especially, her niece Matilda Mary, indicates her significance, both as a pioneer in life writing and a case study in the dynamics of reputation and literary afterlife.

## Notes

1 Mary Hays, *Cursory Remarks on an Enquiry into the Expediency and Propriety of Public or Social Worship*, 2nd edn (London: Thomas Knott, 1792), p. 3.

2 On William Law, see R. K. Webb, 'Religion', in *An Oxford Companion to the Romantic Age: British Culture 1776–1832*, ed. Iain McCalman (Oxford: Oxford University Press, 1999), p. 99.

3   Gina Luria Walker, *Mary Hays (1759–1843):The Growth of a Woman's Mind* (Aldershot: Ashgate, 2006), p. 46.

4   'Cursory Remarks on an Enquiry into the Expediency and Propriety of Public or Social Worship', *Critical Review*, 4 (February 1792), p. 231.

5   E, 'Art. V. Cursory Remarks on an Enquiry into the Expediency and Propriety of Public or Social Worship', *Monthly Review*, 8 (May 1792), p. 36.

6   Barbara Taylor, 'Feminism and Enlightened Religious Discourses: Introduction', in *Women, Gender and Enlightenment*, ed. Sarah Knott and Barbara Taylor (Hampshire: Palgrave Macmillan, 2005), p. 414.

7   Laura Mandell, 'Prayer, Feeling, Action: Anna Barbauld and the Public Worship Controversy', *Studies in Eighteenth Century Culture*, 38:1 (2009), p. 118.

8   William Frend to Mary Hays, 16 April 1792, in *The Correspondence of Mary Hays (1779–1843), British Novelist*, ed. Marilyn L. Brooks (Lewiston, NY: Edwin Mellen Press, 2004), pp. 269–70.

9   Hays, *Cursory Remarks*, pp. 20–1.

10  Gilbert Wakefield to William Frend, qtd in Walker, *The Growth of a Woman's Mind*, p. 51.

11  Gina Luria Walker, '"Energetic Sympathies of Truth and Feeling": Mary Hays and Rational Dissent', *Enlightenment and Dissent*, 26 (2010), p. 266.

12  Mary Waters, '"The First of a New Genus": Mary Wollstonecraft as a Literary Critic and Mentor to Mary Hays', *Eighteenth Century Studies*, 37:3 (2004), p. 424.

13  Mary Wollstonecraft to Mary Hays, 25 November 1792, in *The Correspondence of Mary Hays*, p. 302.

14  Marilyn L. Brooks, *The Correspondence of Mary Hays (1779–1843), British Novelist*, ed. Marilyn L. Brooks (Lewiston, NY: Edwin Mellen, 2004), p. 249; p. 477. See also Walker, '"Energetic Sympathies"', p. 277.

15  Theophilus Lindsey to Mary Hays, 15 April 1793, in *The Correspondence of Mary Hays*, p. 280.

16  Gina Luria Walker, 'Mary Hays (1759–1843): An Enlightened Quest', in *Women, Gender and Enlightenment*, ed. Sarah Knott and Barbara Taylor (Hampshire: Palgrave Macmillan, 2005), p. 501.

17  Walker, *The Growth of a Woman's Mind*, p. 66. Walker, 'Mary Hays (1759–1843): An Enlightened Quest', p. 501. Mary Spongberg identifies *Cursory Remarks* as Hays's first feminist work. See 'Mary Hays and Mary Wollstonecraft and the Evolution of Dissenting Feminism', *Enlightenment and Dissent*, 26 (2010), p. 239.

18  Timothy Whelan, 'Mary Hays, William Godwin, and the Dissenting Tradition of Women's Correspondence', Research Seminar, Queen Mary, University of London, 22 March 2017.

19  Eleanor Ty, *Unsex'd Revolutionaries: Five Women Novelists of the 1790s* (Toronto: University of Toronto Press, 1993), p. 47.

20  Walker, *The Growth of a Woman's Mind*, p. 67.

21  On the politicisation of texts in the 1790s, see Janet Todd, *The Sign of Angellica: Women, Writing and Fiction, 1660–1800* (London: Virago, 1989), p. 224.

22  'Art. IV. Letters and Essays, Moral and Miscellaneous', *English Review*, 22 (October 1793), p. 253; p. 255.

23  *Ibid.*, p. 254; p. 255.

24  'Letters and Essays, Moral and Miscellaneous', *Critical Review*, 8 (August 1793), p. 434.

25  Marilyn Butler, *Romantics, Rebels and Reactionaries: English Literature and Its Background 1760–1830* (Oxford: Oxford University Press, 1981), p. 94.

26  Walker, *The Growth of a Woman's Mind*, p. 74. See D. M., 'Art. LXII.', *Analytical Review*, 16:4 (August 1793), pp. 464–7.

27  'Letters and Essays, Moral and Miscellaneous', *Critical Review*, 8 (August 1793), p. 433.

28  'Art. IV. Letters and Essays, Moral and Miscellaneous', *English Review*, 22 (October 1793), p. 253.

29  Eleanor Ty, 'Introduction', in *Memoirs of Emma Courtney*, ed. Eleanor Ty (Oxford: Oxford University Press, 1996), p. xii.

30  Brooks, *The Correspondence of Mary Hays*, pp. 384–5.

31  Whelan, 'Mary Hays, William Godwin, and the Dissenting Tradition of Women's Correspondence'.

32  Norma Clarke (incorrectly) suggests that Hays met both Wollstonecraft and Joseph Johnson through Godwin. B. P. Pollin implies that Godwin functioned as a gateway to Hays's journalistic work. See Norma Clarke, *The Rise and Fall of the Woman of Letters* (Pimlico: Random House, 2004), p. 328, and B. P. Pollin, 'Mary Hays on Women's Rights in "The Monthly Magazine"', *Études Anglaises*, 24:3 (1971), p. 272.

33  Waters, '"The First of a New Genus"', p. 432.

34  *Ibid.*, p. 425.

35  Pollin, 'Mary Hays on Women's Rights', pp. 276–7. See also Walker, *The Growth of a Woman's Mind*, p. 171.

36  Walker, *The Growth of a Woman's Mind*, p. 171.

37  Whelan, 'Mary Hays, William Godwin, and the Dissenting Tradition of Women's Correspondence'.

38  Brooks, *The Correspondence of Mary Hays*, p. 245.

39  Ty, 'Introduction', pp. xiii–xiv. Ty questions the supposed one-sidedness of the romance.

40  Mary Hays to William Godwin, 6 February 1796, in *The Correspondence of Mary Hays*, p. 430.

41  On literature as therapy, see Todd, *The Sign of Angellica*, p. 252. See also Ty, 'Introduction', p. xv; Spongberg, 'Mary Hays and Mary Wollstonecraft', p. 243.

42  Mary Hays to William Godwin, 11 May 1796, in *The Correspondence of Mary Hays*, p. 457.

43  Mary Hays to William Godwin, 6 February 1796, in *The Correspondence of Mary Hays*, p. 425.

44  Spongberg, 'Mary Hays and Mary Wollstonecraft', p. 245.

45  Mary Hays to William Godwin, 6 February 1796, in *The Correspondence of Mary Hays*, p. 425; p. 425; p. 428.

46  David McCracken, 'Introduction', in *Caleb Williams*, ed. David McCracken (Oxford: Oxford University Press, 1970), p. viii.

47  Mary Hays to William Godwin, 6 February 1796, in *The Correspondence of Mary Hays*, pp. 428–9.

48  Peter Melville Logan, *Nerves & Narratives: A Cultural History of Hysteria in 19th-Century British Prose* (London: University of California Press, 1997), p. 2; p. 67.

49  Mary Hays to William Godwin, 11 May 1796, in *The Correspondence of Mary Hays*, p. 458.

50  Tilottama Rajan, 'Autonarration and Genotext in Mary Hays's "Memoirs of Emma Courtney"', *Studies in Romanticism*, 32:2 (1993), p. 153; p. 159. See also Eleanor Ty, 'Editor's Introduction', in *The Victim of Prejudice*, ed. Eleanor Ty (Toronto: Broadview, 1994), p. ix.

51 See Gina Luria Walker, 'The Invention of Female Biography', *Enlightenment and Dissent*, 29 (2014), p. 92; Spongberg, 'Mary Hays and Mary Wollstonecraft', p. 243; Walker, '"Energetic Sympathies"', p. 271; Walker, *The Growth of a Woman's Mind*, p. 134.

52 Ruth Perry, *Women, Letters, and the Novel* (New York, NY: AMS, 1980), p. 130.

53 *Ibid.*, p. 130.

54 Butler, *Romantics, Rebels and Reactionaries*, p. 37.

55 Lucy Newlyn, *Reading, Writing, and Romanticism: The Anxiety of Reception* (Oxford: Oxford University Press, 2000), p. 320.

56 Hays, *Memoirs of Emma Courtney*, ed. Eleanor Ty (Oxford: Oxford University Press, 1996), p. 4.

57 Vivien Jones, '"The Tyranny of the Passions": Feminism and Heterosexuality in the Fiction of Wollstonecraft and Hays', in *Political Gender: Texts and Contexts*, ed. Sally Ledger, Josephine McDonagh and Jane Spencer (London: Harvester Wheatsheaf, 1994), p. 182.

58 Walker, '"Energetic Sympathies"', p. 279. Although the novel is autobiographical, there is no evidence that Hays offered herself to Frend in the way that Emma does.

59 Tay, 'Art. XV. Memoirs of Emma Courtney', *Monthly Review*, 22 (April 1797), p. 449.

60 'Half-Yearly Retrospect of the State of Domestic Literature', *Monthly Magazine*, 3:12 (January 1797), p. 47.

61 L. M. S., 'Art. XV. Memoirs of Emma Courtney', *Analytical Review*, 25:2 (February 1797), p. 177; p. 178.

62 Tay, 'Art. XV. Memoirs of Emma Courtney', *Monthly Review*, 22 (April 1797), p. 443; p. 449.

63 'Memoirs of Emma Courtney', *Critical Review*, 19 (January 1797), pp. 110–11.

64 'Art. 20. Memoirs of Emma Courtney', *British Critic*, 9 (March 1797), p. 314.

65 Henry Crabb Robinson, *Henry Crabb Robinson: On Books and Their Writers*, ed. Edith J. Morley, 3 vols (London: Dent, 1938), I, p. 5.

66 Wollstonecraft mentions Robinson's reaction to *Emma Courtney* in a letter to Hays: 'She has read your novel, and was <u>very much</u> pleased with the <u>main</u> story.' Mary Wollstonecraft to Mary Hays, [December 1796], in *The Correspondence of Mary Hays*, pp. 309–10. Wollstonecraft's allusion to her own 'privileged peep behind the curtain' confirms her knowledge (and Robinson's ignorance) of the events on which Hays based the story.

67 Amelia Alderson to Mary Wollstonecraft, 15 December 1796, qtd in Walker, *The Growth of a Woman's Mind*, p. 162.

68 Amelia Alderson to William Godwin, 22 December 1796, qtd in Walker, '"Energetic Sympathies"', p. 280.

69 Mary Wollstonecraft to Mary Hays, [early 1797], in *The Correspondence of Mary Hays*, p. 310.

70 Theophilus Lindsey to Rev. John Rowe, 23 December 1796, qtd in Walker, '"Energetic Sympathies"', p. 280. Hays must have been aware of the possibility of such attacks, as she had previously noted that Godwin was often assumed to be an atheist. See Mary Hays to William Godwin, 20 November 1795, in *The Correspondence of Mary Hays*, p. 409.

71 Thomas Holcroft to Mary Hays, 20 September 1797, in *The Correspondence of Mary Hays*, pp. 315–16.

72  Jon Mee, *Romanticism, Enthusiasm, and Regulation: Poetics and the Policing of Culture in the Romantic Period* (Oxford: Oxford University Press, 2003), p. 10.

73  Mee, *Romanticism, Enthusiasm, and Regulation*, p. 15.

74  Hays, *Emma Courtney*, p. 86; p. 97.

75  Mee, *Romanticism, Enthusiasm, and Regulation*, p. 30.

76  Whelan, 'Mary Hays, William Godwin, and the Dissenting Tradition of Women's Correspondence'.

77  Walker, *The Growth of a Woman's Mind*, p. 60.

78  Charles Lamb to Thomas Manning, 8 February 1800, in *The Correspondence of Mary Hays*, p. 326.

79  Robert Southey to Enid Southey, 15 May 1799, in *The Correspondence of Mary Hays*, p. 324; Samuel Taylor Coleridge to Robert Southey, 25 January 1800, in *The Correspondence of Mary Hays*, p. 325. Lloyd was known as a 'dangerous acquaintance' liable to gossip, back-stab, or quarrel, and his behaviour towards Hays fits with private accounts of a man would later suffer from mental illness. See Walker, *The Growth of a Woman's Mind*, p. 199.

80  Robinson, *On Books and Their Writers* I, p. 5.

81  Henry Crabb Robinson to Catherine Clarkson, 23 January 1800, reproduced in Timothy Whelan, 'Mary Hays and Henry Crabb Robinson: Reconstructing a "Female Biography"', Research Seminar, Dr. Williams's Centre for Dissenting Studies, 17 June 2015.

82  *Ibid.*

83  Robinson, *On Books and Their Writers*, I, p. 5.

84  Pollin, 'Mary Hays on Women's Rights', p. 280.

85  R. M. Janes, 'On the Reception of Mary Wollstonecraft's *A Vindication of the Rights of Woman*', *Journal of the History of Ideas*, 39:2 (April–June 1978), p. 297.

86  Walker, *The Growth of a Woman's Mind*, p. 163.

87  Amelia Alderson to Mary Wollstonecraft, 28 August 1796, qtd in Walker, *The Growth of a Woman's Mind*, p. 179; Samuel Taylor Coleridge to Robert Southey, qtd in *The Correspondence of Mary Hays*, p. 325.

88  Walker, *The Growth of a Woman's Mind*, p. 161; p. 163. Robinson, *On Books and Their Writers*, I, p. 131.

89  Robinson, *On Books and Their Writers*, I, p. 235.

90  Robert Southey to Joseph Cottle, 13 March 1797, qtd in Walker, *The Growth of a Woman's Mind*, p. 163.

91  Charles Lloyd, *Edmund Oliver*, 2 vols (Oxford: Woodstock Books, 1990), I, pp. 47–8.

92  Richard C. Allen, 'Charles Lloyd, Coleridge, and *Edmund Oliver*', *Studies in Romanticism*, 35:2 (1996), p. 247.

93  M. Ray Adams, 'Mary Hays, Disciple of William Godwin', *PMLA*, 55:2 (1940), p. 481.

94  Lloyd, *Edmund Oliver*, I, pp. vii–x.

95  *Ibid.*, p. 57.

96  Luisa Calè, 'Periodical Personae: Pseudonyms, Authorship and the Imagined Community of Joseph Priestley's *Theological Repository*', *19: Interdisciplinary Studies in the Long Nineteenth Century*, 3 (2006), p. 1, www.19.bbk.ac.uk

97  Ty, *Unsex'd Revolutionaries*, p. 13.

98  Richard Polwhele, *The Unsex'd Females: A Poem, Addressed to the Author of the Pursuits of Literature* (London: Cadell and Davies, 1798), l, p. 12.

99  *Ibid.*, ll, pp. 103–4.

100 'The Reviewers Reviewed', *Anti-Jacobin Review*, 3:11 (May 1799), p. 55.

101 *Ibid.*, p. 56.

102 *Ibid.*, p. 58.

103 *Ibid.*, p. 57.

104 Elizabeth Hamilton, *Memoirs of Modern Philosophers*, ed. Claire Grogan (Hertfordshire: Broadview, 2000), p. 40; p. 47; p. 72; p. 101.

105 Ty, *Unsex'd Revolutionaries*, pp. 26–7.

106 Hamilton, *Modern Philosophers*, p. 272.

107 On Bridgetina's diseased reading practices, see Katherine Binhammer, 'The Persistence of Reading: Governing Female Novel-Reading in Memoirs of Emma Courtney and Memoirs of Modern Philosophers', *Eighteenth-Century Life*, 27:2 (2003), p. 17.

108 Claire Grogan, 'Introduction', in *Memoirs of Modern Philosophers*, ed. Claire Grogan (Hertfordshire: Broadview, 2000), p. 17.

109 Hamilton, *Modern Philosophers*, p. 385.

110 *Ibid.*, p. 364.

111 *Ibid.*, p. 36. Their unsteady personal relationship also undercuts Hamilton's statement. The two women had been friends until Hamilton took offence at a harsh 1796 *Analytical* review of Hamilton's first novel written by Hays. See Walker, *The Growth of a Woman's Mind*, pp. 173–4.

112 Ty, *Unsex'd Revolutionaries*, p. 45.

113 Mary Hays, *The Victim of Prejudice*, ed. Eleanor Ty (Hertfordshire: Broadview, 1994), p. 131.

114 *Ibid.*, p. 52.

115 Jean-Jacques Rousseau, 'Duties of Women', in *The Portable Enlightenment Reader*, ed. Isaac Kramnick (London: Penguin, 1995), p. 575.

116 Robinson, *On Books and Their Writers*, I, p. 5.

117 A Woman, 'Remarks on A.B.'s Strictures on the Talents of Women', *Monthly Magazine*, 2:6 (July 1796), pp. 469–70 (p. 470).

118 Walker, '"Energetic Sympathies"', p. 273.

119 William Godwin, 'Of History and Romance', in *Political and Philosophical Writings of William Godwin*, ed. Mark Philp, 7 vols (London: William Pickering, 1993), V, p. 293.

120 Mary Hays, 'To the Editor of the Monthly Magazine', *Monthly Magazine*, 1:5 (June 1796), pp. 386–7.

121 Harriet Guest, *Women, Learning, Patriotism, 1750–1810* (Chicago, IL: University of Chicago Press, 2000), p. 50.

122 *Ibid.*, p. 59.

123 *Ibid.*, p. 67.

124 Walker, *The Growth of a Woman's Mind*, p. 218.

125 [Mary Hays], 'Memoirs of Mary Wollstonecraft', in *The Annual Necrology for 1797–8* (London: Richard Phillips, 1800), p. 454.

126 Spongberg, 'Mary Hays and Mary Wollstonecraft', p. 250; p. 251; p. 253.

127 Hays, 'Memoirs of Mary Wollstonecraft', p. 455.

128 William Godwin, *Memoirs of the Author of a Vindication of the Rights of Woman*, ed. Pamela Clemit and Gina Luria Walker (Toronto: Broadview, 2001), p. 107.

129 Greg Kucich, 'Women's Historiography and the (Dis)embodiment of Law: Ann Yearsley, Mary Hays, Elizabeth Benger', *Wordsworth Circle*, 33:1 (2002), p. 3.

130 *Ibid.*, p. 3. See also Gary Kelly, 'Romanticism and the Feminist Uses of History', in *Romanticism, History, Historicism: Essays on an Orthodoxy*, ed. Damian Walford

Davies (Abingdon: Routledge, 2009), pp. 163–81; Greg Kucich, 'The History Girls: Charlotte Smith's *History of England* and the Politics of Women's Educational History', in *Rethinking British Romantic History, 1770–1845*, ed. Porscha Fermanis and John Regan (Oxford: Oxford University Press, 2014), pp. 35–53; Miriam Elizabeth Burstein, *Narrating Women's History in Britain, 1770–1902* (Aldershot: Ashgate, 2004).

131  Hays was the only woman who had known and admired Wollstonecraft to defend her publicly. See Harriet Jump, 'Introduction', in *Lives of the Great Romantics III: Godwin, Wollstonecraft & Mary Shelley By Their Contemporaries,* ed. Harriet Jump, 3 vols (London: Pickering & Chatto, 1999), II, p. xv.

132  Walker, '"Energetic Sympathies"', p. 270.

133  Miriam L. Wallace, 'Writing Lives and Gendering History in Mary Hays's *Female Biography* (1803)', in *Romantic Autobiography in England*, ed. Eugene Stelzig (Farnham: Ashgate, 2009), p. 65.

134  Hays, 'To the Editor of the Monthly Magazine', p. 180.

135  Mary Hays, *Female Biography; or, Memoirs of Illustrious and Celebrated Women, Of All Ages and Countries,* 6 vols (London: Richard Phillips, 1803), I, pp. iii–iv.

136  Gina Luria Walker, 'General Introduction', in *Memoirs of Women Writers, Part II,* ed. Gina Luria Walker, 3 vols (London: Pickering and Chatto, 2013), I, p. xii.

137  Gary Kelly, *Women, Writing and Revolution 1790–1827* (Oxford: Clarendon Press, 1993), p. 234; p. 236.

138  Barbara Brandon Schnorrenberg, 'Mary Hays', in *An Encyclopedia of British Women Writers,* ed. Paul Schlueter and June Schlueter (New Brunswick, NJ: Rutgers University Press, 1998), p. 312.

139  Wallace, 'Writing Lives', p. 66.

140  Spongberg, 'Mary Hays and Mary Wollstonecraft', p. 235.

141  Felicity James, 'Writing *Female Biography*: Mary Hays and the Life Writing of Religious Dissent', in *Women's Life Writing, 1700–1850: Gender, Genre and Authorship* (Basingstoke: Palgrave Macmillan, 2012), p. 131.

142  Spongberg, 'Mary Hays and Mary Wollstonecraft', p. 235. Critics such as Wallace and Walker do discuss form.

143  Cynthia Richards, 'Revising History, "Dumbing Down", and Imposing Silence: The Female Biography of Mary Hays', *Eighteenth-Century Women: Studies in Their Lives, Work and Culture,* 3 (2003), p. 270.

144  Though more often considered a conduct book or a pedagogical text, *Letters and Essays* also has auto/biographical elements. See James, 'Writing *Female Biography*', pp. 124–5, for a discussion of 'The Story of Melville and Cecilia' as a portrait of Robert Robinson in the Unitarian minister Theron, and of Hays herself in Cecilia.

145  Jeanne Wood, '"Alphabetically Arranged": Mary Hays's *Female Biography* and the Biographical Dictionary', *Genre,* 31 (1998), p. 118. For Wood, Hays's broad selection of subjects and use of alphabetical arrangement make *Female Biography* a biographical dictionary. I stress its status as a 'reference work' as a way of foregrounding contemporary material engagement with the text. It can also, of course, be considered as a work of historiography, life writing, and/or political intervention.

146  'Preface' to *General Biography* (1800), qtd in Wood, '"Alphabetically Arranged"', p. 121.

147  Richard Yeo, 'Encyclopaedic Collectors: Ephraim Chambers and Sir Hans Sloane', in *Enlightening the British: Knowledge, Discovery and the Museum in the Eighteenth Century,* ed. Robert Geoffrey William Anderson (London: British Museum Press,

2003), p. 31; Richard Yeo, 'Reading Encyclopedias: Science and the Organization of Knowledge in British Dictionaries of Arts and Sciences, 1730–1850', *Isis*, 82:1 (1991), p. 27.

148 Hays knew Andrew Kippis, and many other scholars, writers and educators with an interest in historical biography, through her Unitarian network. See Walker, 'The Invention of Female Biography', p. 92.

149 Elaine Bailey, 'Lexicography of the Feminine: Matilda Betham's *Dictionary of Celebrated Women*', *Philological Quarterly*, 83:4 (2004), p. 396.

150 Samuel Taylor Coleridge, who attacked alphabetical organisation for its inability to direct the order of study, chose this 'rational' arrangement for his *Encyclopedia Metropolitana* (1817–45). The commercial failure of this text derived, in part, from its inability to cater to Romantic-period reading habits. See Yeo, 'Reading Encyclopedias', pp. 38–9.

151 On the *renvois*, see Janie Vanpée, '*La Femme Mode d'Emploi*: How to Read the Article FEMME in the *Encyclopédie*', in *Using the Encyclopédie: Ways of Knowing, Ways of Reading*, ed. Daniel Brewer and Julie Chandler Hayes (Oxford: Voltaire Foundation, 2002).

152 Hays, *Female Biography*, I, p. 173; p. 170.

153 *Ibid.*, p. 173.

154 *Ibid.*, p. 146; p. 147.

155 *Ibid.*, p. 152; p. 156.

156 *Ibid.*, p. 170; p. 172.

157 *Ibid.*, p. 166.

158 *Ibid.*, p. 167.

159 Stephen Werner, 'The *Encyclopédie* "Index"', in *Using the Encyclopédie: Ways of Knowing, Ways of Reading*, ed. Daniel Brewer and Julie Candler Hayes (Oxford: Voltaire Foundation, 2002), p. 266.

160 *Ibid.*, p. 267.

161 Wallace, 'Writing Lives', p. 66; p. 76. Hays's aims (and methodology) link to concerns in *Letters and Essays* (1793) to get young women to read more widely and actively.

162 Hays, *Female Biography*, I, pp. 10–11.

163 *Ibid.*, IV, p. 63.

164 *Ibid.*, p. 62; p. 63.

165 *Ibid.*, I, p. 11; p. 12.

166 *Ibid.*, p. 12.

167 *Ibid.*, p. 11. On the depiction of Agrippina by Hays and Hamilton, see Burstein, *Narrating Women's History*, pp. 69–70.

168 Wallace, 'Writing Lives', p. 74.

169 Kucich, 'The History Girls', p. 44.

170 Margaret J. M. Ezell, *Writing Women's Literary History* (Baltimore, MD and London: Johns Hopkins University Press, 1993), pp. 21–2.

171 Kucich, 'The History Girls', p. 36; p. 46. For more on this shift, see James Chandler, 'History', in *An Oxford Companion to the Romantic Age*, ed. Iain McCalman (Oxford: Oxford University Press, 1999), p. 354, and Anne K. Mellor and Susan J. Wolfson, 'Romanticism, Feminism, History, Historicism: A Conversation', in *Romanticism, History, Historicism*, p. 148.

172 Chandler, 'History', p. 354. See also Kelly, 'Romanticism and the Feminist Uses of History', p. 177.

173 Michael Bentley, *Modern Historiography: An Introduction* (London: Routledge, 1999), p. 26.

174 James, 'Writing *Female Biography*', p. 117.

175 Chambers, qtd in Yeo, 'Reading Encyclopedias', p. 28.

176 Hays, *Female Biography*, VI, p. 371.

177 *Ibid.*, p. 381.

178 *Ibid.*, p. 381.

179 Le Breton, *Memoirs*, p. 126, qtd in Spongberg, 'Mary Hays and Mary Wollstonecraft', p. 236.

180 Jacqueline Pearson, *Women's Reading in Britain, 1750–1835: A Dangerous Recreation* (Cambridge: Cambridge University Press, 1999), p. 51; Mark Salber Phillips, *Society and Sentiment: Genres of Historical Writing in Britain, 1740–1820* (Princeton, NJ: Princeton University Press, 2000), p. 116.

181 Hays, *Female Biography*, I, p. 90; p. 91.

182 *Ibid.*, III, p. 433.

183 *Ibid.*, IV, p. 439.

184 *Ibid.*, VI, p. 456.

185 Wallace similarly identifies recurring 'patterns' that appear in *Female Biography*, though she is most interested in the entries that 'undercut the concept of "biography"' by becoming '*composite* biography'. See 'Writing Lives', pp. 74–5.

186 Wallace, 'Writing Lives', p. 73.

187 Greg Kucich, 'Romanticism and Feminist Historiography', *The Wordsworth Circle*, 24 (1993), p. 137; Greg Kucich, '"This Horrid Theatre of Human Sufferings": Gendering the Stages of History in CM and PBS', in *Lessons of Romanticism: A Critical Companion*, ed. Thomas Pfau and Robert F. Gleckner (Durham, NC and London: Duke University Press, 1998), p. 453.

188 Though Kelly only mentions Hays in passing, his wider argument is relevant here. See 'Romanticism and the Feminist Uses of History', p. 177.

189 Walker, 'General Introduction', p. xxiv.

190 Mary Spongberg, *Writing Women's History Since the Renaissance* (Basingstoke: Palgrave Macmillan, 2002), p. 180; Arianne Chernock, 'Gender and the Politics of Exceptionalism in the Writing of British Women's History', in *Making Women's Histories: Beyond National Perspectives*, ed. Pamela S. Nadell and Kate Haulman (New York, NY and London: New York University Press, 2013), p. 127.

191 Wallace, 'Writing Lives', p. 70; Spongberg, *Writing Women's History*, p. 118.

192 Hays, *Female Biography*, I, pp. 233–4.

193 *Ibid.*, II, pp. 48–9.

194 *Ibid.*, III, p. 396.

195 *Ibid.*, p. 396.

196 *Ibid.*, I, p. 234; p. 236.

197 *Ibid.*, II, p. 48; *Ibid.*, III, p. 395.

198 *Ibid.*, I, p. 233.

199 *Ibid.*, II, pp. 47–8.

200 Spongberg, *Writing Women's History*, p. 118.

201 Phillips, *Society and Sentiment*, p. 26.

202 *Ibid.*, p. 26.

203 *Ibid.*, p. 98. See also Kucich, 'The History Girls'.

204 Phillips, *Society and Sentiment*, p. 23.

205 Kucich, 'Women's Historiography', p. 4.

206  Kucich, 'The History Girls', p. 45.

207  Hays, *Female Biography*, I, p. 236.

208  *Ibid.*, III, p. 397.

209  James, 'Writing *Female Biography*', p. 131.

210  Rajan, 'Autonarration and Genotext in Mary Hays's', p. 160; p. 175.

211  James, 'Writing *Female Biography*', p. 131.

212  Walker, 'Mary Hays (1759–1843): An Enlightened Quest' p. 507.

213  Wallace, 'Writing Lives', p. 76.

214  Walker, 'General Introduction', p. xxiv.

215  Devoney Looser, *Women Writers and Old Age in Great Britain, 1750–1850* (Baltimore, MD: Johns Hopkins University Press, 2008), p. 71.

216  Hays, *Female Biography*, V, p. 292.

217  *Ibid.*, p. 292.

218  *Ibid.*, p. 292.

219  *Ibid.*, p. 287; p. 294.

220  M, 'Female Biography', *European Magazine & London Review*, 44 (August 1803), p. 118.

221  'Art. VII. Female Biography', *Critical Review*, 37 (April 1803), p. 418; p. 424.

222  *Ibid.*, p. 424.

223  ManS, 'Art. 12. Female Biography', *Monthly Review*, 43 (January 1803), p. 93; p. 92.

224  'Female Biography', *London Review*, 43 (June 1803), p. 451.

225  'Female Biography', *Monthly Register*, 2:11 (March 1803), p. 418, italics in original. The *Monthly Register* plainly endorses *Female Biography*: 'we recommend it to our readers' (418).

226  Spongberg claims *Female Biography* was 'not well reviewed, perhaps because it moved so boldly beyond the women worthies model'. See 'Female Biography', in *Companion to Women's Historical Writing*, ed. Mary Spongberg, Barbara Caine and Ann Curthoys (Basingstoke: Palgrave Macmillan, 2005), pp. 179–80. In her entry on Mary Hays in the same volume, she suggests *Female Biography* was 'tepidly reviewed'. See 'Hays, Mary 1760–1840', in *Companion to Women's Historical Writing*, pp. 237–8. I find both of these statements misleading.

227  Walker, '"Energetic Sympathies"', p. 283.

228  *Ibid.*, p. 283. Hays was able to buy herself a house with the proceeds.

229  Kucich, 'The History Girls', pp. 46–7.

230  Robinson, *On Books and Their Writers*, III, p. 843.

231  *Ibid.*, I, p. 235.

232  Spongberg, 'Hays, Mary 1760–1843', p. 238.

233  Walker, 'The Invention of Female Biography', p. 120.

234  *Ibid.*, p. 121.

235  Whelan, 'Mary Hays, William Godwin, and the Dissenting Tradition of Women's Correspondence'. Whelan has documented Hays's places of residence between 1759 and 1843. He argues that the size, neighbourhood and company of these residences suggest that Hays did not need to write for money, and that she maintained an active social life (often living with or near friends and family). I follow Whelan in contesting Spongberg's assertion that Hays retired from public life after the poor reception of *Female Biography*. Hays continued to write history, publishing works for children such as the third volume of Charlotte Smith's *History of England* (1806).

236  Whelan, 'Mary Hays, William Godwin, and the Dissenting Tradition of Women's Correspondence'.

237 Marilyn L. Brooks, 'Hays, Mary (1759–1843)', in *Oxford Dictionary of National Biography* (Oxford: Oxford University Press, 2004), http://www.oxforddnb.com/view/article/37525 (accessed 27 March 2015).

238 Both James ('Writing *Female Biography*', p. 131) and Walker ('"Energetic Sympathies"', p. 283) make this point.

239 Walker, '"Energetic Sympathies"', p. 283.

240 *Ibid.*, p. 283.

241 See Walker, *The Growth of a Woman's Mind*, p. 236.

242 Walker, '"Energetic Sympathies"', p. 285. James suggests that Hays's later work, particularly *Female Biography*, makes up this 'link' and emphasises that Victorian authors remember Hays primarily as a biographer. See James, 'Writing *Female Biography*', p. 132.

243 On Hays's idea of mentorship as an intellectual and affective relationship, see Margaret Kathryn Sloan, 'Mothers, Marys, and Reforming "The Rising Generation": Mary Wollstonecraft and Mary Hays', in *Mentoring in Eighteenth-Century British Literature and Culture*, ed. Anthony W. Lee (Farnham: Ashgate, 2010), p. 225.

244 See Edmund Kell, qtd in *The Idea of Being Free: A Mary Hays Reader*, ed. Gina Luria Walker (Plymouth: Broadview, 2006), p. 307.

245 Lisa Merrill, 'Hays, Matilda Mary (1820?–1897)', *Oxford Dictionary of National Biography* (Oxford: Oxford University Press, 2004), www.oxforddnb.com/view/article/57829 (accessed 10 April 2018).

246 'Advertisement: "English Edition of George Sand's Works"', *Publishers' Circular and Booksellers' Record* (15 December 1845), p. 388.

247 Matilda M. Hays, 'Introduction', in *The Works of George Sand*, 6 vols (London: Churton, 1847), I, n.p.

248 There is also a fourth paratext: Elizabeth Barrett Browning's lines, 'To George Sand', which celebrate the French author's 'woman-heart'.

249 Matilda M. Hays, 'Advertisement', in *The Works of George Sand*, VI, n.p.

250 Mazzini, 'Introduction', in *The Works of George Sand*, VI, pp. 6–7, italics in original.

251 *Ibid.*, p. 5.

252 George Sand, 'Preface', *Letters of a Traveller*, in *The Works of George Sand*, VI, p. 17.

253 *Ibid.*, p. 19.

254 Merrill, 'Hays, Mary Matilda'.

255 Elizabeth Barrett Browning, qtd in Merrill, 'Hays, Matilda Mary'.

256 'Love in a Haze', *Littell's Living Age*, 73 (April, May, June 1862), p. 632.

257 *Ibid.*, p. 632.

258 Kenneth R. Johnston, 'Whose History? My Place or Yours?', in *Romanticism, History, Historicism*, p. 88.

# Coda: Virginia Woolf's *Common Reader* essays and the legacy of women's life writing

ALTHOUGH VIRGINIA WOOLF OCCUPIES a longstanding and uncontested place in the canon of British novelists, her reception as a writer of non-fiction has been more precarious. Like Mary Wollstonecraft and countless other women of the long nineteenth century who cut their writing teeth on the anonymous pages of the periodical press, Woolf the essayist, both in her lifetime and afterwards, underwent periods of obscurity, fame and critical neglect. [1] Recent interest in her non-fiction oeuvre has meant increased attention to her *Common Reader* collections, published in 1925 and 1932, but these volumes have rarely been classed as life writing or interpreted as such. [2] Yet it is in these essays, even more than in her *Diary* proper, that Woolf not only reads and reflects on a range of life writing but also devises her own hybrid subgenre: a mixture of literary criticism, biographical sketch and personal response. Woolf herself originally referred to this material as her 'Reading book', and Hermione Lee argues that the *Common Reader* comprises 'the autobiography of a reader'. [3] In fact, the *Common Reader* essays are as concerned with biography as autobiography, with writing as reading, with recalling the literary past as inhabiting its present. Woolf's essays offer a perfect opportunity to draw some conclusions about women's life writing in the long nineteenth century, in its literary, historical and generic dimensions.

Like Samuel Johnson, whose 'common reader' she borrows for the title and central figure of these volumes, Woolf sees reading as a conversation that takes place between author and audience across time and space. For Woolf, a book becomes 'a dangerous & exciting game, which it takes two to play at',[4] and reading becomes an endeavour as active, expressive and interpretive as writing. Woolf emphasises reading as a symbiotic process in which reader and writer are 'twins indeed, one dying if the other dies, one flourishing if the other flourishes' and suggests that 'the fate of literature depends upon their happy alliance'.[5] Throughout the *Common Reader* collections, Woolf forges this dialogic 'alliance' with writers of the past, both male and female, canonical and non-canonical. As she ruminates on their novels, poems and personal documents, Woolf immerses herself in their fictional or historical worlds and visualises their writing processes. She also evaluates their writing, comparing it with other works of its kind. Throughout, she features reading – like writing – as an experience at once cerebral, tactile and emotional.

Woolf's connection with authors of the past is often most palpable, however, when she engages with what critics call emergent, non-literary or genre-breaking forms, such as diaries, memoirs and letters.[6] For Woolf, life writing of these kinds remains significant for two main, yet paradoxical, reasons. On the one hand, these texts invite us to enter into the world and thoughts of another person, to be transported to another historical time and place. In 'Dorothy Osborne's "Letters"', for example, Woolf relishes the playful and intimate 'record of life' that allows her not only to 'picture' Dorothy Osborne 'in [her] mind's eye' but to take 'a seat in the depths of Dorothy's mind,     at the heart of the pageant which unfolds itself'.[7] Woolf likewise praises the 'prosaic precision' of Dorothy Wordsworth's journals, which gradually 'unfurl in the mind and open a whole landscape before us' so that 'if we look exactly along the line that it points we shall see precisely what she saw'.[8] In these instances, Woolf's reading is powered by curiosity and interest, and her imaginative engagement with the texts allows her almost to merge with the authors. The 'truthful' and 'descriptive' detail of these works is key.

On the other hand, though, Woolf also delights in life writing precisely because of its untruthfulness. In 'Outlines', Woolf praises biographical scrapbooks like *Mary Russell Mitford and her Surroundings* because they 'license mendacity. One cannot believe what Miss Hill says about Miss Mitford, and thus one is free to invent Miss Mitford for oneself'.[9] Similarly, in 'The Lives of the Obscure', as Woolf reads memoirs of 'forgotten worthies', she explains:

> It is so difficult to keep, as we must with highly authenticated people, strictly to the facts. It is so difficult to refrain from making scenes which, if the past could be recalled, might perhaps be found lacking in accuracy. … Certain scenes have the fascination which belongs rather to the abundance of fiction than to the sobriety of fact.[10]

Works that mask, omit or tell only partial truths hold a 'fascination' for Woolf, sparking her curiosity and giving her room to exercise her own faculties of invention. Instead of being subsumed into the worldview of the writer, these texts invite a creative, yet still sympathetic, imagination of the past. As Hermione Lee suggests, Woolf figures reading as 'a curious mixture of association, memory, dreaming and responsiveness'.[11] Ultimately, reading life writing involves two equally important, if opposite, processes: a dissolution of individual identity, and an affirmation of it.[12]

These processes might be said to exist in the reading of any kind of text, but they are especially important for Woolf with respect to life writing. In her discussion of the *Memoirs of Mrs Pilkington*, Woolf stresses that she likes 'romantically to feel [herself] a deliverer advancing with lights across the waste of years to the rescue of some stranded ghost – a Mrs Pilkington, a Reverend Henry Elman, a Mrs Ann Gilbert'.[13] She envisages Laetitia Pilkington as a 'cross between Moll Flanders and Lady Ritchie', a woman who nevertheless belongs 'in the great tradition of English women of letters'.[14] Her reading of Pilkington therefore functions as an act of empathic personal 'communication' but also as one of literary recovery. According to Juliet Dusinberre, Woolf 'searches the past in order to discover a tradition [to which] she and other women might belong, of common readers and common writers'.[15] In this tradition, Woolf both explicitly and implicitly places writers of unorthodox genres, many of whom were women. She is especially interested in those texts that 'touch realities denied by accepted forms'.[16] She figures her own emotional, aesthetic and intellectual reactions to these texts, and in doing so places herself in a literary lineage that dates from these earlier writers to herself in the present day and stretches forwards to her future readers as well. Rosenberg has suggested that for Woolf, 'what is needed is a tradition that can give women the dialogue of voices needed to construct their own voices'.[17] Life writing deserves a place in literary history, at least in part because it makes more visible the place of *women* in literary history. Woolf's fascination with life writing comprises an essential aspect of her feminism, which joins gender and genre.

This book has discussed the intersection of women's life writing, reputation and genre formation in the nineteenth century. My chapters have traced the authorial careers of four Romantic women writers and have argued that the publication of life writing proved pivotal in their reception both in their lives and afterwards. In paying attention to a wide range of life writing penned by and about Burney, Wollstonecraft, Robinson and Hays, I have highlighted the mixture of strategic personal revelation and generic innovation that makes these texts significant in literary as well as aesthetic terms. In each chapter I have offered a new model for understanding the careers and legacies of these women, and I have suggested the significant, complex and often surprising effects of their life writing within these trajectories. My arguments have been built on the analysis of the life writing itself but also on the myriad nineteenth-century responses to these women and their lives (across forms as diverse as periodical essays, satirical fiction, collective biographies, private letters, commissioned memoirs, poetry and illustrated adaptations) and on quantitative indicators of reception and authorial status (print runs, publishing patterns, sales figures and prices, for example). Throughout the book, I have used this mixture of qualitative and quantitative sources to gauge reputation. However, as I mentioned in my introduction, a reputation remains a slippery thing, dependent on the opinions of other people about a writer rather than on any intrinsic quality of that writer or her work. Reputations vary over time, and can not only be made or broken, but made over, repaired or reformed. They are complex, changing and sometimes contradictory. This is because they comprise not only moral and literary judgements but also affective responses. Ultimately, an individual's reputation rests on how other people *feel* about that person.

Burney, Wollstonecraft, Robinson and Hays understood this, and so did Woolf. This fact should come as no surprise given that so many of Woolf's critical approaches derive from her encounter with the eighteenth century.[18] Echoing Johnson's notion of the common reader, Woolf advocated (and everywhere in the *Common Reader* essays performed) a model of reading which proceeds via the certainty of individual feeling: 'by the common sense of readers, uncorrupted by literary prejudices, after all the refinements of subtilty and the dogmatism of learning, must be finally decided all claim to poetical honours'.[19] Woolf was interested in the effects of books on readers' feelings, and she assigned literary value to those works which continue to evoke a response from readers over time. Yet she understood that books make readers as much as readers make books.[20] In 'The Patron and the Crocus', she emphasises that the author must know – or anticipate – the audience for whom she writes.

This proleptic quality, moreover, is not confined to works traditionally deemed as high literature, for Woolf recognises it even in those life writings which are meant to be artless and/or 'private'. Frances Burney, Woolf acknowledges, was acutely aware of the potential for 'indiscretion' in keeping a diary, and Pilkington's *Memoirs* show her 'wish to entertain' as well as 'to conceal'.[21] Woolf stresses that Dorothy Osborne, 'without admitting it', likewise 'took pains with her own writing', and that Constance Hill had several 'considerations' to juggle when she penned her biography of Mary Russell Mitford.[22] Despite professing that *Mary Russell Mitford and her Surroundings* 'is not a good book', Woolf finds 'something plausible and even ingenious in her approaches'.[23] Woolf's language suggests that she finds these writers of diaries, scrapbooks, memoirs and biographies shrewd and effective in anticipating their effects on future readers.

Andrew Bennett, as we saw in the Introduction, has suggested that this fascination with and desire for a future audience remains 'a specifically masculine phenomenon'.[24] Nonetheless, the life writers discussed in this book seem not only to have engaged later readers emotionally, intellectually and imaginatively, but also, to use Woolf's words, seem to have 'hear[d] [them] coming'.[25] Their texts invite – and shape – active, 'common', empathic readers, though they do so in ways different from works traditionally accorded status as canonical. In the *Common Reader* collections, Woolf's essays on these 'sub-literary' texts sit alongside those on novels, poems and plays already generally accepted as high art. She thus implicitly revises the literary hierarchy, validating innovative representations of female identity and celebrating the new relationships forged between these texts and their readers. Carl Sagan has marvelled at the intersubjective capacity of books:

> What an astonishing thing a book is. It's a flat object made from a tree with flexible parts on which are imprinted lots of funny dark squiggles. But one glance at it and you're inside the mind of another person, maybe somebody dead for thousands of years. Across the millennia, an author is speaking clearly and silently inside your head, directly to you. Writing is perhaps the greatest of human inventions, binding together people who never knew each other, citizens of distant epochs. Books break the shackles of time. A book is proof that humans are capable of working magic.[26]

Woolf understands the democratic nature of this 'magic', that it can and must be worked in different ways, that to ignore any of its past 'citizens' is to shut out some of its present and future 'citizens' as well. Women's life writing marks one strain of this magic that needs to be put back into the nineteenth-century spellbook. Only when we register its reach, variety and complexity can we begin to apprehend the interplay of gender, reputation and cultural value in the long nineteenth century.

## Notes

1 Hermione Lee, 'Virginia Woolf's Essays', in *The Cambridge Companion to Virginia Woolf*, ed. Sue Roe and Susan Sellers (Cambridge: Cambridge University Press, 2000), p. 91.

2 For discussions of these essays as life writing, see Lee, 'Virginia Woolf's Essays', and Morag Shiach, 'On or about December 1930', *Angelaki*, 22:1 (2017), pp. 279–88.

3 Lee, 'Virginia Woolf's Essays', p. 106.

4 Woolf, ms. 189, qtd in Beth Rigel Daugherty, 'Readin', Writin' and Revisin': Virginia Woolf's "How Should One Read a Book"', in *Virginia Woolf and the Essay*, ed. Beth Carole Rosenberg and Jeanne Dubino (Basingstoke: Palgrave Macmillan, 1997), p. 170.

5 Virginia Woolf, 'The Patron and the Crocus', in *The Common Reader*, ed. Andrew McNeillie (London: Vintage, 2003), pp. 208–9.

6 See Juliet Dusinberre, *Virginia Woolf's Renaissance: Woman Reader or Common Reader?* (Basingstoke: Palgrave Macmillan, 1997), p. 16; p. 165; Lee, 'Virginia Woolf's Essays', p. 96.

7 Virginia Woolf, 'Dorothy Osborne's "Letters"', in *The Second Common Reader*, ed. Andrew McNeillie (London: Harcourt, 1986), p. 62.

8 Woolf, 'Four Figures', in *The Second Common Reader*, pp. 166–7.

9 Woolf, 'Outlines', in *The Common Reader*, p. 183.

10 Woolf, 'The Lives of the Obscure', in *The Common Reader*, p. 113.

11 Lee, 'Virginia Woolf's Essays', p. 99.

12 On these opposing processes, see Kate Flint, 'Reading Uncommonly: Virginia Woolf and the Practice of Reading', *The Yearbook of English Studies*, 26 (1996), p. 196.

13 Woolf, 'The Lives of the Obscure', pp. 106–7.

14 *Ibid.*, p. 118.

15 Dusinberre, *Virginia Woolf's Renaissance*, p. 165.

16 Gillian Beer, qtd in Lee, 'Virginia Woolf's Essays', p. 97.

17 Beth Carole Rosenberg, *Virginia Woolf and Samuel Johnson* (New York, NY: St. Martin's Press, 1995), p. 75.

18 *Ibid.*, p. xv.

19 Woolf, 'The Common Reader', in *The Common Reader*, p. 1.

20 Lee, 'Virginia Woolf's Essays', p. 91.

21 Woolf, 'Dr. Burney's Evening Party', in *The Second Common Reader*, p. 108; Woolf, 'The Lives of the Obscure', p. 118.

22 Woolf, 'Dorothy Osborne's "Letters"', p. 61; Woolf, 'Outlines', p. 186.

23 Woolf, 'Outlines', p. 184.

24 *Ibid.*, p. 66.

25 Woolf, 'The Lives of the Obscure', p. 107.

26 Carl Sagan, *Cosmos*, Episode 11: The Persistence of Memory (1980), in A. Malone (Producer and Director) *Cosmos: A Personal Journey*.

# Select bibliography

## Primary sources

Burney, Frances, *Diary and Letters of Madame D'Arblay, 1778–1840*, ed. Charlotte Barrett, rev. Austin Dobson, 6 vols (London: Palgrave Macmillan, 1904)

Burney, Frances, *Early Journals and Letters of Fanny Burney*, ed. Lars E. Troide, 6 vols (Oxford: Oxford University Press; Montreal: McGill-Queen's University Press, 1988)

Burney, Frances, *Evelina*, ed. Edward A. Bloom (Oxford: Oxford University Press, 2002)

Burney, Frances, *The Journals and Letters of Fanny Burney (Madame D'Arblay)*, ed. Joyce Hemlow, 12 vols (Oxford: Clarendon Press, 1984)

Burney, Frances, *Memoirs of Doctor Burney: Arranged from His Own Manuscripts, from Family Papers, and from Personal Recollections*, 3 vols (London: Edward Moxon, 1832)

*The Correspondence of Mary Hays (1779–1843), British Novelist*, ed. Marilyn L. Brooks (Lewiston, NY: Edwin Mellen, 2004)

Godwin, William, *The Enquirer: Reflections on Education, Manners, and Literature* (New York, NY: August M. Kelley, 1965)

Godwin, William, *Memoirs of the Author of A Vindication of the Rights of Woman*, ed. Pamela Clemit and Gina Luria Walker (Toronto: Broadview Press, 2001)

Godwin, William, 'Of History and Romance', in *Political and Philosophical Writings of William Godwin*, ed. Mark Philp, 7 vols (London: William Pickering, 1993), V, pp. 290–301

Hamilton, Elizabeth, *Memoirs of Modern Philosophers*, ed. Claire Grogan (Hertfordshire: Broadview, 2000)

Hays, Mary, *Cursory Remarks on an Enquiry into the Expediency and Propriety of Public or Social Worship: Inscribed to Gilbert Wakefield, as Eusebia*, 2nd edn (London: Thomas Knott, 1792)

Hays, Mary, *Female Biography; or, Memoirs of Illustrious and Celebrated Women, Of All Ages and Countries*, 6 vols (London: Richard Phillips, 1803)

Hays, Mary, *Letters and Essays, Moral and Miscellaneous* (London: Thomas Knott, 1793)

Hays, Mary, *Memoirs of Emma Courtney*, ed. Eleanor Ty (Oxford: Oxford University Press, 1996)

Hays, Mary, 'Memoirs of Mary Wollstonecraft', in *The Annual Necrology for 1797–8* (London: Richard Phillips, 1800), pp. 411–60

Hays, Mary, *Memoirs of Queens, Illustrious and Celebrated* (London: T. and J. Allman, 1821)

*Lives of the Great Romantics III: Godwin, Wollstonecraft & Mary Shelley By Their Contemporaries*, ed. Harriet Jump, 3 vols (London: Pickering & Chatto, 1999)

*Mary Robinson: Selected Poems*, ed. Judith Pascoe (Toronto: Broadview, 2000)

*Mary Wollstonecraft: Political Writings*, ed. Janet Todd (London: William Pickering, 1993)

Paul, Charles Kegan, 'Mary Wollstonecraft. A Vindication', *Fraser's Magazine* (June 1878): 748–62

Paul, Charles Kegan, 'Prefatory Memoir', in *Mary Wollstonecraft: Letters to Imlay* (New York, NY: Haskell House Publishers, 1971), pp. v–lxiii

Paul, Charles Kegan, *William Godwin: His Friends and Contemporaries*, 2 vols (London: Henry S. King, 1876)

Polwhele, Richard, *The Unsex'd Females: A Poem, Addressed to the Author of the Pursuits of Literature* (London: Cadell and Davies, 1798)

*Radical Writing on Women, 1800–1850: An Anthology*, ed. Kathryn Gleadle (Basingstoke: Palgrave Macmillan, 2002)

Robinson, Henry Crabb, *Henry Crabb Robinson: On Books and Their Writers*, ed. Edith J. Morley, 3 vols (London: J. M. Dent & Sons, 1938)

Robinson, Mary, *Memoirs of the Late Mrs. Robinson, Written by Herself, With Some Posthumous Pieces*, 4 vols (London: Richard Phillips, 1801)

Robinson, Mary, *Memoirs of the Late Mrs. Robinson, Written by Herself*, ed. Martin J. Levy (London: Peter Owen, 1994)

Robinson, Mary Elizabeth, *The Wild Wreath* (London: Richard Phillips, 1804)

Wollstonecraft, Mary, *Letters Written During a Short Residence in Sweden, Norway and Denmark*, in *A Short Residence in Sweden & Memoirs of the Author of 'The Rights of Woman'*, ed. Richard Holmes (London: Penguin, 1987), pp. 59–200

Wollstonecraft, Mary, *Mary and the Wrongs of Woman*, ed. Gary Kelly (Oxford: Oxford University Press, 1998)

Wollstonecraft, Mary, *A Vindication of the Rights of Men, in a Letter to the Right Honourable Edmund Burke*, in *Mary Wollstonecraft: Political Writings*, ed. Janet Todd (London: William Pickering, 1993), pp. 1–66

Wollstonecraft, Mary, *A Vindication of the Rights of Woman with Strictures on Political and Moral Subjects*, in *Mary Wollstonecraft: Political Writings*, ed. Janet Todd (London: William Pickering, 1993), pp. 67–296

Woolf, Virginia, *The Common Reader*, ed. Andrew McNeillie (London: Vintage, 2003)

Woolf, Virginia, *The Second Common Reader*, ed. Andrew McNeillie (London: Harcourt, 1986)

## Secondary sources

Asleson, Robyn, 'Introduction', in *Notorious Muse: The Actress in British Art and Culture 1776–1812*, ed. Robyn Asleson (New Haven, CT: Yale University Press, 2003), pp. 1–21

Ayers, Brenda, 'Introduction; or, *What You Will*', in *Biographical Misrepresentations of British Women Writers: A Hall of Mirrors and the Long Nineteenth Century*, ed. Brenda Ayers (Basingstoke: Palgrave Macmillan, 2017), pp. 1–16

Bailey, Elaine, 'Lexicography of the Feminine: Matilda Betham's *Dictionary of Celebrated Women*', *Philological Quarterly*, 83:4 (2004): 389–413

Barchas, Janine, *Graphic Design, Print Culture, and the Eighteenth-Century Novel* (Cambridge: Cambridge University Press, 2003)

Bartolomeo, Joseph F., *A New Species of Criticism: Eighteenth-Century Discourse on the Novel* (London: Associated University Presses, 1994)

Batchelor, Jennie, '"[T]o strike a little out of a road already so much beaten": Gender, Genre, and the Mid-Century Novel', in *The History of British Women's Writing, 1750–1830*, ed. Jacqueline Labbe (Basingstoke: Palgrave Macmillan, 2010), pp. 84–101

Batchelor, Jennie, *Women's Work: Labour, Gender, Authorship, 1750–1830*, (Manchester: Manchester University Press, 2010)

Bennett, Andrew, *Romantic Poets and the Culture of Posterity* (Cambridge: Cambridge University Press, 1999)

Binhammer, Katherine, 'The Persistence of Reading: Governing Female Novel-Reading in Memoirs of Emma Courtney and Memoirs of Modern Philosophers', *Eighteenth-Century Life*, 27:2 (2003): 1–22

Blodgett, Harriet, *Centuries of Female Days: Englishwomen's Private Diaries* (New Brunswick: Rutgers University Press, 1988)

Botting, Eileen Hunt, and Christine Carey, 'Wollstonecraft's Philosophical Impact on Nineteenth-Century American Women's Rights Advocates', *American Journal of Political Science*, 48:4 (2004): 707–22

Bour, Isabelle, 'A New Wollstonecraft: The Reception of the *Vindication of the Rights of Woman* and of *The Wrongs of Woman* in Revolutionary France', *Journal for Eighteenth-Century Studies*, 36:4 (2013): 575–87

Brant, Clare, 'Varieties of Women's Writing', in *Women and Literature in Britain, 1700–1800*, ed. Vivien Jones (Cambridge: Cambridge University Press, 2000), pp. 285–305

Braudy, Leo, *The Frenzy of Renown: Fame & Its History* (Oxford: Oxford University Press, 1986)

Breashears, Caroline, 'The Female Appeal Memoir: Genre and Female Literary Tradition in Eighteenth-Century England', *Modern Philology*, 107:4 (2010): 607–31

Brewer, William D., 'General Introduction', in *The Works of Mary Robinson*, ed. William D. Brewer, 8 vols (London: Pickering & Chatto, 2009), I, pp. xv–xxxi

Brock, Claire, *The Feminization of Fame, 1750–1830* (Basingstoke: Palgrave Macmillan, 2006)

Burstein, Miriam Elizabeth, *Narrating Women's History in Britain, 1770–1902* (Aldershot: Ashgate, 2004)

Butler, Marilyn, 'Introductory Essay', in *Burke, Paine, Godwin, and the Revolution Controversy*, ed. Marilyn Butler (Cambridge: Cambridge University Press, 1984), pp. 1–17

Butler, Marilyn, *Jane Austen and the War of Ideas* (Oxford: Oxford University Press, 1975)

Butler, Marilyn, *Romantics, Rebels and Reactionaries: English Literature and Its Background 1760–1830* (Oxford: Oxford University Press, 1981)

Caine, Barbara, *English Feminism: 1780–1980* (Oxford: Oxford University Press, 1997)

Calé, Luisa, 'Periodical Personae: Pseudonyms, Authorship and the Imagined Community of Joseph Priestley's *Theological Repository*', *19: Interdisciplinary Studies in the Long Nineteenth Century*, 3 (2006): 1–25. http://doi.org/10.16995/ntn.447

Campbell, Gina, 'How to Read Like a Gentleman: Burney's Instructions to Her Critics in *Evelina*', *ELH*, 57 (1990): 557–83

Chaney, Christine, 'The Intimate Familiar: Essay as Autobiography in Romanticism', in *Romantic Autobiography in England*, ed. Eugene Stelzig (Farnham: Ashgate, 2009), pp. 195–209

Chernock, Arianne, 'Gender and the Politics of Exceptionalism in the Writing of British Women's History', in *Making Women's Histories: Beyond National Perspectives*, ed. Pamela S. Nadell and Kate Haulman (New York, NY: New York University Press, 2013), pp. 115–36

Chisholm, Kate, 'The Burney Family', in *The Cambridge Companion to Frances Burney*, ed. Peter Sabor (Cambridge: Cambridge University Press, 2007), pp. 7–22

Civale, Susan, 'The Literary Afterlife of Frances Burney and the Victorian Periodical Press', *Victorian Periodicals Review*, 44:3 (2011): 236–66

Clarke, Norma, *The Rise and Fall of the Woman of Letters* (Pimlico: Random House, 2004)

Clemit, Pamela, and Gina Luria Walker, 'Introduction', in *Memoirs of the Author of A Vindication of the Rights of Woman*, ed. Pamela Clemit and Gina Luria Walker (Toronto: Broadview Press, 2001), pp. 11–36

Cockshut, Anthony O. J., *Truth To Life: The Art of Biography in the Nineteenth Century* (London: Collins, 1974)

Cook, Daniel, 'An Authoress to Be Let: Reading Laetitia Pilkington's *Memoirs*', in *Women's Life Writing, 1700–1850: Gender, Genre and Authorship*, ed. Daniel Cook and Amy Culley (Basingstoke: Palgrave Macmillan, 2012), pp. 39–54

Cook, Daniel, and Amy Culley, 'Introduction', in *Women's Life Writing, 1700–1850: Gender, Genre and Authorship*, ed. Daniel Cook and Amy Culley (Basingstoke: Palgrave Macmillan, 2012), pp. 1–8

Corbett, Mary Jean, *Representing Femininity: Middle-Class Subjectivity in Victorian and Edwardian Women's Autobiographies* (Oxford: Oxford University Press, 1992)

Cross, Ashley, *Mary Robinson and the Genesis of Romanticism: Literary Dialogues and Debts, 1784–1821* (Abingdon: Routledge, 2017)

Crouch, Kimberly, 'The Public Life of Actresses: Prostitutes or Ladies?' in *Gender in Eighteenth-Century England: Roles, Representations, and Responsibilities*, ed. Hannah Barker and Elaine Chalus (London: Longman, 1997), pp. 58–78

Culley, Amy, *British Women's Life Writing, 1760–1840: Friendship, Community, and Collaboration* (Basingstoke: Palgrave Macmillan, 2014)

Curran, Stuart, 'Charlotte Smith, Mary Wollstonecraft, and the Romance of Real Life', in *The History of British Women's Writing, 1750–1830*, ed. Jacqueline Labbe (Basingstoke: Palgrave Macmillan, 2010), pp. 194–206

Curran, Stuart, 'Mary Robinson's *Lyrical Tales* in Context', in *Re-Visioning Romanticism: British Women Writers, 1776–1837*, ed. Carol Shiner Wilson and Joel Haefner (Philadelphia, PA: University of Pennsylvania Press, 1994), pp. 17–35

Darcy, Jane, *Melancholy and Literary Biography, 1640–1816* (Basingstoke: Palgrave Macmillan, 2013)

Davenport, Hester, 'Introduction', in *The Works of Mary Robinson*, ed. William D. Brewer, 8 vols (London: Pickering & Chatto, 2009), VII, pp. xi–xxxiii

Delafield, Catherine, 'Barrett Writing Burney: A Life among the Footnotes', in *Women's Life Writing, 1700–1850: Gender, Genre and Authorship*, ed. Daniel Cook and Amy Culley (Basingstoke: Palgrave Macmillan, 2012), pp. 26–38

Delafield, Catherine, *Women's Diaries as Narrative in the Nineteenth-Century Novel* (Aldershot: Ashgate, 2009)

Demoor, Marysa, *Their Fair Share: Women, Power and Criticism in the Athenaeum, From Millicent Garrett Fawcett to Katherine Mansfield, 1870–1920* (Aldershot: Ashgate, 2000)

Denlinger, Elizabeth Campbell, *Before Victoria: Extraordinary Women of the British Romantic Era* (New York, NY: Columbia University Press, 2005)

Donoghue, Frank, *The Fame Machine: Book Reviewing and Eighteenth-Century Literary Careers* (Stanford, CA: Stanford University Press, 1996)

Doody, Margaret Anne, *Frances Burney: The Life in the Works* (New Brunswick, NJ: Rutgers University Press, 1988)

Dowd, Michelle M., and Julie A. Eckerle, 'Introduction', in *Genre and Women's Life Writing in Early Modern England*, ed. Michelle M. Dowd and Julie A. Eckerle (Aldershot: Ashgate, 2007), pp. 1–14

Dugaw, Dianne, 'General Introduction', in *Memoirs of Scandalous Women*, ed. Dianne Dugaw, 5 vols (London: Pickering & Chatto, 2011), I, pp. xi–xxi

Eckerle, Julie A., 'Prefacing Texts, Authorizing Authors, and Constructing Selves: The Preface as Autobiographical Space', in *Genre and Women's Life Writing in Early Modern England*, ed. Michelle M. Dowd and Julie A. Eckerle (Aldershot: Ashgate, 2007), pp. 97–113

Eckroth, Stephanie, 'Celebrity and Anonymity in the *Monthly Review*'s Notices of Nineteenth-Century Novels', in *Women Writers and the Artifacts of Celebrity in the Long Nineteenth Century*, ed. Ann R. Hawkins and Maura Ives (Aldershot: Ashgate, 2012), pp. 13–32

Engel, Laura, *Fashioning Celebrity: Eighteenth-Century Actresses and Strategies for Image Making* (Columbus, OH: Ohio State University Press, 2011)

Epstein, Julia, *The Iron Pen: Frances Burney and the Politics of Women's Writing* (Madison, WI: University of Wisconsin Press, 1989)

Erickson, Lee, *The Economy of Literary Form: English Literature and Industrialization of Publishing, 1800–1850* (Baltimore, MD: Johns Hopkins University Press, 1996)

Ezell, Margaret J. M., *Writing Women's Literary History* (Baltimore, MD: Johns Hopkins University Press, 1993)

*Fanny Burney: An Annotated Bibliography*, ed. Joseph A. Grau (London: Garland, 1981)

Favret, Mary, *Romantic Correspondence: Women, Politics and the Fiction of Letters* (Cambridge: Cambridge University Press, 1993)

Feldman, Paula, 'Women Poets and Anonymity in the Romantic Era', *New Literary History*, 33:2 (2002): 279–89

Fergus, Jan, and Janice Farrar Thaddeus, 'Women, Publishers, and Money, 1790–1820', *Studies in Eighteenth-Century Culture*, 17 (1987): 191–207

Flint, Christopher, *The Appearance of Print in Eighteenth-Century Fiction* (Cambridge: Cambridge University Press, 2011)

Flint, Christopher, 'The Eighteenth-Century Novel and Print Culture', in *A Companion to the Eighteenth-Century English Novel and Culture*, ed. Paula R. Backscheider and Catherine Ingrassia (Oxford: Blackwell, 2005), pp. 343–64

Flint, Kate, 'Reading Uncommonly: Virginia Woolf and the Practice of Reading', *The Yearbook of English Studies*, 26 (1996): 187–98

Fraser, Hilary, and Daniel Brown, *English Prose of the Nineteenth Century* (London: Addison Wesley Longman, 1996)

Fraser, Hilary, Stephanie Green, and Judith Johnston, *Gender and the Victorian Periodical* (Cambridge: Cambridge University Press, 2003)

Furniss, Tom, 'Mary Wollstonecraft's French Revolution', in *The Cambridge Companion to Mary Wollstonecraft*, ed. Claudia L. Johnson (Cambridge: Cambridge University Press, 2002), pp. 59–81

Gallagher, Catherine, *Nobody's Story: The Vanishing Acts of Women Writers in the Marketplace, 1670—1820* (Oxford: Clarendon Press, 1994)

Gamer, Michael, *Romanticism, Self-Canonization, and the Business of Poetry* (Cambridge: Cambridge University Press, 2017)

Gamer, Michael, and Terry F. Robinson, 'Mary Robinson and the Dramatic Art of the Comeback', *Studies in Romanticism*, 48:2 (2009): 219–56

Garside, Peter, James Raven, and Rainer Schöwerling, *The English Novel 1770–1829: A Bibliographical Survey of Prose Fiction Published in the British Isles*, 2 vols (Oxford: Oxford University Press, 2000)

Genette, Gerard, *Paratexts: Thresholds of Interpretation*, trans. Jane E. Lewin (Cambridge: Cambridge University Press, 1997)

Gordon, Lyndall, *Mary Wollstonecraft: A New Genus* (London: Little Brown, 2005)

Guest, Harriet, *Small Change: Women, Learning, Patriotism, 1750–1810* (Chicago, IL: University of Chicago Press, 2000)

Harman, Claire, *Fanny Burney: A Biography* (London: Flamingo, 2000)

Hemlow, Joyce, *The History of Fanny Burney* (Oxford: Clarendon Press, 1958)

Higgins, David, *Romantic Genius and the Literary Magazine: Biography, Celebrity, Politics* (New York, NY: Routledge, 2005)

Hodson, Jane, *Language and Revolution in Burke, Wollstonecraft, Paine, and Godwin* (Aldershot: Ashgate, 2007)

Holmes, Richard, 'Introduction', in *A Short Residence in Sweden & Memoirs of the Author of 'The Rights of Woman'* (London: Penguin, 1987), pp. 9–55

*The Idea of Being Free: A Mary Hays Reader*, ed. Gina Luria Walker (Plymouth: Broadview, 2006)

Jackson, Heather J., *Those Who Write for Immortality: Romantic Reputations and the Dream of Lasting Fame* (New Haven, CT: Yale University Press, 2015)

James, Felicity, 'Writing *Female Biography*: Mary Hays and the Life Writing of Religious Dissent', in *Women's Life Writing, 1700–1850: Gender, Genre and Authorship*, ed. Daniel Cook and Amy Culley (Basingstoke: Palgrave Macmillan, 2012), pp. 117–32

Janes, R. M., 'On the Reception of Mary Wollstonecraft's *A Vindication of the Rights of Woman*', *Journal of the History of Ideas*, 39:2 (April–June 1978): 293–302

Janowitz, Anne, *Women Romantic Poets: Anna Barbauld and Mary Robinson* (Horndon: Northcote House Publishers, 2004)

Johnson, Claudia, *Equivocal Beings: Politics, Gender and Sentimentality in the 1790s – Wollstonecraft, Radcliffe, Burney, Austen* (Chicago, IL: University of Chicago Press, 1995)

Johnston, Kenneth R., 'Whose History? My Place or Yours?', in *Romanticism, History, Historicism: Essays on an Orthodoxy*, ed. Damian Walford Davies (Abingdon: Routledge, 2009), pp. 79–102

Jones, Vivien, 'Mary Wollstonecraft and the Literature of Advice and Instruction', in *The Cambridge Companion to Mary Wollstonecraft*, ed. Claudia L. Johnson (Cambridge: Cambridge University Press, 2002), pp. 119–40

Jump, Harriet, 'Introduction', in *Lives of the Great Romantics III: Godwin, Wollstonecraft & Mary Shelley By Their Contemporaries*, ed. Harriet Jump, 3 vols (London: Pickering & Chatto, 1999), II, pp. ix–xxiv

Jump, Harriet, 'Introduction', in *Mary Wollstonecraft and the Critics 1788–2001*, ed. Harriet Devine Jump, 2 vols (London: Routledge, 2003), I, pp. 1–20

Jump, Harriet, '"One Cry for Justice": Virginia Woolf Reads Mary Wollstonecraft', in *The Monstrous Debt: Modalities of Romantic Influence in Twentieth-Century Literature*, ed. Damian Walford Davies and Richard Marggraf Turley (Detroit, MI: Wayne State University Press, 2006), pp. 41–60

Justice, George, 'Burney and the Literary Marketplace', in *The Cambridge Companion to Frances Burney*, ed. Peter Sabor (Cambridge: Cambridge University Press, 2007), pp. 147–62

Kaplan, Cora, 'Mary Wollstonecraft's Reception and Legacies', in *The Cambridge Companion to Mary Wollstonecraft*, ed. Claudia Johnson (Cambridge: Cambridge University Press, 2002), pp. 246–70

Keane, Angela, *Women Writers and the English Nation in the 1790s: Romantic Belongings* (Cambridge: Cambridge University Press, 2000)

Keen, Paul, *The Crisis of Literature in the 1790s: Print Culture and the Public Sphere* (Cambridge,: Cambridge University Press, 1999)

Kelly, Gary, *Revolutionary Feminism: The Mind and Career of Mary Wollstonecraft* (Basingstoke: Palgrave Macmillan, 1992)

Kelly, Gary, 'Romanticism and the Feminist Uses of History', in *Romanticism, History, Historicism: Essays on an Orthodoxy*, ed. Damian Walford Davies (Abingdon: Routledge, 2009), pp. 163–81

Kelly, Gary, *Women, Writing and Revolution 1790–1827* (Oxford: Clarendon Press, 1993)

Kittredge, Katharine, 'Introduction', in *Lewd and Notorious: Female Transgression in the Eighteenth Century*, ed. Katharine Kittredge (Ann Arbor, MI: University of Michigan Press, 2003), pp. 1–17

Kucich, Greg, 'The History Girls: Charlotte Smith's *History of England* and the Politics of Women's Educational History', in *Rethinking British Romantic History, 1770–1845*, ed. Porscha Fermanis and John Regan (Oxford: Oxford University Press, 2014), pp. 35–53

Kucich, Greg, '"This Horrid Theatre of Human Sufferings": Gendering the Stages of History in CM and PBS', in *Lessons of Romanticism: A Critical Companion*, ed. Thomas Pfau and Robert F. Gleckner (Durham, NC: Duke University Press, 1998), pp. 448–65

Kucich, Greg, 'Romanticism and Feminist Historiography', *The Wordsworth Circle*, 24 (1993): 133–40

Kucich, Greg, 'Women's Historiography and the (Dis)embodiment of Law: Ann Yearsley, Mary Hays, Elizabeth Benger', *Wordsworth Circle*, 33:1 (2002): 3–7

Kurtz, Rita J., and Jennifer L. Womer, 'The Novel as Political Marker: Women Writers and their Female Audiences in the Hookham and Carpenter Archives, 1791–1798', *Cardiff Corvey*, 13 (2004): 47–65

Labbe, Jacqueline M., 'A Family Romance: Mary Wollstonecraft, Mary Godwin, and Travel', *Genre*, 25 (1992): 211–28

Lamb, Jonathan, *The Evolution of Sympathy in the Long Eighteenth Century* (London: Pickering & Chatto, 2009)

Lee, Hermione, *Body Parts: Essays on Life-Writing* (London: Chatto & Windus, 2005)

Lee, Hermione, 'Virginia Woolf's Essays', in *The Cambridge Companion to Virginia Woolf*, ed. Sue Roe and Susan Sellers (Cambridge: Cambridge University Press, 2000), pp. 91–108

Lejeune, Philippe, 'The Autobiographical Contract', in *French Literary Theory Today: A Reader*, ed. Tzvetan Todorov (Cambridge: Cambridge University Press, 1982), pp. 192–223

Levy, Michelle, *Family Authorship and Romantic Print Culture* (Basingstoke: Palgrave Macmillan, 2008)

Levy, Michelle, 'Women and Print Culture, 1750–1830', in *The History of British Women's Writing, 1750–1830*, ed. Jacqueline M. Labbe (Basingstoke: Palgrave Macmillan, 2010), pp. 29–46

Logan, Peter Melville, *Nerves & Narratives: A Cultural History of Hysteria in 19th-Century British Prose* (London: University of California Press, 1997)

Looser, Devoney, *Women Writers and Old Age in Great Britain, 1750–1850* (Baltimore, MD: Johns Hopkins University Press, 2008)

Marcus, Laura, *Auto/biographical Discourses: Criticism, Theory, Practice* (Manchester: Manchester University Press, 1994)

*Mary Wollstonecraft: An Annotated Bibliography*, ed. Janet Todd (New York, NY: Garland, 1976)

*Mary Wollstonecraft Godwin 1759–1797: A Bibliography of First and Early Editions*, ed. John Windle, 2nd edn, rev. Karma Pippin (New Castle: Oak Knoll Press, 2000)

McDayter, Ghislaine, 'On the Publication of William Godwin's *Memoirs of the Author of a Vindication of the Rights of Woman*, 1798', *BRANCH*, http://www.branchcollective.org/?ps_articles=ghislaine-mcdayter-on-the-publication-of-william-godwins-memoirs-of-the-author-of-a-vindication-of-the-rights-of-woman-1798 (accessed 25 March 2013).

McGann, Jerome, *The Poetics of Sensibility: A Revolution in Literary Style* (Oxford: Clarendon Press, 1996)

McInnes, Andrew, *Wollstonecraft's Ghost: The Fate of the Female Philosopher in the Romantic Period* (London: Routledge, 2017)

McInnes, Andrew, 'Wollstonecraft's Legion: Feminism in Crisis, 1799', *Women's Writing*, 20:4 (2013): 479–95

McLay, Molly, 'From Wollstonecraft to Mill: Varied Positions and Influences of the European and American Women's Rights Movements', *Constructing the Past*, 7:1 (2006): 110–19

Mee, Jon, *Romanticism, Enthusiasm, and Regulation: Poetics and the Policing of Culture in the Romantic Period* (Oxford: Oxford University Press, 2003)

Mellor, Anne K., 'Mary Robinson and the Scripts of Female Sexuality', in *Representations of the Self from the Renaissance to Romanticism*, ed. Patrick Coleman, Jayne Lewis and Jill Kowalik (Cambridge: Cambridge University Press, 2000), pp. 230–59

Mellor, Anne K., 'Mary Wollstonecraft's *A Vindication of the Rights of Woman* and the Women Writers of Her Day', in *The Cambridge Companion to Mary Wollstonecraft*, ed. Claudia L. Johnson (Cambridge: Cambridge University Press, 2002), pp. 141–59

Mellor, Anne K., 'On Romanticism and Feminism', in *Romanticism and Feminism*, ed. Anne K. Mellor (Bloomington, IN: Indiana University Press, 1988), pp. 3–9

Mellor, Anne K., *Romanticism & Gender* (London: Routledge, 1993)

Mole, Tom, *Byron's Romantic Celebrity: Industrial Culture and the Hermeneutic of Intimacy* (Basingstoke: Palgrave Macmillan, 2007)

Mole, Tom, 'Introduction', in *Romanticism and Celebrity Culture, 1750–1850*, ed. Tom Mole (Cambridge: Cambridge University Press, 2009), pp. 1–18

Mole, Tom, 'Mary Robinson's Conflicted Celebrity', in *Romanticism and Celebrity*, ed. Tom Mole (Cambridge: Cambridge University Press, 2009), pp. 186–206

Mole, Tom, *What the Victorians Made of Romanticism: Material Artifacts, Cultural Practices, and Reception History* (Princeton, NJ: Princeton University Press, 2017)

Myers, Mitzi, 'Mary Wollstonecraft's Literary Reviews', in *The Cambridge Companion to Mary Wollstonecraft*, ed. Claudia Johnson (Cambridge: Cambridge University Press, 2002), pp. 82–98

Myers, Mitzi, 'Sensibility and the "Walk of Reason": Mary Wollstonecraft's Literary Reviews as Cultural Critique', in *Sensibility in Transformation: Creative Resistance to Sentiment from the Augustans to the Romantics*, ed. Syndy McMillen Conger London (London: Associated University Presses, 1990), pp. 120–44

Newlyn, Lucy, *Reading, Writing, and Romanticism: The Anxiety of Reception* (Oxford: Oxford University Press, 2000)

Nixon, Cynthia L., '"Stop a Moment at this Preface": The Gendered Paratexts of Fielding, Barker, and Haywood', *Journal of Narrative Theory*, 22:2 (2002): 123–53

Nussbaum, Felicity A., *The Autobiographical Subject: Gender and Ideology in Eighteenth-Century England* (Baltimore, MD: Johns Hopkins University Press, 1989)

Nussbaum, Felicity A., 'Eighteenth-Century Women's Autobiographical Commonplaces', in *The Private Self: Theory and Practice of Women's Autobiographical Writings*, ed. Shari Benstock (London: Routledge, 1988), pp. 147–76

Nyström, Per, *Mary Wollstonecraft's Scandinavian Journey* (Gothenburg: Acts of the Royal Society of Arts and Sciences of Gothenburg, Humaniora No. 17: 1980)

Parisian, Catherine M., *Frances Burney's* Cecilia*: A Publishing History* (Aldershot: Ashgate, 2012)

Parke, Catherine N., 'What Kind of Heroine Is Mary Wollstonecraft?', in *Sensibility in Transformation: Creative Resistance to Sentiment from the Augustans to the Romantics*, ed. Syndy McMillen Conger (London: Associated University Presses, 1990), pp. 103–19

Parker, Mark, *Literary Magazines and British Romanticism* (Cambridge: Cambridge University Press, 2001)

Pascoe, Judith, 'Introduction', in *Mary Robinson: Selected Poems*, ed. Judith Pascoe (Toronto: Broadview, 2000), pp. 19–62

Pascoe, Judith, 'Mary Robinson and the Literary Marketplace', in *Romantic Women Writers: Voices and Countervoices*, ed. Paula R. Feldman and Theresa M. Kelley (Hanover, NE: University Press of New England, 1995), pp. 252–68

Pascoe, Judith, *Romantic Theatricality: Gender, Poetry, and Spectatorship* (Ithaca, NY: Cornell University Press, 1997)

Pearson, Jacqueline, 'Mothering the Novel: Frances Burney and the Next Generation of Women Novelists', *Corvey CW3 Journal*, 1 (2004), https://www2.shu.ac.uk/corvey/cw3journal/Issue%20one/pearson.html (accessed 2 November 2013).

Pearson, Jacqueline, *Women's Reading in Britain, 1750–1835: A Dangerous Recreation* (Cambridge: Cambridge University Press, 1999)

Perry, Gill, 'Ambiguity and Desire: Metaphors of Sexuality in Late Eighteenth-Century Representations of the Actress', in *Notorious Muse:*

*The Actress in British Art and Culture 1776–1812*, ed. Robyn Asleson (New Haven, CT: Yale University Press, 2003), pp. 57–80

Perry, Gill, *Spectacular Flirtations: Viewing the Actress in British Art and Theatre 1768–1820* (New Haven, CT: Yale University Press, 2007)

Perry, Gill, with Joseph Roach and Shearer West, *The First Actresses: Nell Gwyn to Sarah Siddons* (Ann Arbor, MI: University of Michigan Press, 2011)

Perry, Ruth, *Women, Letters, and the Novel* (New York, NY: AMS, 1980)

Peterson, Linda H., 'Becoming an Author: Mary Robinson's *Memoirs* and the Origins of the Woman Artist's Autobiography', in *Re-Visioning Romanticism: British Women Writers, 1776–1837*, ed. Carol Shiner Wilson and Joel Haefner (Philadelphia, PA: University of Pennsylvania Press, 1994), pp. 36–56

Peterson, Linda H., *Becoming a Woman of Letters: Myths of Authorship and Facts of the Victorian Market* (Princeton, NJ: Princeton University Press, 2009)

Peterson, Linda H., *Traditions of Victorian Women's Autobiography: The Poetics and Politics of Life Writing* (Charlottesville, VA: University Press of Virginia, 1999)

Phillips, Mark Salber, *Society and Sentiment: Genres of Historical Writing in Britain, 1740–1820* (Princeton, NJ: Princeton University Press, 2000)

Pink, Emma E., 'Frances Burney's *Camilla*: "To Print My Grand Work ... by Subscription"', *Eighteenth-Century Studies*, 40 (2006): 51–68

Poovey, Mary, *The Proper Lady and the Woman Writer: Ideology as Style in the Works of Mary Wollstonecraft, Mary Shelley, and Jane Austen* (Chicago, IL: University of Chicago Press, 1984)

Rajan, Tilottama, 'Autonarration and Genotext in Mary Hays's "Memoirs of Emma Courtney"', *Studies in Romanticism*, 32:2 (1993): 149–76

Rajan, Tilottama, 'Framing the Corpus: Godwin's "Editing" of Wollstonecraft in 1798', *Studies in Romanticism*, 39 (2000): 511–31

Rajan, Tilottama, *Romantic Narrative: Shelley, Hays, Godwin, Wollstonecraft* (Baltimore, MD: Johns Hopkins University Press, 2010)

Raven, James, 'Historical Introduction: The Novel Comes of Age', in *The English Novel, 1770–1829: A Bibliographical Survey of Prose Fiction Published in the British Isles*, ed. Peter Garside, James Raven and Rainer Schöwerling, 2 vols (Oxford: Oxford University Press, 1998), I, pp. 21–56

Richards, Cynthia, 'Revising History, "Dumbing Down", and Imposing Silence: The Female Biography of Mary Hays', *Eighteenth-Century Women: Studies in Their Lives, Work and Culture*, 3 (2003), pp. 263–94

Richards, Sandra, *The Rise of the English Actress* (Basingstoke: Palgrave Macmillan, 1993)

Robinson, Daniel, *The Poetry of Mary Robinson: Form and Fame* (Basingstoke: Palgrave Macmillan, 2011)

Robertson, Ben P., *Elizabeth Inchbald's Reputation: A Publishing and Reception History* (London: Pickering & Chatto, 2013)

Roper, Derek, *Reviewing before the Edinburgh: 1788–1802* (Newark, NJ: University of Delaware Press, 1978)

Rosenberg, Beth Carole, *Virginia Woolf and Samuel Johnson* (New York, NY: St. Martin's Press, 1995)

*A Routledge Literary Sourcebook on Mary Wollstonecraft's A Vindication of the Rights of Woman*, ed. Adriana Craciun (London: Routledge, 2002)

Runge, Laura L., 'Mary Robinson's Memoirs and the Anti-Adultery Campaign', *Modern Philology*, 101:4 (2004): 563–86

Saglia, Diego, 'Commerce, Luxury, and Identity in Mary Robinson's "Memoirs"', *Studies in English Literature*, 49:3 (2009): 717–39

Samuelian, Kristin Flieger, *Royal Romances: Sex, Scandal, and Monarchy in Print, 1780–1821* (Basingstoke: Palgrave Macmillan, 2010)

Sapiro, Virginia, *A Vindication of Political Virtue: The Political Theory of Mary Wollstonecraft* (Chicago, IL: University of Chicago Press, 1992)

Schellenberg, Betty A., 'From Propensity to Profession: Female Authorship and the Early Career of Frances Burney', *Eighteenth-Century Fiction*, 14:3–4 (2002): 345–70

Schellenberg, Betty A., *The Professionalization of Women Writers in Eighteenth-Century Britain* (Cambridge: Cambridge University Press, 2005)

Schellenberg, Betty A., 'Writing Eighteenth-Century Women's Literary History, 1986 to 2006', in *Literature Compass*, 4:6 (2007): 1538–60

Scott, Joan W., 'Fantasy Echo: History and the Construction of Identity', *Critical Inquiry*, 27:2 (2001): 284–304

Setzer, Sharon, 'The Gothic Structure of Mary Robinson's *Memoirs*', in *Romantic Autobiography in England*, ed. Eugene Stelzig (Farnham: Ashgate, 2009), pp. 31–47

Shattock, Joanne, 'The Construction of the Woman Writer', in *Women and Literature in Britain, 1800–1900*, ed. Joanne Shattock (Cambridge: Cambridge University Press, 2001), pp. 8–34

Sherman, Stuart, 'Diary and Autobiography', in *The Cambridge History of English Literature, 1660–1780*, ed. John Richetti (Cambridge: Cambridge University Press, 2012), pp. 649–72

Simons, Judy, *Diaries and Journals of Literary Women from Fanny Burney to Virginia Woolf* (Basingstoke: Palgrave Macmillan, 1990)

Sireci, Fiore, '"Defects of Temper": Mary Wollstonecraft's Strategies of Self-Representation', in *Called to Civil Existence: Mary Wollstonecraft's A*

*Vindication of the Rights of Woman*, ed. Enit Karafili Steiner (Amsterdam: Rodopi, 2014), pp. 71–92

Skolnik, Christine M., 'Wollstonecraft's Dislocation of the Masculine Sublime: A Vindication', *Rhetorica: A Journal of the History of Rhetoric*, 21:4 (2003): 205–23

Sloan, Margaret Kathryn, 'Mothers, Marys, and Reforming "The Rising Generation": Mary Wollstonecraft and Mary Hays', in *Mentoring in Eighteenth-Century British Literature and Culture*, ed. Anthony W. Lee (Farnham: Ashgate, 2010), pp. 225–43

Smith, Sidonie, and Julia Watson, *Reading Autobiography: A Guide for Interpreting Life Narratives*, 2nd edn (Minneapolis, MN: University of Minneapolis Press, 2001)

Spacks, Patricia Meyer, *Imagining a Self: Autobiography and Novel in Eighteenth-Century England* (Cambridge, MA: Harvard University Press, 1976)

Spacks, Patricia Meyer, *Privacy: Concealing the Eighteenth-Century Self* (Chicago, IL: University of Chicago Press, 2003)

Spongberg, Mary, 'Female Biography', in *Companion to Women's Historical Writing*, ed. Mary Spongberg, Barbara Caine and Ann Curthoys (Basingstoke: Palgrave Macmillan 2005), pp. 172–82

Spongberg, Mary, 'Mary Hays and Mary Wollstonecraft and the Evolution of Dissenting Feminism', *Enlightenment and Dissent*, 26 (2010): 230–58

Spongberg, Mary, 'Remembering Wollstonecraft: Feminine Friendship, Female Subjectivity and the "Invention" of the Feminist Heroine', in *Women's Life Writing, 1700–1850*, ed. Daniel Cook and Amy Culley (Basingstoke: Palgrave Macmillan, 2012), pp. 165–80

Spongberg, Mary, *Writing Women's History Since the Renaissance* (Basingstoke: Palgrave Macmillan, 2002)

Stelzig, Eugene, 'Introduction', in *Romantic Autobiography in England*, ed. Eugene Stelzig (Farnham: Ashgate, 2009), pp. 1–30

St Clair, William, *The Reading Nation in the Romantic Period* (Cambridge: Cambridge University Press, 2004)

Swaab, Peter, 'Romantic Self-Representation: The Example of Mary Wollstonecraft's *Letters in Sweden*', in *Mortal Pages, Literary Lives: Studies in Nineteenth-Century Autobiography*, ed. Philip Shaw and Vincent Newey (Aldershot: Scolar Press, 1996), pp. 13–30

Taylor, Barbara, 'Feminism and Enlightened Religious Discourses: Introduction', in *Women, Gender and Enlightenment*, ed. Sarah Knott and Barbara Taylor (Basingstoke: Palgrave Macmillan, 2005), pp. 410–15

Taylor, Barbara, *Mary Wollstonecraft and the Feminist Imagination* (Cambridge: Cambridge University Press, 2003)

Taylor, Barbara, 'Mary Wollstonecraft and the Wild Wish of Feminism', *History Workshop*, 33 (1992): 197–219

Temple, Kathryn, *Scandal Nation: Law and Authorship in Britain, 1750–1832* (Ithaca, NY: Cornell University Press, 2003)

Thaddeus, Janice Farrar, *Frances Burney: A Literary Life* (London: Palgrave Macmillan, 2000)

Thompson, Leslie M., and John R. Ahrens, 'Criticism of English Fiction 1780–1810: The Mysterious Powers of the Pleading Preface', *Yearbook of English Studies*, 1:1 (1971): 125–34

Thompson, Lynda M., *The 'Scandalous Memoirists': Constantia Phillips, Laetitia Pilkington and the Shame of 'Publick Fame'* (Manchester: Manchester University Press, 2000)

Todd, Janet, *The Sign of Angellica: Women, Writing and Fiction, 1660–1800* (London: Virago, 1989)

Treadwell, James, *Autobiographical Writing and British Literature, 1783–1834* (Oxford: Oxford University Press, 2005)

Trott, Nicola, 'Sexing the Critic: Mary Wollstonecraft at the Turn of the Century', in *1798: The Year of the Lyrical Ballads*, ed. Richard Cronin (Basingstoke: Palgrave Macmillan, 1998), pp. 32–67

Ty, Eleanor, 'Editor's Introduction', in *The Victim of Prejudice*, ed. Eleanor Ty (Toronto: Broadview, 1994), pp. vii–xxxvii

Ty, Eleanor, 'Engendering a Female Subject: Mary Robinson's (Re)presentations of the Self', *English Studies in Canada*, 21:4 (1995): 407–28

Ty, Eleanor, 'Introduction', in *Memoirs of Emma Courtney*, ed. Eleanor Ty (Oxford: Oxford University Press, 1996), pp. vii–xxxvii

Ty, Eleanor, *Unsex'd Revolutionaries: Five Women Novelists of the 1790s* (Toronto: University of Toronto Press, 1993)

Walker, Gina Luria, '"Energetic Sympathies of Truth and Feeling": Mary Hays and Rational Dissent', *Enlightenment and Dissent*, 26 (2010): 259–85

Walker, Gina Luria, 'The Invention of Female Biography', *Enlightenment and Dissent*, 29 (2014): 79–136

Walker, Gina Luria, 'Mary Hays (1759–1843): An Enlightened Quest', in *Women, Gender and Enlightenment*, ed. Sarah Knott and Barbara Taylor (Basingstoke: Palgrave Macmillan, 2005), pp. 493–518

Walker, Gina Luria, *Mary Hays (1759–1843): The Growth of a Woman's Mind* (Aldershot: Ashgate, 2006)

Walker, Gina Luria, 'Mary Hays's "Love Letters"', *Keats-Shelley Journal*, LI (2002), 94–115

Wallace, Miriam L., 'Writing Lives and Gendering History in Mary Hays's *Female Biography* (1803)', in *Romantic Autobiography in England*, ed. Eugene Stelzig (Farnham: Ashgate, 2009), pp. 63–78

Wanko, Cheryl, 'Patron or Patronised? "Fans" and the Eighteenth-century English Stage', in *Romanticism and Celebrity Culture, 1750–1850*, ed. Tom Mole (Cambridge: Cambridge University Press, 2009), pp. 209–26

Wanko, Cheryl, *Roles of Authority: Thespian Biography and Celebrity in Eighteenth-Century Britain* (Lubbock, TX: Texas Tech University Press, 2003)

Waters, Mary A., *British Women Writers and the Profession of Literary Criticism, 1789–1832* (Basingstoke: Palgrave Macmillan, 2004)

Waters, Mary A., '"The First of a New Genus": Mary Wollstonecraft as a Literary Critic and Mentor to Mary Hays', *Eighteenth Century Studies*, 37:3 (2004): 215–34

Wilkes, Joanne, *Women Reviewing Women in Nineteenth-Century Britain: The Critical Reception of Jane Austen, Charlotte Brontë and George Eliot* (Aldershot: Ashgate, 2010)

Wilson, Lisa M., 'From Actress to Authoress: Mary Robinson's Pseudonymous Celebrity', in *The Public's Open to Us All: Essays on Women and Performance in Eighteenth-Century England* (Newcastle: Cambridge Scholars Publishing, 2009), pp. 156–75

# Index

Milton Keynes UK
Ingram Content Group UK Ltd.
UKHW021440240823
427422UK00015B/75

'This carefully researched, clearly-written monograph makes an invaluable and original contribution to life studies, to women's writing and to Romanticism.'

Ashley Cross, *Nineteenth-Century Gender Studies*

*Romantic women's life writing* explores how the publication of women's life writing influenced the reputation of its writers and of the genre itself during the long nineteenth century. It provides case studies of Frances Burney, Mary Wollstonecraft, Mary Robinson and Mary Hays – four writers who authored and/or inspired works of life writing and whose names were caught up in the debates surrounding the moral and literary respectability of publishing the 'private' through diaries, letters, memoirs and (auto) biography.

Focusing on gender, genre and authorship, the book examines key works such as Frances Burney's *Diary and Letters of Madame D'Arblay* (1842–46), Mary Wollstonecraft's *Letters Written During a Short Residence in Sweden, Norway, and Denmark* (1796), William Godwin's *Memoirs of the Author of a Vindication of the Rights of Woman* (1798), Mary Robinson's *Memoirs* (1801) and Mary Hays's *Female Biography* (1803), as well as responses to these texts in essays, reviews, fiction, poetry and other life writing. It also considers print runs, circulation figures, pricing and reprinting patterns. The book argues for the importance of life writing – a crucial site of affective and imaginative identification – in shaping authorial reputation and afterlife, and reveals the innovative contributions of these women to the genre of life writing. Ultimately, it constructs a fuller, more varied picture of the literary field in the long nineteenth century, and the role of both women writers and their life writing within it.

**Susan Civale** is Reader in Romanticism at Canterbury Christ Church University

Cover image:
Vintage graphic by The Graphics Fairy

Manchester University Press

ISBN 978-1-5261-7466-6

9 781526 174666

www.manchesteruniversitypress.co.uk